PATRONAGE
An American Tradition

PATRONAGE
An American Tradition

ANNE FREEDMAN
Roosevelt University

NELSON-HALL PUBLISHERS
Chicago

Library of Congress Cataloging-in-Publication Data

Freedman, Anne E.
    Patronage: an American tradition / Anne Freedman.
      p.   cm.
    Includes bibliographical reference (p.   ) and index.
    ISBN 0-8304-1287-5
    1. Patronage, Political--United States.   2. Patronage, Political-
-United States--History.   I. Title.
JK736.F68   1993   93-1962
324.2'04--dc20   CIP

Manufactured in the United States of America

10 9 8 7 6 5 4 3 2 1

The paper used in this book meets the minimum requirements of American National Standard for Information Sciences—Permanence of Paper for Printed Library Materials, ANSI Z39.48-1984.

CONTENTS

PREFACE

This is a book about patronage in America today. Of course, there are some who would argue that patronage is largely a thing of the past and is no longer a significant part of the nation's politics. However, there are many who suspect that patronage is still a feature of the American political landscape.

Unfortunately, with few exceptions, those who are in the know don't want to talk. Patronage has gone underground. No one wants to admit to a practice that bears the taint of corrupt machine politics. And, now that many forms of patronage have become illegal as a result of a series of laws and Supreme Court decisions, openly discussing patronage has become even more foolhardy.

Probably because of the obstacles involved, the literature on patronage is quite sparse. Moreover, most of the more detailed studies, including the Susan and Martin Tolchin's anecdotal book, date back to the 1970s or even earlier.[1] The literature on political parties and on state and local politics provides some information, but there is little in the way of a systematic study of patronage. David Mayhew's state by state documentation of city and county level party structure is in all likelihood the most comprehensive work, but it is primarily a picture of machine-like party organizations in the 1960s. It is instructive that to paint that portrait Mayhew had to search through a multitude of published and unpublished sources, including newspaper stories and that he ended up with a "blend of general, undiscriminating evidence on the lower-level electoral environments of whole states, and particular evidence on cities and counties that are large enough or whose politics has otherwise been eye-catching enough to draw the attention of writers."[2] A similar blend is the best that a researcher trying to survey patronage today could expect. Indeed, I have searched through the published sources as well as through many unpublished materials and a number of newspapers and have interviewed experts in a number of states. I will introduce some of the information I gleaned where it's relevant and illuminating. However, an understanding of patronage in America requires more than just adding up bits of information. I believe case studies can provide some of the depth that is missing from a survey. I have therefore chosen to concentrate on three cases of large-scale patronage operations in order to show: (1) How these patronage systems operated and managed to persist long after patronage was supposed to be dead and (2) How reformers, working primarily through the courts in combination with the changing political and economic environment, have affected these systems and altered the practice of patronage.

The first chapter is designed to provide background and to frame the case studies. It opens with a discussion of the 1990 Rutan case in which the Supreme Court ruled patronage hiring unconstitutional, continues with a brief history of patronage in the United States, and ends with a case study of patronage in Mayor Koch's New York.

Chapter 2 focuses on the legendary Chicago machine which is often described as the most long-lived and powerful of all American machines. Because of its fame and size it has been extensively studied and it is possible to get a good understanding of how the Cook County Democratic Party organization has functioned from its heyday under the first Mayor Richard Daley to the present. However, I chose Chicago primarily because it is in the Windy City that modern-day reformers have had their greatest success in using the federal courts as a weapon against patronage. While the story of the nineteenth-century reformers legislative successes has often been told, the saga of Michael Shakman's battle with King Richard's patronage army is virtually unknown outside of Chicago. The story is one that deserves to be known because it involves the governance of the nation's third largest city and because it sheds light on the role that the federal courts can play in changing political institutions.

The courts also play a central role in the second case study, that of the state of Illinois during the administration of Governor James Thompson. This case, presented in Chapter 3, is significant because it shows how a governor used patronage to increase his power *and* because it was the Illinois system which was challenged in the landmark Rutan case. From a practical point of view, the Illinois state system, like that of Chicago, is also a good subject because its involvement in a court case resulted in many facts being brought to light which might otherwise have been buried.

Finally, in Chapter 4 I look at a less well known, but all the same, very successful patronage operation. The Nassau County Republican machine is significant both because of its scale and because it succeeded in an affluent suburban environment which many believe is not fertile soil for machine politics. Again, there were practical reasons for choosing Nassau. Like Chicago and the state of Illinois, some operations of the machine were exposed in the course of federal court action. More critically, the Long Island daily *Newsday* has over the years devoted considerable resources to investigating the Republican patronage mill. Although I interviewed a number of Nassau County politicians and political experts and conducted a library search, I could not have written the case study without the *Newsday* material. It is valuable work and deserves an audience outside Long Island.

The fifth and last chapter is devoted to evaluating and taking stock: how much patronage remains; "new" forms of patronage; the parties and patronage; the impact of Rutan; and the future of the American tradition of patronage.

Notes

1. Among the most frequently cited studies are: Frank J. Sorauf's "State Patronage in a Rural County," *American Political Science Review*, 50 (1956), pp. 1046-56 and "The Silent Revolution in Patronage," *Public Administration Review*, 20 (1960), pp. 28-34; Daniel Patrick Moynihan and James Q. Wilson, "Patronage in New York State, 1955-1959," *American Political Science Review*, 58 (1964), pp. 286-301; W. Robert Gump, "The Functions of Patronage in American Party Politics: An Empirical Reappraisal," *Midwest Journal of Political Science*, 15 (1971), pp. 81-107 and Michael Johnston, "Patrons and Clients, Jobs and Machines: A Case Study of the Uses of Patronage," *American Political Science Review*, 73 (1979), pp. 385-98. The Tolchin's book is *To The Victor* (New York: Random House, 1972).

2. David Mayhew, *Placing Parties in American Politics* (Princeton: Princeton University Press, 1986), pp. 7-8.

CHAPTER 1
FROM THE BEGINNING

To the victor belong the spoils of the enemy.
—*New York Senator William Learned Marcy, 1832*

To the victor belong only those spoils that may be constitutionally obtained.
—*Justice William Brennan, Opinion of the court in Rutan v. Republican Party of Illinois, 1990.*

The Rutan Suit

The words of Justice Brennan are etched on a plaque fixed prominently on the wall above Mary Lee Leahy's desk in the turn-of-the-century Victorian house used by her three woman Springfield law firm. The plaque was a Christmas present from a grateful state rehabilitation counselor named Cynthia Rutan to the lawyer who had fought the state of Illinois and its Republican governor, James Thompson, on her behalf. Rutan sued the state claiming that she had been denied a promotion she deserved solely because she did not support the Illinois Republican party. Her suit was combined with those of four others who also said they were discriminated against because they were not Republicans. One of them said he was not hired at all; another alleged he was not promoted or given a transfer to an office nearer his home; and two said they were not recalled to work from a layoff.

The Rutan suit had gradually made its way up from the federal District Court in Danville, Illinois to the Seventh Circuit Court of

1

Appeals in Chicago to the Supreme Court. There Mary Lee Leahy found herself pitted against Thomas Sullivan, a former United States Attorney who argued for the state. Thompson was unwilling to entrust the case to the lawyers employed by the state and had hired Sullivan's firm of Jenner and Block, a legal giant with more than 300 partners and associates. The governor and the state's Republican party officials were anxious to win in Rutan because the case posed a fundamental threat to their massive patronage system.* If Mary Lee Leahy could convince a majority of the justices that hiring people on the basis of their party affiliation violated the First Amendment, Thompson and the party would no longer be able to use state jobs to reward Republican supporters. They would lose a powerful weapon in the partisan struggle.

Springfield likes to call itself Mr. Lincoln's hometown. Wherever one turns there are signs of the great man—the law offices he shared with Billy Herndon; the Old State Capitol where he gave his "House Divided" speech; the home he shared with Mary Todd Lincoln and their rambunctious children; and the railroad station from which he left for the White House and to which his body was returned. In view of Lincoln's use of the patronage powers of the presidency, "Big Jim" Thompson might be forgiven for thinking that he was merely following in the footsteps of our most venerated president. Lincoln had in his five years on Pennsylvania Avenue raised the practice of spoils politics to new heights, replacing more government employees than any of his predecessors. He believed that his use of spoils preserved the fledging Republican party and thereby helped save the Union. Still, he found spoils politics distasteful and complained about being hounded by office seekers. The story is told that once, when he was lying in bed suffering from a mild pox, he ordered his secretary to "invite the job seekers in, for at last I have something to give all of them."[1]

If Abraham Lincoln could play patronage politics, there didn't seem to be any reason why Governor Thompson couldn't use jobs for political purposes. The defendants did not expect an increasingly con-

---

* The Rutan case dealt with patronage in the form of jobs. Although many scholars use a broader definition, I have adopted the definition used by Beck and Sorauf and made a distinction between patronage and preferments. Thus, patronage refers to appointments to government jobs as a reward for political support, while preferments involve the discretionary granting of governmental favors to political supporters. See Paul Allen Beck and Frank J. Sorauf, *Party Politics in America*, 7th ed. (New York: HarperCollins, 1992), pp. 115–116.

servative Supreme Court to reject political hiring. They were confident of winning even though the Court had ruled in the 1976 Elrod case, and again in the 1980 Branti case, that firing nonpolicymaking employees for political reasons was unconstitutional. Their confidence was based on the fact that the Elrod decision was clearly limited to political firing. As Justice Potter Stewart put it: the "single substantive question" in the case was "whether a nonpolicymaking, non-confidential government employee can be discharged or threatened with discharge from a job that he is satisfactorily performing upon the sole ground of his political beliefs."[2] The Supreme Court implied, and subsequently other federal courts explicitly stated, that a person losing a job suffered much greater harm than one who merely failed to get a job.

In the Rutan case the Seventh Circuit had decided in favor of the state. It ruled that politically based hiring in lower level jobs doesn't do great harm because the applicant isn't deprived of his livelihood. The court maintained that political discrimination simply lowers the individual's "chances for receiving employment with one of many potential employers." The damage to the jobseeker wasn't serious enough to justify the court's intervention; the federal courts should not preside as "Platonic Guardians over state employment systems." The only patronage practices which should be considered unconstitutional according to the Seventh Circuit are dismissals and actions which are the "substantial equivalent of a dismissal."[3]

But five justices of the Supreme Court did not agree with the Seventh Circuit. To the surprise and dismay of Governor Thompson and many other politicians, the Supreme Court accepted Leahy's arguments and declared that politically based hiring—patronage—was unconstitutional. Justice Brennan, who wrote the opinion of the Court, argued that there was no compelling government interest which could justify denying the First Amendment rights of individuals applying for government jobs. Patronage hiring, as much as political firing and other patronage practices related to jobs, deprives an individual of his right to freedom of speech, belief and association. He asked how an individual could be considered free to make political choices if he knows that he can only get or keep a government job by supporting a particular party and its candidates? For Justice Brennan conditioning "employment on political activity pressures employees to pledge political allegiance to a party with which they prefer not to associate, to work for the election of political candidates they do not support, and to contribute money to be used to further policies with which they do not agree." In his view this is "tantamount to coerced belief."[4]

3

Unlike the Seventh Circuit judges, Justice Brennan was not impressed by the supposedly great differences between political hiring and firing. As he saw it, patronage hiring does harm to the person rejected and places "burdens on free speech and association." He reasoned: "A state job is valuable. Like most employment, it provides regular pay checks, health insurance, and other benefits. In addition, there may be openings with the State when business in the private sector is slow. There are also occupations for which the government is a major (or the only) source of employment, such as social workers, elementary school teachers, and prison guards. Thus denial of a state job is a serious privation."[5]

To Justice Brennan the issue was clear. None of the purported benefits of patronage could justify taking away the individual's vital First Amendment freedoms. One by one he dismissed the pro-patronage arguments.

First he dealt with the contention that patronage is needed to insure that government workers are efficient and that the government will function effectively. Patronage proponents maintain that if people are hired who don't support the party of the chief executive, they will not be motivated to work effectively and they may even be tempted to try to subvert the incumbent administration's programs.

Brennan summarily rejected this contention, saying he was "not persuaded." He went on:

> The inefficiency resulting from the wholesale replacement of large numbers of public employees every time political office changes hands belies this justification. And the prospect of dismissal after an election in which the incumbent party has lost is only a disincentive to good work. Further, it is not clear that dismissal in order to make room for a patronage appointment will result in replacement by a person more qualified to do the job since appointment often occurs in exchange for the delivery of votes, or other party service, not job capability.

In any case, Brennan found it doubtful that employees are motivated to perform poorly because they are of a different "political persuasion"; besides the government could always discharge "employees for good cause, such as insubordination or poor job performance."[6]

In the same vein, Brennan dismissed the argument that patronage is needed to insure that employees will be loyal and will faithfully implement policies. He pointed out that the Court would permit an administration to put its own people into confidential and policymaking positions. As the Court ruled in Branti, patronage appointments are permissible for those positions for which "the hiring authority can demonstrate that party affiliation is an appropriate requirement for the effective performance of the public office involved."[7] There would seem to be no reason why a clerk or a truck driver should be required to belong to a particular party.

Finally, Brennan refused to accept the argument that patronage is necessary to maintain political parties and preserve the democratic process. In his view the loss of patronage as a result of the Rutan decision would not kill the parties. They have, after all, managed to survive up to now even though the establishment of civil service systems substantially reduced their patronage. As for the democratic process, Brennan thought it might actually be better off without patronage because patronage can result in one party rule; one party becomes so entrenched that other parties never have a chance.

What was clear to Justice Brennan was not necessarily clear to others. The Rutan decision met with a decidedly mixed reception. It was applauded by reformers and other good government types. In Chicago, Terrence Brunner, the executive director of the crusading Better Government Association trumpeted that the Rutan ruling was "like the Emancipation Proclamation for public employees." In New York the head of the state Commission on Government Integrity proclaimed that now "people who are victims of patronage abuses will have a claim based on the Constitution to do something about it." The director of a Philadelphia group which monitors government predicted that there would be litigation from disgruntled city employees.[8] In Springfield many state employees joined Cynthia Rutan and Mary Lee Leahy in rejoicing that this was a victory for the people. Leahy marvelled that her tiny law firm had even been able to get a case to the Supreme Court. As she saw it, her victory "didn't depend on clout or money, but on the merit of the issues."[9] Cynthia Rutan hoped that she would finally be able to get the promotion she felt she deserved without anyone bothering to check how she had voted in the last primary.[10]

Not surprisingly, some of the people who had benefitted from patronage did not join Cynthia Rutan in celebrating. Chicagoan Jim Weyrich, a clerk who got his job in the Cook County Treasurer's office through patronage told the *New York Times* that "this is the way that ordinary working people have gotten ahead. If doing a little work for the precinct captain helps people to get a job, what's wrong with that?"[11]

Mr. Weyrich's reaction was relatively mild compared to those who foresaw dire consequences flowing from the Rutan decision. Governor Thompson exclaimed: "This turns politics on its head. . . .

This will strike a severe blow at whatever is left of political parties in America. The Supreme Court is naive when it thinks that patronage has no basis in strengthening political parties. That's just wrong. It brings willing adherents to your cause."[12] He warned that "If you take hiring away from politicians you're going to be giving a lot of power to special interests, unions and the bureaucracy. And then you'll really see a lot of somebody's cousin getting on the payroll."[13]

As strong as his language was, the Governor's opinions seem measured when compared to those voiced by Justice Antonin Scalia. In his dissenting opinion in Rutan, Scalia predicted that the decision could have "disastrous consequences" for the political system. By accelerating the disintegration of the parties and fostering the spread of civil service systems, Rutan would contribute to the trend towards making elected government increasingly "helpless . . . unprotected by 'party discipline', before the demands of small and cohesive interest groups." The two party system would be undermined; candidates unable to "rely upon patronage-based party loyalty for their campaign support, would have to attract workers and raise funds by appealing to various interest groups." As parties lose power, interest groups will gain in influence; each office holder will have to reach an accommodation with competing interest groups and political parties may be prevented from enacting their programs into law.[14]

In Scalia's doomsday scenario the death of patronage would have other negative effects. No longer would racial and ethnic minorities be able to use patronage as an avenue of upward mobility. To abolish patronage would "prevent groups that have only recently obtained political power, especially blacks, from following this path to economic and social advancement."

While Scalia recognized that patronage has some "disadvantages," he insisted that it is not up to the courts to decide whether the disadvantages outweigh the advantages in any particular situation. In every case "the desirability of patronage is a policy question to be decided by the people's representatives."

Scalia shocked many legal experts by arguing that Elrod and Branti (as well as Rutan) should be reversed. The Supreme Court, he argued, has no business limiting patronage hiring or, for that matter, patronage firing because patronage is a "venerable and accepted tradition." Patronage existed when the First Amendment was adopted; there is no evidence that it was intended at that time to be used to strike down patronage. Therefore, the Court should not do so now. "When a practice not expressly prohibited by the text of the Bill of Rights bears the endorsement of a long tradition of open, widespread and unchallenged use that dates back to the beginning of the Republic, we have no proper basis for striking it down."

Scalia would leave it to the voters to determine the "appropriate mix of patronage and civil service jobs; to do anything else would open the courts to a flood of litigation." In his view, the Supreme Court failed dismally when it tried in Branti to enunciate a standard for distinguishing between those jobs which can properly be filled on a political basis and those which cannot. The Courts of Appeal have been unable to agree on how to apply the Branti standard. Scalia argued that uncertainty and confusion will inevitably result as long as the Court tries to draw the line because there is "no right line that can be nationally applied and that is known to judges."

In light of Scalia's agonizing over the folly of the Court, it may be surprising that some political observers and politicians reacted to Rutan with a degree of indifference. The indifferent fell into two distinct groups. To one group Rutan was largely irrelevant because they believed that patronage jobs were already in sharp decline and that the few which were left were not essential to the parties or officeholders. As one political scientist put it, the Rutan ruling was unnecessary because the number of patronage positions had already "significantly decreased in virtually every state."[15] Or, as a Pennsylvania party director observed, patronage was a part of the state's "colorful past." Today, he said, "I don't do jobs. We can't run a political party in Pennsylvania based on jobs. And I don't want to be a personnel manager."[16] In Ohio officials said they didn't think the ruling would have much impact on them because they didn't have an ingrained patronage system.[17] (Still, it should be noted, many officials were reexamining their hiring procedures and in the months after Rutan it did appear that many were exercising more caution in making appointments.)[18]

However, some of those who were being more careful were not really trying to eliminate patronage; they just wanted to avoid detection and litigation. This group viewed Rutan not so much as unnecessary, but as fated to be ineffectual. For example, in Springfield Irv Smith, himself the holder of a patronage job, said his role as Sangamon County Republican chairman was to build the party and that he would continue to use jobs for that purpose. Because of Rutan he no longer would give out state employment applications with Republican party membership applications stapled to them, but he would not stop helping Republicans get jobs. He vowed that if the state changes its hiring system, he'll "learn the system and become adroit at the system. . . . I don't think they can take politics out of the government."[19] A New Jersey Republican county chairman echoed Smith, saying "This ruling will just make people a little more wary, a little more nervous. . . . But I'll tell you this: if a Republican calls me tomorrow and wants help for a job for a wife or husband or daughter, I will absolutely try to help them."[20]

On Long Island some stalwarts of the Nassau County Republican machine said that they didn't think Rutan would affect them because they were careful not to leave any "smoking guns." One official told *Newsday* "we're well past the days where someone would threaten you and say if you don't help out in this campaign, you're not going to get a certain job. We've gotten better at it. We're more sophisticated. . . . If you have eyes to see, you notice the people making their moves through the system are those who are the most politically active." A former head of New York's state civil service system agreed that, "This is a very easy decision to evade. Within the arena of discretionary hiring . . . there is always going to be a fairly broad opportunity for decision-making, and there it will be very hard to be sure one has excluded partisan considerations."[21]

Many political scientists and historians also agreed that, as one put it, the "Supreme Court decision is going to be devilishly difficult to enforce" and that it was unlikely that patronage would disappear in the United States where it is so much an "accepted part of the landscape."[22]

What then, one might well ask, does Rutan mean? What is the status of patronage in the nation? What is happening to patronage in America? Is patronage as beneficial to the system as Justice Scalia claims? Or should it be seen as Justice Brennan sees it, as an impediment to individual freedom? These are the questions to which this book is devoted. To begin to deal with them, we have to first look at the history of patronage in the United States.

Patronage Before Reform

In his Rutan dissent Justice Scalia wrote that patronage "bears the endorsement of a long tradition of open, widespread, and unchallenged use that dates back to the beginning of the Republic." It is, in sum, a "venerable and accepted tradition."[23] To this, Justice Stevens, in a concurring opinion retorted that: "if the age of a pernicious practice were a sufficient reason for its continued acceptance, the constitutional attack on racial discrimination would, of course, have been doomed to failure." For him "the tradition that is relevant in this case is the American commitment to examine and reexamine past and present practices against the basic principles in the Constitution."[24]

Leaving aside the intricacies of the constitutional arguments, it does seem clear that patronage is an American traditon, but not that it is, as Justice Scalia would have it, an accepted or venerated practice. While there have been periods when patronage achieved widespread acceptance and the practice has at all times had its defenders, for much of our history patronage has been considered undemocratic and unsavory if not downright corrupt and immoral. At the height of the outcry against patronage in the late nineteenth century, it was virtually equated with murder because a disappointed office seeker had shot President Garfield in order to put a spoilsman into the presidency. After firing twice, the assassin shouted that he was a Stalwart (the pro-patronage faction of the Republican party) and that "Arthur was President now." When Garfield finally died after lingering in agony for two months, his suffering was used to promote the cause of civil service reform. Posters appeared around the country trumpeting that Garfield had "died . . . a martyr to the fierceness of factional politics and the victim of that accursed greed for spoils of office which was the bane of his brief conscious existence as President, and is the gravest peril that threatens the future of his country."[25]

In fact resentment of spoils actually predates the constitution. Patronage was entrenched in England at the time the colonies were established and the king naturally extended the practice to the New World. Surely some of the Englishmen who bought their positions were exemplary public servants but many were not, and the colonists had to suffer under corrupt, lazy and inept administrators who milked their offices for profits which they sent back to the motherland.[26] In the Declaration of Independence the aggrieved colonists cited as proof of the King's "absolute Tyranny" the "Fact" that "he has erected a multitude of New Offices, and sent hither swarms of Officers to harass our People, and eat out their substance."

The Revolutionaries did not want to perpetuate the evils of the British tyrant. At the beginning of the Republic they certainly had no thought of using patronage to build and maintain political parties. In fact, they had a very dim view of parties and were determined to keep them out of the United States altogether. As the historian Richard Hofstadter notes:

> Political discussion in eighteenth-century England and America was pervaded by a kind of anti-party cant. Jonathan Swift, in his *Thoughts on Various Subjects,* had said that "Party is the madness of many, for the gain of a few." This maxim, which was repeated on this side of the Atlantic by men like John Adams and William Paterson, plainly struck a deep resonance in the American mind. Madison and Hamilton, when they discussed parties or factions (for them the terms were usually interchangeable) in *The Federalist,* did so only to arraign their bad effects. In the great debate over the adoption of the Constitution both sides spoke ill of parties. The popular sage, Franklin . . . gave an eloquent warning against factions and the "infinite mutual abuse of parties, tearing to

9

pieces the best of characters." George Washington devoted a large part of his political testament, the Farewell Address, to stern warnings against "the baneful effects of the Spirit of Party." His successor, John Adams, believed that "a division of the republic into two great parties . . . is to be dreaded as the greatest political evil under our Constitution."[27]

Because the Founding Fathers hoped to keep parties from forming, there is no mention of them in the Constitution. The Constitution is also largely silent on the question of how government offices are to be filled, leaving it to the executive to nominate and appoint "by and with the Advice and Consent of the Senate . . . Ambassadors, other public ministers and Counsuls, Judges of the Supreme Court, and all other Officers of the United States whose Appointments are not herein otherwise provided for . . . but the Congress may . . . vest the Appointment of inferior offices . . . in the President alone, in the Courts of Law, or in the Heads of Departments."

There are no guidelines for the President to follow in making appointments, but it is safe to say that he wasn't expected to fill offices on a strictly partisan basis since partisanship itself was anathema to the Constitution writers. The Father of the Country opted to use "fitness of character" as measured by "family background, educational attainment, honor and esteem, and, of course, loyalty to the new government—all tempered by a sagacious regard for geographic representation."[28] But, as the split widened between the Hamiltonian and Jeffersonian factions and the Federalist and Democratic Republican (the Democratic party of today) parties emerged, Washington's appointments "became increasingly partisan."[29] Leonard White, the leading chronicler of U.S. administrative history, writes that Washington tried to hold his warring advisers together, but when he failed and Jefferson resigned from the cabinet, he averred that he would not "bring a man into any office of consequence knowingly whose political tenets are adverse to the measures which the general government are pursuing; for this, in my opinion, would be a sort of political Suicide."[30]

Still, Washington's partisanship was very mild. He only considered party in regard to important offices and even for those "offices of consequence" he didn't limit his choices to Federalists; he only eliminated committed opponents of his programs. Since the second president, John Adams, was also a Federalist, the question of removing officials of the "wrong" party did not arise in his administration. In general Adams followed Washington's example although he was somewhat more partisan and felt more hostile towards the Federalists' competitors. Despite that hostility, Adams wrote to his Secretary of the Treasury that "no man's political creed would be an insuperable bar to promotion." However, he added that "Political principles and discretion will always be considered, with all other qualifications, and well weighed, in all appointments."[31]

Adams was followed in office by Thomas Jefferson, the leader of the Democratic Republicans. The new President found himself heading a government staffed with adherents of the opposing party. He resisted temptation (and pressures from office-hungry members of his own party) and refused to get rid of all the Federalists in the government. In the interests of conciliation and fairness he promised that he would not remove job holders on political grounds. "Malconduct," he said, "is a just ground of removal; mere difference of political opinion is not." He anticipated that he would be able to appoint Republicans (as they were called at the time) to fill openings created by death, resignation or the dismissal of incompetents. When enough openings failed to materialize, he began to remove some Federalists, particularly those who were most actively opposed to his administration, on the grounds that fairness required the sharing of offices. He came to feel that the newly elected party was justified in gradually bringing in its people until it had government jobs proportionate to its "numbers in the body politic."[32] One scholar says that Jefferson's policies marked a shift and that from his presidency on "party service was recognized as a reason for appointment to office, and party dissent as a cause for removal,"[33] but this seems unjust since Jefferson removed less than one quarter of the men holding presidential appointment and didn't disturb the lower level workers such as clerks and postal employees at all. The "little people," who are today protected by civil service, were allowed to stay in their jobs.[34]

The real shift in attitudes and policies towards parties and patronage came in 1828 with the election of Andrew Jackson. Congress had already laid the basis for the policy Jackson called rotation in office when it passed the Four Year Law in 1820. This act limited the terms of certain regional officials such as customs collectors and district attorneys to four years and gave Presidents Monroe and John Quincy Adams the opportunity to put their supporters in office.[35] However, Monroe and Adams were unenthusiastic about the prospect and it remained for Jackson to elevate rotation in office into a principle of democratic government. Having been elected with the support of many newly enfranchised voters, the first Westerner to occupy the presidency saw himself as a champion of the common man, and was committed to opening up government service to ordinary Americans.

When Jackson took office high level government posts were pretty much the province of an aristocratic elite. Even low level jobs were dominated by a small segment of the population and once in office individuals tended to stay for life. Not only did clerks and officials come "from an identifiable section of the population; they were not infrequently succeeded by their sons, and they often found places for their relatives; they organized a Provident Society for their mutual benefit; they sometimes developed their own small cliques and they grew old in office."[36]

If all this weren't bad enough, the government at the time of Jackson's inauguration was also pervaded by corruption.[37] Consequently, Jackson's highest priority at the start of his presideny was a program to reform the administration of the government.[38] Old Hickory told Congress that the public service had to change because men who stay too long in office are likely to become indifferent to the public's interests. They regard their office "as a species of property, and government rather as a means of promoting individual interests than as an instrument created solely for the service of the people."[39]

Urging Congress to extend the 1820 Act, Jackson argued:

> In a country where offices are created solely for the benefit of the people no one man has any more intrinsic right to official station than another. Offices were not established to give support to particular men at the public expense. No individual wrong is, therefore, done by removal, since neither appointment to nor continuance in office is a matter of right. The incumbent became an officer with a view to public benefits, and when these require his removal they are not to be sacrificed to private interests. It is the people, and they alone, who have a right to complain when a bad officer is substituted for a good one. He who is removed has the same means of obtaining a living that are enjoyed by the millions who never held office. The proposed limitation would destroy the idea of property now so generally connected with official station, and although individual distress may be sometimes produced, it would, by promoting that rotation which constitutes a leading principle in the republican creed, give healthful action to the system.

For those worried that rotation in office would damage the government's capacities, Jackson asserted that "the duties of all public officers are, or at least admit of being made, so plain and simple that men of intelligence may readily qualify themselves for their performance."

Jackson's actions were more moderate than his words. While estimates vary, at most 20 percent of the total number of civil servants were fired during the Jackson presidency. According to the leading Jackson biographer, only 9 percent of all office holders were removed during the entire two terms Old Hickory served.[40] This seems to be in line with Jackson's instructions to his cabinet to remove only those individuals who had, in his words, been "appointed against the manifest will of the people" or who worked against the "freedom of state elections." Further, he told the department heads that they were to fill the empty slots with men who would "set examples of fidelity and honesty," thereby elevating the character of government and purifying the morals of the nation.[41]

Although Jackson himself was far from being a complete spoilsman, his administration is seen as marking a turning point in American political life. The local party official began to replace the university trained eastern patricians in the government; these new organization men came to "define" the "character of politics and administration" in the country.[42]

Unlike some of his contemporaries, Jackson's motives in promoting rotation in office were not purely partisan. Of course, he recognized the role that jobs, especially in the post office, played in building his party, but he also seems to have been concerned with the moral character of the civil service. Matthew Crenson maintains that the Jacksonians believed that appointing party politicians who were men of power and position at the local level would bolster the government's legitimacy and in turn its effectiveness. The citizens were less likely to defy the government officials when these officials were people they knew and respected. However, because the officials might not always be the most qualified and might be tempted to garner illegal riches, the Jacksonians also introduced bureaucratic systems of organization and control into the operation of the federal government.[43]

Whatever Jackson's true motivation, his critics in Congress saw his policies as a grab for power at the expense of the legislature and the opposition party. William Marcy of New York surely did not help matters when he tried to defend Jackson in a Senate debate. Marcy proclaimed: "It may be, sir, that the politicians of New York are not as fastidious as some gentlemen are as to disclosing the principles on which they act. They boldly preach what they practice. When they are not contending for victory, they avow their intention of enjoying the fruits of it. . . . If they are successful, they claim, as a matter of right, the advantages of success. They see nothing wrong in the rule, that to the victor belong the spoils of the enemy."[44]

It should be added that the legislators' own motives in fighting Jackson's appointments were themselves suspect as part of the continuing tug of war between the executive and the Congress for control of patronage.

Old Hickory was followed in office by Martin Van Buren, who was a party man through and through. Van Buren, as part of a new generation of leaders, rejected the Founding generation's negative view of political parties. For him, parties were a legitimate instrument of government and the principled struggle of opposing parties helped advance the cause of democracy. He considered patronage necessary for securing the loyalty of party men and maintaining the unity of the party organization, and expected that loyalty would be cemented by those career opportunities the party gave its adherents rather than by its ideology.[45]

Despite the increasingly brazen use of patronage by the presidents who followed Van Buren, there was little public opposition to the spoils system before the Civil War. The distribution of offices to a wider range of people was popular and usually it was only the out of office politicians who raised any objections to patronage. Once these politicians were in office themselves, they quickly abandoned their protests and forthwith gave jobs to their own backers.[46] Each president yielded to pressure from his supporters and played the patronage game. When James Buchanan, a Democrat, succeeded fellow Democrat Franklin Pierce in 1857, the country was treated to the spectacle of a president sweeping members of his own party from office. Reportedly, even William Marcy found this a bit hard to swallow. "I," he said, "certainly should never recommend the policy of pillaging my own camp."[47]

Buchanan was followed in office by Abraham Lincoln, a good party man who used patronage with the "virtuoso skill of an inveterate spoilsman" in order to weld his "heterogenous new party into an effective instrument of government."[48] Observing Lincoln, the satirist Artemus Ward was led to remark that the Union's retreat from Bull Run could be blamed on a rumor of three vacancies at the New York Custom House.[49]

However unseemly it may have been, Lincoln's use of patronage helped him in winning reelection so it could be said that patronage helped to save the Union. Still, Lincoln evidently had some qualms; after his second inauguration, he refused to replace the officeholders he had appointed in his first term, perhaps because, as he once remarked, he thought the spoils system might in time prove more dangerous to the health of the union than the rebellion itself.[50]

14

The Reform Movement

At the same time that patronage was becoming a prominent and (for the time) generally accepted feature of the national political landscape, it was also taking hold at the local level. Actually, patronage had been established in many cities and states even before the Jacksonians brought it to the federal government. By 1829 northern and western politicians, particularly in New York and Pennsylvania, had begun building party organizations with the jobs and money provided by the spoils system. Only the south, where the tradition of aristocratic rule was maintained, resisted the trend.[51] That peculiarly American institution, the "machine," had also begun to take shape by the mid-nineteenth century; the infamous William Marcy Tweed had been elected chairman of the Democratic central committee for New York County in 1860 and in 1863 he was elevated to the leadership of Tammany Hall.

Tammany was the prototype of the big city machine which also exemplified the corruption that often went hand-in-hand with machine politics. That corruption and the inefficiencies of governments run by jobholders who qualified for jobs by working a precinct, eventually fueled the growth of a movement to reform the civil service by replacing the spoils system with a merit system. Naturally, the Tammany men fought reform. To them, politics without patronage was inconceivable. As George Washington Plunkitt, a turn of the century Tammany sachem, put it, "you can't keep an organization together without patronage. Men ain't in politics for nothin'. They want to get somethin' out of it."[52]

As Plunkitt saw it, civil service reform threatened the very survival of the nation. He exclaimed:

> It is the curse of the nation. There can't be no real patriotism while it lasts. How are you goin' to interest our young men in their country if you have no offices to give them when they work for their party? Just look at things in this city today. There are ten thousand good offices, but we can't get more than a few hundred of them. How are we goin' to provide for the thousands of men who worked for the Tammany ticket? It can't be done. These men were full of patriotism a short time ago. They expected to be servin' their city, but when we tell them that we can't place them, do you think their patriotism is goin' to last? Not much. They say: "What's the use of workin' for your country anyhow? There's nothin' in the game." And what can they do? I don't know, but I'll tell you what I do know. I know more than one young man in past years who worked for the ticket and was just overflowin' with

patriotism, but when he was knocked out by the civil service humbug he got to hate his country and became an Anarchist.

This ain't no exaggeration. I have good reason for sayin' that most of the Anarchists in this city today are men who ran up against civil service examinations. Isn't it enough to make a man sour on his country when he wants to serve it and won't be allowed unless he answers a lot of fool questions about the number of cubic inches of water in the Atlantic and the quality of sand in the Sahara desert? There was once a bright young man in my district who tackled one of these examinations. The next I heard of him he had settled down in Herr Most's saloon smokin' and drinkin' beer and talkin' socialism all day. Before that time he had never drank anything but whiskey. I knew what was comin' when a young Irishman drops whiskey and takes to beer and long pipes in a German saloon. That young man is today one of the wildest Anarchists in town. And just to think! He might be a patriot but for that cussed civil service.[53]

Unfortunately for them, the Plunkitts of the world did not understand that their calculating and materialistic view of the nature of patriotism had helped their enemies—the advocates of "snivel service" reform.[54] This reform movement drew support from many quarters for many different reasons. The 1883 Congress which passed the Pendleton Act establishing a national merit system did so primarily for political reasons. The Republicans feared that their losses in the 1882 congressional elections presaged a loss in the 1884 presidential election and were anxious to give tenure to the government workers they had put in place.[55] The Democrats in Congress accepted the Republican payrollers in return for eliminating the kickbacks these payrollers contributed to the party. Probably, there were also some politicians who realized that the battle over spoils could shatter a party's unity. As Jefferson ruefully remarked, every appointment created nine enemies and one ingrate.[56]

Many businessmen supported reform because they hoped that it would eliminate the disruption wrought by the constant turnover of workers and would insure a more qualified and better disciplined workforce. Businessmen increasingly needed efficient government operations. They were, for example, disturbed by the wasteful, incompetent operations of some post offices. In New York City a newly appointed postmaster who was sent in to clean up the organization was appalled to find that some "400 to 600 neglected bags of mail were scattered throughout the building."[57]

Some of the professionals—newspaper editors, lawyers, doctors, clergymen and professors—who were the leaders of the reform

16

movement supported it because they resented their own loss of influence and prestige in the Gilded 'Age. By attacking patronage, they could weaken the parties and take the reins of power away from the lower classes and the Irish bosses. However, the major force propelling civil service reform was moral outrage at the greedy excesses of the spoilsmen. Even in Jackson's day patronage had been tainted by corruption. To cite one infamous example, in 1837 Samuel Swartwout, who had been named Collector of the Customs in New York by Jackson, retired from office and sailed to Europe. Investigators from the Treasury Department discovered that more than one and a quarter million dollars was missing; this sum was equivalent to 5 percent of the entire United States budget for a year.[58] The corruption of the urban machine was perhaps best symbolized by the 65% cut that William Marcy Tweed demanded from contractors hired to work on the New York County Courthouse. After thirteen years of construction and the expenditure of the then astronomical sum of thirteen million dollars, the courthouse was still unfinished in 1871 when a muckraking campaign by the *New York Times* brought down the Tweed ring.[59]

While Boss Tweed went to jail, his spirit lived on. Plunkitt, who rose from butcher boy to millionaire, bragged that he "had grown rich in politics" through "honest graft." He declared, "I seen my opportunities and I took 'em." Honest graft, as opposed to "dishonest graft," involves a political insider making money by trading on his knowledge. If, for example, Plunkitt was tipped off that the city was going to build a new bridge, he'd go out and buy as much property as he could in the area that would have to be used for the approaches. "Later on," he said, "I sell at my own price and drop some more money in the bank."[60]

The reform bill adopted in 1883 did not interfere directly with the machines and their graft, but it did begin the process of taking the control of government jobs away from party organizations. A bipartisan Civil Service Commission, its members appointed by the president and confirmed by the Senate, was created to supervise hiring. Individuals would not be hired on the basis of their party loyalties, but on the basis of their merit as measured by open, competitive exams. The exams were supposed to be practical in character rather than academic; applicants were not to be quizzed about ancient Greek history or the poetry of Wordsworth. Like the British civil service on which it was modeled, the American service was supposed to be politically neutral. No one was to be removed for partisan reasons or forced to do political work. The bill also contained provisions designed to end the system of political assessments which had entered national politics at the same time as the spoils system. Workers who owed their jobs to the party were expected to contribute a percentage of their salaries, often 2 percent, to the national party and sometimes another percentage to state or local party units. Supposedly, Lincoln himself had once written to a payroller reminding him to make his contribution. Although the parties sometimes tried to represent these contributions as voluntary, employees learned there were penalties for not paying. A Virginia postmaster who paid his assessment with a Confederate bill lost his job; when his neighbors expressed sympathy for him, the post office was closed.[61]

After Pendleton

The passage of the Pendleton Act hardly signified total victory for reform. Initially only 13,924 positions, about 11 percent of the total, in the federal government were covered by the provisions of the act. However, the numbers included in the merit system gradually increased as successive presidents used the power the law gave them to extend coverage to new groups of jobs, a process known as "blanketing in." Generally, as a president was about to leave office, he would extend the protections of civil service to those positions his partisan appointees filled. He would thereby preserve those jobs for his party and his supporters since the law excused individuals already doing a job from taking the exams required of new appointees. The incumbents who had gotten their jobs through patronage were allowed to keep those jobs *and* enjoy the freedom from political removal provided by the Pendleton Act for competitive positions. At times presidents also extended merit status to a limited number of positions which required technical training or other expertise. Such jobs as weather bureau scientist or doctor on an Indian reservation were unlikely to be of much use to the party anyway. At the same time that they were "blanketing in" jobs, some presidents were also removing others from the protective umbrella of civil service. The Pendleton Act gave the president this option and several presidents used it to increase their store of patronage jobs. Hard core reformers despaired, but there was little public outcry after 1883 as the public had largely lost interest in the subject of civil service.[62]

All in all, because the fate of reform was left in the hands of the partisan politicians in Congress and the White House, the progress of the merit system was slow and uneven. Seventeen years after the Pendleton Act was passed, almost 95,000 positions were covered by civil service rules and were filled through the examination system, but there were still more than 110,000 positions outside the system which could be used for patronage.[63] The reform movement itself languished and even adherents, once in office, sometimes deserted the cause. For example, when Josiah Quincy, a founder of the National Civil Service League became assistant secretary of state in the second Cleveland administration, he replaced Republican consular officials with men from his own Democratic party. Questioned by other reformers, he "frankly admitted that he had removed former and appointed new United States consuls at a rate more rapid than even before" and confessed that "as far as he was aware, a similar policy of rapid changes had been carried out in all non-competitive positions of other departments." Cleveland, who had wooed reformers when he was running for office, also found spoils useful in bargaining with Congress. As presidents had since the days of Jackson, he gave control of jobs to congressmen in exchange for their support.[64] No president, not even Theodore Roosevelt, who had served on the Civil Service Commission and been a stalwart of reform or the moralistic political science professor Woodrow Wilson, was able to resist the temptation to use patronage as a political tool. As a result, when Franklin Delano Roosevelt became president, there were still approximately 100,000 positions, representing 20 percent of the total federal employment, which were not classified.

Of all the American presidents, it is FDR, not Jackson, who deserves to be known as the King of Spoils. On taking office, Roosevelt mounted a patronage operation of unprecedented scale. Conveniently, the 100,000 non-civil service jobs which did not require examinations had been listed in a Congressional publication formally titled *Positions not Under Civil Service*, but informally known as the Plum Book. Postmaster James Farley, the patronage chief, was able to make use of these jobs and of another 100,000 positions which were subsequently exempted from civil service in the many agencies created as part of the New Deal. The proportion of merit jobs continued to decline during Roosevelt's entire first term. By 1936 there were almost 400,000 patronage jobs (60 percent of the total number of federal jobs) at the president's disposal. Roosevelt, the master politician, astutely used this cache of jobs in his dealings with Congress. He "rewarded and punished to support his social program and to bring together the discordant party he had inherited."[65]

In light of its massive dimensions, it is not surprising that there was some corruption and a good deal of inefficiency in the New Deal patronage operation. However, a great many of the people who entered government service were highly trained, very competent and dedicated. As Paul Van Riper notes, "The great influx of personnel into the federal government in the thirties contained a smaller than usual proportion of ex-precinct workers, party hacks and unemployables." This was, no doubt, a reflection of the fact that Roosevelt and his inner circle, while willing to deal with the local party organizations, were not primarily interested in helping the organizations, but in achieving the goals of the New Deal. Theirs was a different kind of patronage, an "intellectual and ideological patronage" and it attracted people who believed in the president and the New Deal. One New Dealsman called FDR's system "a kind of Phi Beta Kappa version of Tammany Hall."

Congress was a willing partner in all this until the 1938 elections. Opposition to the patronage operation had been building for some time. The League of Women Voters began a campaign against it in 1934; other good government groups followed suit and there were pamphlets published and hearings held. By 1936 a Gallup poll found that 88% of the public supported giving jobs to those who got the highest grades on civil service exams; only 12 percent wanted jobs to go to those who helped put their party in office. For all the good it did him, Alf Landon came out in favor of merit principles in the 1936 presidential campaign. The turning point in Congressional attitudes clearly came in 1938 when FDR tried to use his control of patronage to unseat Democrats who had not backed him in the court-packing fracas. Although the president failed to influence the primary results, Congress came to the realization that patronage had become a presidential tool which could be used against it. Led by the Chairman of the House Civil Service Committee, Richard Ramspeck of Georgia, Congress began to extend civil service coverage in the federal government and even in state and local governments through the device of requiring that all employees working for federally funded welfare programs had to be included in a state merit system. Since FDR was sensitive to public opinion, he went along. Besides, by 1939 the expansion of government was nearly finished and there weren't many new jobs being created. Later, Roosevelt "blanketed in" most of the remaining civil service exempt positions in order to protect his appointees.

Congress struck a more telling blow against the presidency when it passed the Hatch Acts of 1939 and 1940. These made it illegal for virtually all federal employees, whether or not they were under civil service, to engage in partisan activities including campaigning, fund raising and running for party or public office. Only top level policymakers were excluded from the Hatch prohibitions. The 1940 Act also "Hatched in" state and local employees whose salaries were paid, even if only partially, by the federal government. They too were forbidden to take part in partisan politics. With the passage of the Hatch Acts, the president was denied access to thousands of potential campaign workers.

Through the years the Hatch Acts have withstood political and constitutional challenges. Twice, the Supreme Court has rejected arguments that the Acts violate the First Amendment rights of federal employees. On the political front, Congress has made some minor changes, but repeated attempts to repeal the Acts have failed. President Bush vetoed one of the more recent repeal bills on the grounds that it would lead to a repoliticization of the civil service.

Presidents and Patronage

Because there are several separate merit systems and different categories of government employees, it is impossible to give an exact figure, but it's quite clear that over 99 percent of the approximately three million federal employees are covered by a merit system. This leaves the president with much less patronage than many of his predecessors had. The report of the National Commission on the Public Service chaired by former Federal Reserve chief Paul Volcker speaks of 3,000 presidential appointees.[66] Bradley Patterson Jr. in his authoritative book on the White House staff, says that as of early 1988, the president's "patronage universe" included almost 6,300 positions. This number is misleading, however, because it includes 860 federal judgeships, but no president gets to make all of these lifetime appointments. The president's patronage operation, the Office of Presidential Personnel, actually only concerns itself with 5,000 available positions, some 1,500 of which are part-time (many unpaid) on boards and commissions.[67]

While the number of political appointees in the federal government appears to have been on the increase since 1978, at most a few hundred positions have been added[68] and in an absolute sense the patronage available to the president is very limited. The Volcker Commission and many other public administration experts have complained that even 3,000 presidential appointees are too many and Volcker wants the number cut by at least a third. The Commission points out that "new governments in Britain, France or Germany operate with fewer than 100 new appointees, and yet often implement more sweeping policy changes than in the United States" and argues that the US government would operate more effectively and efficiently if it followed the European example.[69] There is considerable debate in academic and policy-making circles about the impact political appointees have on administration, the proper relationship between political and career executives, and the uses presidents can and should make of their appointees to control the bureaucracy and influence policy.[70] Whatever the merits of the various sides in that debate, it is clear that from a political standpoint the president's patronage today is too small to be of major importance in the struggle between the parties. There simply aren't enough jobs for the president to be able to build a nationwide political machine or significantly affect local party organizations. Since FDR no president has really tried to go down that road. Recent presidents have all appointed more members of their own party than of the opposition party and the White House personnel office has had some sort of political clearance process in which party officials and congressmen are consulted, but the party has not controlled presidential patronage and partisan concerns have to compete with other presidential priorities.[71] Pressures from party leaders are only one of the many that are brought to bear in the appointment process. There is buffeting from "Congress, organized special interests . . . prominent friends and supporters of the president—and at times even foreign governments."[72] Those in charge of presidential personnel operations speak with feeling of the "tidal wave of people" coming at them, of having people "crammed down their throats" and of tiptoeing through a "minefield."[73] This may sound like Lincoln complaining of being besieged by jobseekers, but there is a crucial difference. In the words of Hugh Heclo:

> It is important to recognize the difference between the political executive realm that has evolved in recent times and the classic system of nineteenth-century political patronage. . . . Political patronage was a method of oiling the gears of party machinery through the mass distribution of public jobs. This jobbery, which so bedeviled nineteenth-century presidents, focused on the large number of routine tasks in custom houses, post offices, and so on which ordinary party supporters could be expected to fill. The modern in-and-outer system is different. To be sure, one can on occasion find tinges of old-fashioned jobbery in Washington—the presidential campaign worker whose only claim to gainful public employment is past service as a faithful go-for, the displaced congressman in need of maintaining his lifestyle, the benighted relative of some important personage, or the friend of a friend. But these instances are only the pale imitation of a real patronage system. They are treated as a necessary evil by presidential personnel managers, and the positions are sometimes referred to disparagingly as "jobs for slobs."[74]

Today's appointees, the in-and-outers, may belong to the president's party, but they are not professional party politicians. They are called on to play "challenging roles as policy managers and administrative leaders"; their qualifications are "technocratic"[75] and, especially in the

Reagan administration, ideological. Statistics indicate that Reagan appointed fewer members of the opposition party than any of the other last ten presidents.[76] Yet he did so for ideological and programmatic, rather than partisan, reasons. The Reagan administration was looking first and foremost for people ideologically committed to Reaganism and loyal to Reagan. Even competence and professional credentials took a back seat. As long-time Reagan political operative Lyn Nofziger explained, "We have told members of the Cabinet we expect them to help us place people who are competent. . . . As far as I'm concerned any one who supported Reagan is competent."[77] Most of these people turned out to be Republicans because parties are now more divided on ideological lines and conservatives attracted to Reagan are almost always Republicans.

When George Bush succeeded Reagan, he reverted in part to Jimmy Carter's practice of allowing the Cabinet secretaries to fill slots in their own departments. The new President did look for people loyal to him, but he was much less concerned with ideological purity than Reagan. Moreover, even though Bush had once been the national chairman of the Republican party, he was not particularly sensitive to the party's interests. For example, he failed to take full advantage of the opportunity to use the hundreds of thousands of temporary census jobs as patronage. The 1978 Civil Service Reform Act had put these jobs under Civil Service for the first time in United States history, but the law had a loophole allowing the president to waive the civil service requirement. Jimmy Carter had signed a waiver for the 1980 census, reportedly in order to use the jobs as a weapon in his fight for the nomination against Senator Edward Kennedy. In 1989 Congressional Republicans, hungry for some patronage, repeatedly asked the Bush White House for the waiver, but in the words of one of the legislators, there was a "total and complete screw-up." The President didn't sign the waiver order until two thirds of the 2,700 managers (who would be responsible for hiring 300,000 to 400,000 door-to-door census takers) had been hired through civil service.[78]

Patronage at the State and Local Level

Once the Pendleton Act was passed, civil service reformers turned their attention to the states and cities where patronage abounded. The bosses whom the reformers detested depended on local patronage even more than on the federal variety; local jobs were more "numerous, lucrative and regularly assessed. The New York County clerk, for instance, retained as part of his annual salary $80,000 in fees."[79]

Most politicians were not overly enthusiastic about civil service reform, but in the wake of public emotion aroused by the Garfield assassination, bills modeled after Pendleton were passed in New York and Massachusetts. A number of cities including Albany, Buffalo, New York, Chicago, Boston, and Seattle also adopted merit systems although these often only covered a portion of the municipalities' employees—usually clerks, police and firefighters.[80]

However, this first civil service movement was led by the "gentlemen reformers" of the National Civil Service Reform League. It did not really have mass support, and reform began to lose steam almost as soon as Pendleton was enacted. A few years later, in the early part of the twentieth century, reform was revived as part of the Progressives' agenda. Some cities, counties and states like Wisconsin became strongholds, but once again the movement stalled. By 1935 only nine states had civil service systems. Then the picture began to change. In that year of 1935 the federal government launched Social Security. The historic law that created the Social Security system also gave the states grants for a variety of welfare and employment assistance programs. However, the states proved incapable of handling the administrative burdens thrust upon them. There were complaints of waste and inefficiency and of the "political use of employees and welfare recipients." As a result, in 1939 Congress amended the Social Security Act to require that states establish merit systems as a condition of receiving federal funds. As has generally been the case in American history, the national legislators did not act out of some moralistic urge, but to protect their own political interests. Many congressmen were disturbed that some of the states' governors were using federal patronage and money to increase their own power. In particular, the Senate was outraged by one governor who first collected 2 percent of the salaries of the state employees and then, a week before the election, sent these employees from the state capital to their home counties to promote the governor in his primary battle against the incumbent senator.[81]

After 1939 dozens of federal programs included provisions requiring merit systems of grant recipients. Some states responded to the federal mandates by putting all of their employees under civil service. Other states established dual systems, continuing their old patronage practices, but creating a merit system just for workers in federally funded programs. Recent figures indicate that thirty-five states now have comprehensive merit systems; in the other fifteen there are partial systems. In addition, the Hatch Act covers all of the employees in programs getting federal money. All of the states have also enacted their own "Little Hatch Acts" although thirty-three of these are not as strict as the federal version.[82]

At the same time that Washington was prodding the states to adopt civil service systems, the states were pushing local governments to do the same. Because of these pressures and other factors, including local reform activities, most larger (over 50,000) and many smaller cities and towns now have civil service systems for at least some of their employees. Counties throughout the nation have also established civil service systems although they have lagged behind the cities and states.[83]

If the statistics on merit systems were the whole story, there wouldn't be any reason to write a book on patronage. The statistics, clearly, only tell part of the story.[84] Many of the merit systems are incomplete and/or riddled with loopholes. Even when a civil service law looks good on paper, it is often evaded (in ways described in later chapters). In the real world, there are no foolproof systems.

Unquestionably, patronage has been on the decline and the party machines which depended on patronage to reward their followers are fading. It is also true that civil service reform has been a major cause of the decline of patronage and of the machines (although only one of many causes as will be seen in the chapters on Chicago's Democratic machine and Nassau County's Republican one). Still, even with civil service reform, elements of machine politics, including patronage, persist. The disappearance of cohesive, centralized, hierarchical party organizations like Tammany Hall doesn't necessarily mean that machine politics, in which jobs and other material incentives are exchanged for political support, has also disappeared.[85] For example, Tammany Hall and its last boss Carmine DeSapio may be certifiably dead, *but* patronage has lived on through successive "reform" regimes. In 1965 John Lindsay came into the New York mayor's office denouncing power brokers and patronage. He soon found that his image as a good government type may have helped him win office, but was little help in building the power he needed to govern and to get reelected. He turned to preferments, i.e. favors, particularly tax abatements, zoning variances, purchasing and consulting contracts, and to patronage jobs. During his first term he increased the number of exempt jobs from 1,500 to 12,800; in his second term he tripled the number of provisional employees (who were hired without taking any exams) to almost 30,000.[86] Defending his actions, he said, "You've got to have people in government who are politically smart. . . . This means they have to understand that part of politics is the art of obligation."[87] In order to win reelection, Lindsay even made a pact with the devil, forming alliances with the Brooklyn, Queens and Manhattan Democratic machines (he was a Republican in 1965), promising them patronage in his second term. In addition to the standard city jobs, they were also to get jobs (and funds) in the federally sponsored anti-poverty programs of that era.[88]

Abe Beame, who followed Lindsay into City Hall, made no pretense of being anything but an old-fashioned organization politician. All appointments which weren't filled by examination had to be cleared through his office and were then distributed directly by the Democratic county organizations. His aide explained that the mayor needed patronage to "revitalize" the Democratic party; "there has to be some inducement for people to go out and ring doorbells."[89] Subsequently, when New York's fiscal crisis forced Beame to fire many lower level patronage appointees, Democratic clubs reported a decline in attendance and the mayor was weakened politically.[90]

When Edward Koch, a liberal congressman with excellent reform credentials, succeeded Beame, it was—to quote Yogi Berra—"deja vu all over again." Koch had first become prominent as the man who had dethroned Carmine DeSapio by defeating the Tammany boss in a Democratic Assembly District leadership election. Although patronage was not a major issue in the 1977 mayoral contest, Koch had criticized Beame for being tied to the party organizations, and once in office the new mayor proclaimed that his administration would be different from the previous one. As Koch tells it, at his first City Hall meeting with the Democratic leaders he said:

> I want everybody to know . . . that my government will not deal in patronage with respect to jobs in government. . . . I'm happy to receive your recommendations, but I will make the determination as to who gets the positions, and will fill jobs on the basis of who's best irrespective of where they come from. I'm happy to have your resumes for the purposes of interviewing people, and I will interview them. But the ultimate selection will be on the basis of who's the most qualified.

Koch says that when he entered office, he also told his commissioners that they could pick whoever they "think is the best" for their subordinates as long as they didn't discriminate. He warned them:

> Don't call me when you hire and don't call me when you fire. . . . I don't want you ever to be in the position that if I find fault with you you will say to me that I prevented you from doing your job because I sent you palookas whom you had to hire. If you have palookas on your staff, they're there because you put them on.[91]

Koch insists that he remained true to his hiring policies and that he "spoiled the system" for the party bosses by making appointments "without regard to the political considerations of the county leaders" (although he says he did let the bosses save face by taking credit for appointments). Playing the martyr, Koch has self-righteously proclaimed that his principled stance on patronage hurt him in his losing bid for the New York governorship in 1982 when "there were few volunteers, and the best people who had been appointed by me in government didn't come out in large numbers to help." Not only didn't the commissioners "feel obliged to work" in the campaign; they didn't "feel obliged to urge others who worked for them to work in the campaign."[92]

Koch has conceded that he knew his commissioner made deals with the county chairmen, but has maintained that he "wasn't part of the practice."[93] Seasoned observers of New York politics agree that Koch successfully insulated himself from his commissioners' patronage, but believe that he allowed patronage to continue to fulfill his part of the bargain he made with the county leaders he once denounced. Both academics and journalists[94] think Koch first reached an accommodation with the county leaders in 1977 and became more tightly allied with them over the years. By his third and last inauguration in 1986 Koch took the oath of office on the steps of City Hall flanked by Donald Manes, the Queens party head and Stanley Friedman, head of the Bronx organization and emissaries of the Brooklyn boss Meade Esposito (who was vacationing in Florida). One of these emissaries was Anthony Ameruso whom Koch had appointed Commissioner of Transportation over the objections of his own blue-ribbon search committee.

Within a few months of the triumphant inaugural, the Koch administration was engulfed in a series of scandals created by the actions of the three county leaders and of men such as Ameruso whom they had placed in various "pockets of patronage" in the city's government.[95] Ultimately, a number of these patronage appointees, as well as Meade Esposito and Stanley Friedman (whom Koch had once described as "one of the smartest, ablest, most loyal people I know"[96]) received jail sentences for their corrupt activities. Donald Manes escaped jail by killing himself. Knowing he was going to be indicted, Manes (during a lull in a telephone conversation with his psychiatrist) seized a kitchen knife and plunged it into his heart. With Manes' suicide, the power he had accumulated dissipated. No longer could you get, as New York Attorney General Robert Abrams once observed, "one-stop service" in Queens; whatever you wanted—a city contract, a judgeship, a job in government, a cable franchise—you "went to Donald Manes."[97]

As indictment followed indictment and the sensational trial of Koch's good friend Bess Meyerson, his Cultural Affairs Commissioner, wound down, Koch was subjected to the further indignity of a state investigation. On a tip from a whistleblower the New York State Commission on Government Integrity which was headed by John Feerick, the Dean of Fordham University's School of Law, began to look at City Hall personnel operations. The commission was particularly interested in the activities of Joseph DeVincenzo, a special assistant to the mayor with close ties to the party organization who was said to be operating a patronage mill out of City Hall. The commission conducted an extensive investigation and held public hearings in January of 1989 and again in April when Koch himself was questioned for more than two hours. Although Koch denied that he knew about or had in any way encouraged the patronage operation, the Commission concluded that his administration was responsible for "shocking" patronage abuses. It laid out the evidence in a report to the governor titled " 'Playing Ball' with City Hall: A Case Study of Political Patronage in New York City."[98]

The abuses could occur because New York's civil service system had loopholes and, most importantly, did not cover all of the city's jobs. During the Koch years both the overall number of city employees and the proportion of employees who were in one way or another hired outside the civil service system increased. By 1988 there were more than 350,000 city employees; of these about 150,000 worked for mayoral agencies and were directly under the control of the mayor. Almost one third of these mayoral employees were catagorized as discretionary, meaning they could be hired without having to take a civil service exam. In the mayoral agencies there were 30,000 provisional employees and another 2,000 working in jobs to which they had been provisionally promoted; in addition there were 12,000 employees in noncompetitive slots and 750 in exempt classifications. The number of provisionals was extraordinarily high and it appeared that the rule limiting provisional appointees to nine months had been widely flouted.

When Abe Beame was mayor there were only 10,000 discretionary employees, representing about 10 percent of those in the mayoral agencies. It is clear that between 1978 when Koch took office and the investigation in 1988-89, the potential pool of patronage workers had grown considerably.

Virtually any personnel action affecting mayoral agency employees—hiring, firing, promotion, awarding raises—had to be reviewed and approved by DeVincenzo in the Mayor's Office. Agencies couldn't act without a letter from DeVincenzo, commonly called a

"Joe D. letter." Beginning in April 1983, the agencies also were required (by a mayoral directive) to notify DeVincenzo's office in writing of any vacancies and to give that office at least 10 working days to refer candidates to them. If for some reason the agency didn't give the job to the referral, it had to submit a written explanation to the mayor's office.

Understandably, the mayoral agencies were very sensitive to Joe D.'s wishes. The departments learned to "play ball" with the Mayor's Office. When an agency had a vacancy, it didn't post or advertise the opening; instead, it informed the Mayor's Office. The Office would forward a list of candidates, many of them referred by political figures; sometimes there would even be a notation on the list indicating the candidate's sponsor. In at least one agency which the Commission investigated, the only people hired for certain types of positions were Mayor's Office candidates. In other cases an agency that cooperated with DeVincenzo and usually hired the referrals would occasionally be allowed to hire someone it wanted for the job. or, the agency might be permitted to "reject some (City Hall) candidates in favor of other candidates from City Hall." Officials from the Department of Transportation testified that they "could and did reject a City Hall candidate who may have 'reek(ed) of alcohol' or 'look(ed) like a bum.' " There were times though when the agencies had to find a place for a referral even if there were no vacancies and the agency had to create a job for the "City Hall Special." Once hired the "must" had to be treated with kid gloves. A Department of Transportation official described these people as being "like bad pennies" that the agency "couldn't get rid of." Another told the committee he particularly remembered a "must" who was behaving very strangely:

> My staff in Appointments and Promotions came out and said that this guy is not too straight, he was rambling and babbling, and I went to the Commissioner and I said, "You know, this guy is a problem, but I understood it to be important to City Hall that he be put on, and he told me to hold off for a while and he would check it out, and at a certain point, he said, "Look, we have to find something for him," and we put him in the Parking Violations Bureau.
>
> After about two weeks, I got a call from them that he was very disruptive, and I went to the Commissioner again and I said, "This guy is very bad, he's obviously not all there," and again I was told . . . that we should give him another chance somewhere else, and we put him in Ferries for a while, and I think he fell down a ferry hatch. . . . He was on Workmen's Compensation. I don't know what happened to him after that.

Between 1983 and 1986 DeVincenzo utilized an operation called the Talent Bank as a conduit for political referrals. The Talent Bank, which was created by the Mayor in 1983, was supposed to be an affirmative action hiring program to bring more women and minorities into the city's work force. Because of its mission, it attracted a young, idealistic New Yorker of Puerto Rican descent named Nydia Padilla-Barham. In 1985 the Yale graduate went to work for Joe D. as the head of the Talent Bank.

Ms. Padilla soon began to learn the truth about the Talent Bank. She discovered that the Bank had no recruiter on its staff and had made almost no effort to recruit minorities and women. So she sent her first proposal to DeVincenzo recommending that a recruiter be hired and that the Talent Bank be publicized and opened up to the general public. His answer was a "sharp no." He told Padilla that the "real purpose (of the Talent Bank) is . . . these political resumes that are submitted to us" and that her "main goal" was to "follow up on resumes referred by political figures to make sure they were referred to vacancies."

Koch had established the Talent Bank after the 1982 gubernatorial primary. The Democratic county organizations had helped him then and it seemed that he was paying them back by providing jobs for their supporters through the Talent Bank. The program's operations were all designed to serve this political purpose. The Bank's computers were programmed to keep track of the progress made in placing people with important political sponsors. The programmer told the Feerick Commission that DeVincenzo was particularly concerned with knowing the referral "source." She said he told her he wanted "to be able to see by referral source who got a job and who didn't, how many jobs people had gotten by referral source." For convenience, the computer-generated lists of pending and hired candidates were gathered into a large three-ring binder known as the Black Book. For a time the Talent Bank's files were also color coded with red folders used for the "hottest" or most important sources whose candidates were to be given top priority, pink for political referrals from less important figures and green for "street" referrals, i.e. people who walked in off the street or sent unsolicited letters asking for jobs. The Talent Bank's staff was under constant pressure from DeVincenzo's office to place the hot candidates and the staff, in turn, pushed the departments to take these people. When lists were sent to the hiring departments, the candidates would be ranked in order of their political priority. In fact one can track the Koch's administration's relationships with the various county leaders through the Talent Bank lists; the organizations close to Koch had the most candidates with the highest priority.

Strictly speaking, the Talent Bank's operations were not illegal; the Supreme Court had not yet ruled that political hiring is unconstitutional. But, without a doubt, the Koch administration would be embarrassed if its cynical manipulations were to become public. When the scandals involving Manes and other county leaders close to Koch began to break, someone decided to get rid of the paper trail. Early in 1986, in one day of frantic activity, the Talent Bank staff acting on instructions from James Hein, Joe D.'s assistant, went through the files, tearing up and throwing out anything that mentioned referral sources. They also destroyed the colored file folders and removed the referral source data from the computer files. The staff was warned to be quiet about all these goings-on; Hein told them it should be off the record, "a day like it never happened." Presumably, the Talent Bank offices didn't have any sophisticated shredding equipment because Hein took the garbage bags containing the discarded material home with him to Yonkers to dispose of them there. (He later explained to the Commission that the office garbage wasn't scheduled to be picked up until the following day and he didn't want "those papers flying all over Chambers Street the next morning.")

Padilla testified that after the purging DeVincenzo showed greater concern about placing women and minorities in jobs and the Talent Bank's dismal record in that respect did improve. However, she found that things gradually slipped back to the way they were before, and with some trepidation, she quit. Soon after the Feerick staff began to look at the city's contracting and personnel practices. Essentially, the staff was engaged in a fishing expedition, talking to dozens of present and past officials. Padilla was scheduled for one of these routine meetings. She decided to blow the whistle on the Koch administration and for the first time the Commission learned about the Koch patronage and the Talent Bank and the attempt to cover it up.

During the investigation that followed both Hein and DeVincenzo were questioned. At the public hearings they both denied that there had been any patronage operation and DeVincenzo insisted that the "alleged" cover-up was merely a routine disposal of materials that were no longer needed. Joe D. insisted that he knew nothing about political referrals and couldn't "recall ever seeing any printouts with political sources on them." When questioned about the colored folders, Hein offered this explanation:

Q. And when you were in charge of the Talent Bank, did you understand that there was a scheme for the colored folders?
A. No, there was no scheme.

31

Q. How about a plan?

A. No.

Q. Any resume was just put in any folder?

A. That's correct. Actually, what happened, they had no meaning at all. The clerks in the office were tired of filing just the same drab folders.

Little wonder that after hearing Hein and DeVincenzo, one of the commission members—Cyrus Vance, the former Secretary of State—commented that the testimony "sounded like Alice in Wonderland" and was "not credible." DeVincenzo was later indicted on eleven counts of perjury; patronage may not be a crime, but lying under oath is.[99] No legal action was taken against DeVincenzo's boss, but the Commission report singled out Koch for blame, saying that the "ultimate responsibility belongs to the Mayor." If the Mayor really did not intend to use the Talent Bank for funnelling patronage and was serious about being committed to affirmative action, he failed to communicate this to his aides or to monitor their performance adequately.

Ironically, the free rein given to the county leaders by Koch helped to bring about their downfall (and his). By 1989 when Koch was fighting his losing battle in the Democratic primary, the bosses were gone and their organizations so weakened as to be "irrelevant." They couldn't help Koch or keep their black lieutenants from supporting his opponent.[100]

Koch is gone from the mayor's office, but there is no reason to believe that patronage has also been swept out. The new mayor, David Dinkins, is a product of clubhouse politics. He has held patronage jobs and has never expressed any opposition to patronage. In this he is no different from most other New York politicians, whose only complaint about patronage has generally been that they aren't getting enough of it. Neither the media nor the public was energized by the Integrity Commission report. Dean Feerick lamented that, "Nobody's done enough," while Cyrus Vance counselled patience: "This is not for the short-winded. One has to keep after it."[101]

Patronage Today

It has always been difficult to track patronage. Many Americans see it as part of the seamy side of the nation's political life so that outside the bastions of old-time machine-type politics most officials don't like to admit openly that they are using patronage. Since Pendleton the tendency has been more and more to mask patronage. In the early 1970s (before any of the Supreme Court decisions against patronage) Martin

Tolchin of the *New York Times* and his wife Susan, a political science professor, tried to measure the amount of patronage available to party leaders. Only 26 percent of their questionnaires were returned.[102] Now that the Supreme Court has declared political hiring and firing in low-level jobs to be unconstitutional, it is doubtful that any party officials would tell a researcher how many jobs they controlled. One can find statistics on the numbers of municipal and state employees who are and are not under civil service, but these figures do not by themselves tell one how many actually got their jobs through patronage. As the case studies in this book reveal, civil service jobs can be used for patronage. Conversely, not all exempt jobs are part of the patronage universe. Various factors, including the technical requirements of a job, may lead a mayor or governor to appoint nonpolitical professionals to some positions even though they could legally give the jobs out on a political basis.

If all of this didn't make for enough difficulties, one also has to reckon with the fact that the states and cities comprise only a fraction of the total number of governments in the United States. There are more than 83,000 separate units of government in the nation ranging from school districts to counties to a host of special districts. Most of these operate in obscurity; many are run by elected boards which have the final say over personnel policies; many have no civil service system and even when they do, the systems are poorly monitored. It would be extremely naive to think that all of the more than 10 million people employed at the local level got their jobs solely on the basis of merit.[103] Occasionally, the curtains part and the public gets a glimpse of the nepotism and political patronage in these governments. In one dramatic case involving an elected community school board in Queens, New York, the superintendent of the district working with investigators secretly recorded his conversations with the board members. He took this unusual step because he was outraged when the board's leaders had tried to bribe him, telling him that if he were a "good boy" and allowed them to take charge of appointments and personnel policies, his contract would be renewed and he could have a long career as superintendent. In one recorded conversation, the board treasurer is heard saying that he is a "political leader" and has "to make sure his people got jobs." He then gave the superintendent, Colman Genn, a list of eleven teaching aides and paraprofessionals he wanted hired. In another conversation this man told Genn to set up a $42,000-a-year job for a Republican politician. According to Genn, the board wasted hundreds of thousands of its $96 million dollar yearly budget; he said he knew of at least 45 paraprofessionals, teaching aides and assistant principals who were collectively paid over $80,000 a month even though they didn't have a "real assignment." James Gill, the chairman of the Joint Commission on Integrity in the Public Schools, commented that the evidence produced by Genn proved that "some community school boards had replaced political clubhouses as patronage dispensaries." He might have added that uncovering and eliminating this patronage will not be easy. In the Queens case, the school board was suspended and more than fifty employees were dismissed. However, whistleblower Genn was subjected to so much harassment that a year after the investigation he quit the school system saying, "I feel ill at ease. I'm tense and worried that I've made a lot of enemies, that people whose toes have been stepped on will come at me in one way or another."[104]

CHAPTER 2
DOING BATTLE WITH THE
PATRONAGE ARMY

Harold Washington, the late Mayor of Chicago, liked to say he had stomped on the grave of patronage, that he went to its grave, jumped up and down and called out: "Patronage, patronage! Are you alive? And patronage didn't answer. It is dead, dead, dead."[1]

In fact, Harold Washington may have won the final battle against the Cook County Democratic Party's legendary patronage army, but as the Mayor himself acknowledged, the victory could not have occurred had it not been for a series of events set in motion by a little known Chicago lawyer named Michael Shakman. Also, the victory extended only to Chicago's traditional political-machine practices; new forms of political rewards were utilized by Mayor Washington to sustain his power base.

In 1969 Michael Shakman became a candidate for delegate to the Constitutional Convention being called to revise the Illinois Constitution. With bachelor's and master's degrees in political science, a law degree from the University of Chicago, and service on the Chicago Bar Association's special committee preparing for the convention, Shakman was well qualified for the delegate's post. However, running as an independent in Chicago, even in the liberal University of Chicago Hyde Park area, Shakman did not have a chance. He found he was competing against candidates backed by the Democratic machine's "patronage army." He reported that "many people with city jobs told me they would gladly vote for me, but they couldn't.

They had to support the party choices and work for them. They weren't free."[2]

Unable to defeat the machine at the polls, Shakman and a friend, Paul M. Lurie, filed a lawsuit challenging the constitutionality of Chicago's patronage system. They argued that their rights as candidates and voters were effectively denied when public employees were required to work for the machine candidates and to contribute a portion of their salaries to the machine war chest. In this situation, the "outs"—independents and Republicans—had little chance against the "ins."

Ironically, the first judge to hear the case was a good friend of Mayor Richard J. Daley, the machine's boss. Judge Abraham Lincoln Marovitz, who owed his position on the federal district court to Daley, dismissed Shakman's suit. However, the Seventh Circuit U.S. Court of Appeals reversed Marovitz, ruling that "the interest of candidates in an equal chance and the interests of voters in having an equally effective voice are rights secured from state action by the equal protection clause of the fourteenth amendment." When the "misuse of official power over public employees creates a substantial, perhaps massive, political effort in favor of the ins against the outs," these interests are "entitled to constitutional protection."[3]

The case went back to the District Court to begin the process of discovery. Dozens of public officials were subpoenaed, but the day before Mayor Daley's secretary at the Democratic Party County Central Committee was scheduled to give a deposition, the defendants let it be known that they were willing to negotiate. However, they demanded that Shakman broaden his suit to include Republican office holders. As Shakman wryly observed, the Democrats weren't willing to submit to "unilateral disarmament."[4]

After long, hard bargaining, Mayor Daley and a number of other government officials, including the Republican governor of Illinois, signed a consent judgment banning politically motivated firing. Employees were allowed to engage in voluntary political activity, but "compulsory or coerced" political financial contributions or activity were prohibited. Once hired, a government employee was to be "free from all compulsory political requirements in connection with his employment."[5]

Although the patronage system was dealt a blow by the 1972 decree, it remained largely intact because jobs were still filled on a political basis. Shakman continued, therefore, to press his suit. In 1979, Federal Judge Nicholas Bua, who had taken over the case, ruled that patronage firing was unconstitutional because it violated both the First and the Fourteenth Amendments.[6] However, Judge Bua deferred issuing an implementing ruling in order to give the parties time to work out an appropriate remedy. Finally, in April 1983, the District Court entered a judgment permanently enjoining the defendants from engaging in political hiring and laying down some general rules to be followed in hiring. Several defendants, led by the President of the Cook County Board of Commissioners, appealed the 1979 ruling, and they refused to accept the 1983 decree. However, other defendants, including the City of Chicago, signed consent judgments accepting the order and began to work out detailed hiring plans to comply with it.[7] In 1984, the city submitted a hiring plan, and in June of 1985 the plan went into effect. By 1987, the city had been using court-approved hiring procedures for two years, and the Shakman decrees had become an accepted part of the city's landscape. Then, much to everyone's surprise, the Seventh Circuit U.S. Court of Appeals handed down a ruling on the appeal filed by the County Board. Although it had ruled in 1970 that Shakman had standing to challenge the constitutionally of patronage, the Circuit Court now found that Shakman did not have standing to challenge patronage hiring. The Court, therefore, dismissed the challenge to the appellants' hiring practices.[8]

While this Appeals Court decision (which did not affect the earlier ruling on firing) clearly permitted the County Board and the other appellants to hire on the basis of political considerations, the city was still bound by the consent decree it had signed. In February 1988, Washington's successor stunned Chicago by announcing that he was asking the Court to vacate the 1983 hiring decree. Mayor Sawyer maintained that he was merely trying to avoid paying fees awarded by the Court to Shakman's attorneys, and he promised to replace the decrees with a legislative ban on political hiring.

Apparently Sawyer didn't expect the ourcry that greeted his announcement. Facing a tough battle in the 1989 election scheduled to decide who would fill the remainder of Washington's second term, Sawyer decided to negotiate a settlement with Shakman. In June he announced that the city had agreed to drop its court challenge and abide by the hiring decree and that the Shakman attorneys accepted a reduction of $2.4 million in the legal fees to be paid them by the city. The City Council ratified the pact, approving the payment of $1 million to the Shakman lawyers.

Despite his trying to assume Harold Washington's reform mantle, Sawyer could not hold on to the Mayor's office. Taking advantage of the disarray within the African-American community which followed Washington's sudden death in November 1987, Richard M. Daley defeated Sawyer and a number of other candidates. While the new mayor was the son of the "boss" himself, he made no move to disturb the Shakman decrees. Even after he was reelected in 1991 to a full four-year term, the son showed no interest in resurrecting his father's patronage army. By then, of course, the Supreme Court had issued the Rutan decision which overrode the 1987 Seventh Circuit's reversal of Shakman. Still, Daley the younger, genuinely seemed to have accepted Shakman and was concentrating on using other tools of power.

Reform Through the Courts

As a reform Democrat[9] in a machine-dominated city, Michael Shakman could not change public policy through legislative or administrative action since the Cook County Democratic Organization controlled both the City Council and the administrative apparatus of the city. Therefore, he turned to the courts to effect reform. His suit and the decrees resulting from it are typical of a new type of litigation which began to take shape in the 1960s. Such "public law litigation" is distinguished from more traditional suits in several ways. In public law litigation, the decision-making process is more akin to that in a legislature than to typical adjudication. The judge plays much more of an "active role in shaping, organizing and facilitating the litigation." Generally, he or she will consult with the parties in drafting an order and may even ask them to prepare a draft of the decree. Outstanding consultants may also be asked for help in designing relief. Usually, extensive negotiations occur before the judge finally issues a decree. Unlike traditional orders, the public law litigation decree "seeks to adjust future behavior, not to compensate for past wrongs. It is deliberately fashioned rather than logically deduced from the nature of the legal harm suffered. It provides for a complex, ongoing regime of performance rather than a simple, one-way transfer. Finally, it prolongs and deepens, rather than terminates, the court's involvement."[10]

In the Shakman Case, the parties engaged in prolonged negotiation, and a consulting firm was eventually called in to draft a detailed hiring plan for the City of Chicago. The decree which resulted is designed to bring about fundamental changes in the city's political system by changing the way in which it hires and fires its employees. To ensure the city's compliance, the Court has remained deeply involved in the case. The city cannot revise its hiring procedures without the Court's permission, and until 1993 it must file quarterly affidavits of compliance and yearly reports of its hiring actions. It must also submit to an annual audit of its hiring practices by a Court-approved outside firm. In addition, any registered voter may go to court with complaints of city violations of the decrees.

The Shakman Case also exemplifies the public lawsuit in that it resulted in a "new partnership" between the federal judiciary and local administrators. With the growth of the administrative state since the New Deal, the courts have carved out a more active role, often becoming "directly involved in the management of public facilities."[11] In the Shakman Case the Court become intimately involved in directing the city's Department of Personnel. To the extent that the detailed hiring plan forced on the city by the Court is faithfully implemented, the Court will have brought about a major overhaul of the city's personnel and political systems.

Patronage and Personnel Under the Machine

Jobs have been the lifeblood of the Cook County Democratic Organization since the machine was begun by Anton Cermak in the early 1930s. In order to maintain itself in power the machine needed votes. To gain votes, it needed to be able to provide services in exchange for votes; to finance its service activities and pay its workers, it needed money. The key to meeting all of these needs was patronage.[12]

In the heyday of the machine during the Daley years (1955-1976) all patronage jobs were personally controlled by Richard J. Daley who was both the mayor and the party chairman. Jobs were allocated to ward and township committeemen in proportion to the individual committeeman's influence and the number of votes his ward delivered for machine candidates. In 1967 the colorful alderman and committeeman of the 25th ward, Vito Marzullo, matter-of-factly ticked off his jobs for a reporter:

> I got an assistant state's attorney, and I got an assistant attorney general. I got an electrical inspector at $10,500-a-year, and street inspectors and surveyors and a $7,900-a-year county highway inspector. I got an administrative assistant to the zoning board, and some bailiffs and some process servers and a county building inspector at $8,400-a-year. . . . I got 59 captains and they all have jobs.[13]

In all, Marzullo calculated that he had about 160 jobs which he distributed to his precinct captains and their assistants. Generally, the committeemen parcelled out the jobs they "owned" to their precinct captains on the basis of the captains' ability to garner votes. If a captain failed to deliver his precinct, he could be "viced" or fired from his job. If his failure were less serious, he might only lose some of the jobs under his control.

Clearly, workers were afraid of being viced. Richard Johnson, a lawyer for Shakman, tells of a case that was "called just before Shakman at one of the many court calls in the patronage litigation." The case "involved the sentencing of a precinct worker for vote fraud. He testified that he committed the fraud because he was afraid that otherwise he would lose his patronage job."[14]

Everyone was expected to work for the party. High level office-holders like Marzullo's assistant attorney general were excused from precinct work of the door-to-door variety, but the alderman expected them to give "service" in the form of "free legal advice to the people of the ward."[15] Job holders also had to buy tickets to various party fund-raising events and were required to contribute a percentage of their salaries to the ward organization. Generally, they were assessed between 2% and 3% of their total pay.

Patronage workers were held strictly accountable for their political performance, but not for their performance on the job. It was understood that political obligations took precedence over their job duties, and that employees with powerful political sponsors couldn't be fired. One woman who got a patronage job scrubbing floors at Cook County Hospital, said her supervisor was "surprised" when she worked hard because "in these jobs . . . it isn't necessary to work very hard. The supervisor can't fire you anyway."[16] Organization members with more clout than the cleaning woman could even get away with doing little or no work.

Friends and foes agree that Harold Washington, in the days when he was a machine worker, seldom showed up for work at his patronage job in the city's corporation counsel's office. One co-worker called him the "original ghost payroller."[17]

Job holders and their families formed a nucleus of support for the machine. Since each jobholder was expected to insure at least 10 more votes,[18] the machine went into any election with a running start of hundreds of thousands of votes. While estimates of the number of Democratic patronage jobs in Cook County vary, the party admitted in stipulation to the U.S. District Court that there were, on average, 250 patronage job holders in each of Chicago's 50 wards and that "preference in hiring of employees for over 20,000 positions" is "given to persons who have sponsorship of a local organization."[19] Other experts claim there were as many as 30,000 to 40,000 patronage-based jobs in city and county government or, sometimes, in the state and federal governments. The party even controlled some private sector jobs. Milton Rakove, a political scientist who worked inside the machine, writes of once applying for a job with Sears Roebuck, whose headquarters was then located in Chicago's 25th ward. The employment office at Sears wouldn't even give him an application until his precinct captain got a letter for Rakove from the ward's alderman. He reports that, "upon presentation of the alderman's letter, the Sears employment office promptly produced a job application for me."[20]

The organization relied on its patronage armies to win the support of voters. In part, the voters were wooed with services. As Alderman Marzullo explained to Rakove, "Anybody in the 25th [ward] needs something, needs help with his garbage, needs his street fixed, needs a lawyer for his kid who's in trouble, he goes first to the precinct captain. . . . If the captain can't deliver, that man can come to me. My house is open every day to him."[21] Even though the modern welfare state provides many of the material benefits the pre-New Deal machines distributed to their supporters, the precinct captains could still make themselves useful to the voters by finding out what they needed, communicating their needs to the proper authorities and guiding them through the bureaucratic maze. According to one committeeman, the party's primary service became one of referral. He says, "People ask, 'How do I get this? Where do I go to get that?' In some instances a letter from me helps and I never turn them down. Some people feel a letter always helps, but I think they would get what they need without it in most cases."[22] Rakove found out personally what the machine could do in the 1950s when he was a University of Chicago graduate student. At the time he was also a "full-time clerk with civil service status at the United States Post Office in Chicago, working forty hours on the night shift."

> He says that he requested a change in status at the post office to substitute clerk, so that I could work only four or five hours a night. After going through all the proper channels in the post office, I was told repeatedly by authorities that such a request could not be granted, that a regular clerk could not be reduced to a substitute mail handler, even at his request. A subsequent brief conversation with my Democratic precinct captain resulted in a note from the ward committeeman to my congressman, who was on the House of Representatives Post Office Committee, a letter from the congressman to the Postmaster of the Chicago Post Office, and a letter from the postmaster to me, notifying me of my immediate reduction to substitute mail handler.[23]

Thomas Guterbock, another University of Chicago graduate student who studied the machine in the 1970s, maintains that by that time the voters had come to expect city services as a matter of right and that support for the regular Democrats was not based on gratitude for services but on "traditional loyalties and on the local attachments of many ward residents." Party men like Marzullo and his precinct captains were intimately involved in local life and would commit "tremendous time and effort to the meetings, rallies, ceremonies, conferences and confrontations which are so much a part of local public life."[24]

One might well ask where the machine got its jobs since Chicago was ostensibly under a civil service system. Indeed Chicago was one of the first cities in the nation to adopt a "merit" system, its Civil Service Commission having been established in 1895. However, as long as the Commission was willing to cooperate with the organization, there were many ways to get around civil service requirements. Martin Kennelly, the mayor who preceded Daley, had been dumped by the machine because, among other sins, he had appointed a strong advocate of merit hiring as president of the Chicago Civil Service Commission. Committeemen were livid because the machine lost control of some 10,000 to 12,000 jobs.[25] As soon as Daley became mayor in 1955, he replaced Kennelly's man; from then on the Civil Service Commission collaborated with the organization to ensure its control of jobs. In a revealing aside, one Commissioner, confessed, "Sure I believe in the civil service, but I think the Democrats should get the jobs."[26]

The machine did its best to insure that Democrats (or, more accurately, the right Democrats) got the jobs. To begin with, the general public was kept from even knowing of the existence of job openings. The party had a list of openings on file at its headquarters, but this information was carefully guarded. Jobs were neither posted nor advertised. Then, in filling openings, the organization took full advantage of a loophole in the state civil service law which allowed a local Commission to make temporary appointments. Such an appointment could be made when there was no one available who had passed a civil service exam for the position. The Commission insured that there would be no one available by giving exams infrequently. In 1965, for example, the city of Chicago gave only 82 civil service exams while Milwaukee, with only one third as many employees, gave 360 exams. Even when exams were given, they were sometimes so difficult that no one would pass and a temporary appointment would have to be made. Or, if an outsider did pass an exam, the Commission would delay issuing the results so applicants without machine sponsorship would be certain to have accepted other jobs.[27]

Once a temporary appointment was made, it could be renewed indefinitely. Some employees held "temporary" jobs for decades. In

1974, the Civil Service Commission admitted to having 8,186 temporary workers among a total of 42,500 city employees, but other sources believe the figure was higher. The Civic Federation, a watchdog taxpayer group, claims that as many as 40 percent of all employees (other than police and fire) were at one time temporaries.[28] During Jane Byrne's administration, a consultant's study showed that there were 25,000 city workers in the civil service system (which was then called the career service). A majority of those (some 15,000) protected by civil service regulations were in sworn police and fire positions. Of the remaining employees, 900 were in exempt (generally policy-making) positions and 14,000 were in temporary or provisional slots; all were patronage workers whose hiring was done through the Mayor's Office.[29] In addition to these city employees, there were many patronage jobholders in various county and state agencies which were either not under civil service systems or which had systems that could be easily evaded. The patronage ranks also included workers in federal programs such as CETA which were not subject to merit system rules as well as the workers in private jobs controlled by the machine.

Top managers in the Department of Personnel argue that prior to the implementation of the Shakman hiring decree, Chicago had a dual employment system.[30] One system involved civil service employees who were hired on the basis of merit by the Department of Personnel. Once they completed a probationary period, these career service employees had job protection and could only be fired for cause. They had a right to a hearing before the Personnel Board which took over this function when the Civil Service Commission was eliminated in the mid-1970s. Conversely, in the second system, the one involving patronage employees, the Department of Personnel played only a minimal, record-keeping role. Although Personnel was occasionally asked to do some candidate screening, the decision to hire was made in the mayor's office. There, a key aide known as the patronage chief was responsible for keeping track of patronage appointments and seeing to it that applicants had the necessary sponsorship. Most of the sponsors were ward committeemen or other important politicians, but at least a "couple of thousand" jobs were controlled by union locals and required a referral letter from the union. Every day the patronage chief would bring Mayor Daley a list of all new employees "down to the window washer, the ditch digger, the garbage collector." Each name would be followed by a notation of the person's sponsor.[31] Everyone had to be approved by Daley who jealously guarded his power over appointments. Dr. Eric Oldberg, who headed the Board of Health for a time during the Daley years, found he had to clear appointments with Daley even though he was an old friend of the mayor's and a nationally known neurosurgeon. He told newsman Len O'Connor:

> If you'd go to him [Daley] with a name of somebody you thought was qualified to fill an opening, he would never give you an answer right at that moment. He would say, "Fine, Doc, I think you have given me a fine name," or something like that. He said he would look into it. And it might be the next day or it might be six months before he appointed your person or somebody else, and in the meantime he wouldn't have said a damned word to you about it. He wanted you to know that giving out jobs was entirely within his hands. . . . All of the decisions on hiring went to the fifth floor, to his office—every damned time. You didn't make any appointments without clearing it with him. You would suggest something or somebody to him, but he made the decision. And, in one way or another, all of the decisions were political.[32]

It is clear that, contrary to the claims of some Department of Personnel officials, the line between career service and patronage employees was blurred in the machine years. The entire personnel system was pervaded by politics and the Department of Personnel was always very weak.[33] Since jobs were not widely advertised and there was very little attempt to recruit individuals who were not in the system, even career posts were often effectively open only to those with connections. In making appointments, department heads (as well as the mayor) regularly bypassed the personnel department and did all of the screening and interviewing themselves. Patronage employees in temporary slots were often moved into career service status when permanent vacancies were filled. Not only would their experience on the job give them an advantage in taking examinations, but they were also given credit for their experience in the temporary job so that their overall scores would be raised. Once they had achieved career status, employees might be temporarily moved to a higher grade. Then, if they failed to fulfill their political obligations, they could be demoted back down to the level of their official career service position. In general, promotions were made on a political basis an the nonpolitical career employees without sponsors were kept at the lower end of the career ladder.[34]

At the end of Mayor Daley's reign, the Chicago personnel system was "reformed." A new personnel ordinance, fashioned after the model law promulgated by the National Civil Service League, replaced the Civil Service Commission with a Personnel Board and a Department of Personnel headed by a director appointed by and responsible to the mayor. This change, together with others which eased some of the rules governing hiring, disciplining and reorganizing the workforce, was supposed to modernize the system by giving the mayor more managerial flexibility. Since the ordinance also called for the elimination of temporaries after two years, it was sold as a "reform." However, the deadline for ending provisional appointments was extended several times and temporary appointments continued to be made until the 1983 Shakman order went into effect. Moreover, the ordinance included a provision which allowed the mayor and department heads to exempt virtually any job from the career service on the grounds of administrative necessity. On balance the so-called reform actually strengthened the Mayor's hold on Chicago's personnel system.[35]

While Daley died in 1976, the machine lived on; Mayors Bilandic and Byrne and the City Council were determined to protect the patronage that nourished the organization. In 1981, the City Council brazenly voted to kill the entire civil service system in order to protect the jobs of patronage workers serving in temporary positions. The workers were afraid they could not pass a written examination that was scheduled to be given by the Personnel department. The vote forced the Personnel Director to cancel the exam, but the Council's ordinance did not survive because of the public outrage it engendered. Mayor Jane Byrne reluctantly vetoed the measure, but the cause of patronage carried the day and the temporaries kept their jobs when the Council later passed a new personnel ordinance proposed by the mayor. This "reform" established a Senior Executive Service (SES) for several hundred high ranking employees and a Departmental Employment Service (DES) for approximately 7,500 unskilled and semi-skilled workers. Both SES and DES employees were exempt from the civil service system and could be summarily fired without a hearing before the Personnel Board. They could be hired directly by the Mayor or department head and were not required to take exams. The ordinance also grandfathered in some 6,000 temporary employees who were to be given career status upon completion of a year's probation. In effect, the DES legitimized and formalized the patronage system which continued to flourish during Byrne's administration.[36]

Shakman I—The 1972 Consent Judgment

In October of 1972 all employees of the city of Chicago received notices signed by Judge Marovitz informing them of the terms of the Shakman consent judgment signed by the city. They were told they could no longer do political work on city time and that "under the judgment you cannot be discharged or demoted, not retained in temporary employment, not promoted or otherwise punished or discriminated against or affected in governmental employment because of your political affiliation, activity or contributions for any party or candidate, or the lack of such affiliation, activity or contributions." Employees were also told that they (or any other registered voter) could bring a complaint to the United States District Court if the terms of the judgment were violated. They were reminded that they did not have to actually be punished for there to be a violation; a threat of punishment also constituted a violation.[37]

Similar notices have been sent to employees periodically since 1972. The Chicago area newspapers and news broadcasts have also given a good deal of coverage to Shakman, so it seems likely that most employees are at least vaguely aware of the judgment. Over the years, about two hundred workers have brought suit in the courts charging that their rights under Shakman were violated. Many of these cases have been settled out of court and employees have lost a number of them, particularly in recent years, but there have also been some well publicized employee victories. Daley and the machine first learned of the power of Shakman when they suffered a symbolically damaging defeat at the hands of a leading black politician who had broken with the mayor over the issue of police brutality. When Congressman Ralph Metcalfe refused to endorse Daley in the 1975 primary, the machine retaliated by taking all new patronage jobs away from Metcalfe. Supervisors in the Department of Streets and Sanitation also tried to force Metcalfe-sponsored employees to get signatures for Daley's nominating petitions. Eighteen of the workers struck back by filing suit under Shakman.[38] The court found the city and the assistant commissioner of Streets and Sanitation in contempt and fined them both. Later, Daley's handpicked black candidate was unable to defeat Metcalfe in the 1976 congressional primary. Many see Metcalfe's victory as a turning point in the machine's fortunes, heralding its eventual citywide loss of black support.

When Jane Byrne tried to play the usual game of patronage politics in the manner of her mentor Richard J. Daley, she found that the rules had changed. High-level police officials resisted pressures from Byrne's patronage office to fire police department employees who had supported her arch political rival, Richard M. Daley, son of the "boss." A Shakman suit was filed and the city and one of Byrne's aides were found in contempt of court and ordered to pay the plaintiff's legal costs. In another case the city was found in contempt for violating the Shakman decree by firing or demoting 17 city employees who had supported Byrne's political opponents; the city was forced to reinstate the employees with full back pay and to pay the workers' legal costs. Encouraged by this victory, another 20 workers filed suit within weeks. Patronage politics was proving expensive for the city. In one two-year period of Mayor Byrne's administration, the city paid $250,000 in legal fees connected to Shakman suits.

Both Mayor Byrne and her successor, Harold Washington, were accused of using layoffs to get rid of employees with political connections to previous administrations. Although both mayors claimed that layoffs were necessary for budgetary reasons, some of the positions were subsequently refilled with allies of the mayors or were resurrected under different job titles and filled by new employees. There is reason to believe that both mayors used reorganizations and reclassifications to get rid of employees who were either considered politically hostile or who were regarded as incompetent and unqualified for jobs they had gained through patronage. Since Washington was generally more cooperative with the court, fewer Shakman suits were brought against his administration. However, Washington was not allowed to forget that Shakman applies to self-professed reformers as well as to machine stalwarts. In the heat of his second campaign for mayor, 200 female city workers appeared at a City Hall press conference called to refute charges by his leading opponent, Jane Byrne, that his administration had done less for women than hers had. Some of the employees later claimed they were coerced into appearing at the conference. They filed a Shakman suit charging the city with violating the prohibitions against making employees do political work and against employees doing political work on city time. Although the mayor did not admit to any wrongdoing, he agreed to an out-of-court settlement in which the administration paid the plaintiffs' legal fees, promised not to require city workers to attend similar press conferences in the future, and agreed to distribute a memo to city departments reminding everyone of the terms of the Shakman decree.

Although Shakman I was costly to the city and placed some limitations on its mayors, the decree did not kill patronage. The machine could still reward the faithful with jobs. It was also able to blunt the order's impact by delaying tactics, subterfuge and, occasionally, outright defiance. Many employees were still too afraid to risk defying their ward committeeman's demands. Since the Shakman decrees, unlike the Hatch Act, did not ban all campaign work, it could always be claimed that employees were doing political work "voluntarily." An employee who does go to the courts may also find it difficult to prove that he or she was fired for political reasons and political reasons alone. The courts have placed the burden of proof on the employee to show that political considerations were the sole motivating factor for the firing.[39] In addition, supervisors can always punish an employee with unpleasant assignments and other moves short of firing, or they can build a dossier on the employee which can then be cited in court as the reason for dismissal.

Despite the limitations of Shakman, many observers of the Chicago scene believe the decree did hurt the machine. Former Alderman Thomas Keane, who had been Daley's chief lieutenant before being convicted of mail fraud, lamented that "the Shakman decree was a thousand times more powerful in curtailing political work performed by the organization than any civil service law that ever existed. . . . The organization depended on the patronage jobholder to work in the precinct at night, to attend meetings, to buy tickets to party functions. [But] gradually the workers lost touch. . . . I used to take a precinct list and sit down with a fellow who had worked and say 'Tell me who lives down the block.' He would name the number of each house and apartment building and tell me who lived [there]. Few precinct captains can do that any longer."[40] Shakman himself thought the firing decree had made a difference in some races. He attributed the Democrat's loss of the State's Attorney's office to defections by blacks who were angered by the machine candidate's handling of a raid against the Black Panthers. According to Shakman, "Black patronage workers, who could have been forced to get out the vote . . . under the old system, just sat on their hands."[41]

Still, Shakman recognized from the beginning that the firing decree could only be "half effective." He noted that hiring is "crucial because you can pre-screen public employees and only hire those who are loyal to your organization, then they're going to feel you have a claim on them. No matter what a federal judge says, some of them are going to be afraid of losing their jobs and others are going to feel obligated to carry out the bargain they've made."[42]

In 1979, after years of delaying tactics by the Daley and Bilandic administrations, the Court at last dealt with the hiring issue. In a long and scholarly opinion, Judge Bua ruled that patronage hiring as practiced in Cook County was unconstitutional. However, this decision, which is known as Shakman II in Chicago political circles, had virtually no immediate impact because there was no implementing order. Citing Abram Chayes on public law litigation, Judge Bua invited the parties to offer suggestions "as to the manner in which [the Court] should proceed in order to determine the proper remedy."[43] Because the hiring opinion broke new ground in an area in which higher courts had not ruled, Bua also agreed to delay until Chicago appealed. Only after the Seventh Circuit refused to review the case before the issuing of an implementing order did Bua hold hearings on a remedy. The plaintiffs brought in a number of leading experts. However, the city called no experts, and it refused to offer suggestions on the grounds that any new hiring system would be too costly. Finally, disregarding the city's protests, Judge Bua issued an implementing order four years after he had written his opinion on hiring.

Shakman III—The Hiring Order

The 1983 order, known as Shakman III, incorporated many of the plaintiff's suggestions. It required Chicago to take immediate steps to open up the recruitment process and to eliminate political sponsorship from influencing hiring. The city was ordered to give public notice of all job openings and to post the notices at least 14 days before the deadline for accepting applications. It also had to mail notices to anyone requesting them and to publish quarterly announcements in the major Chicago newspapers informing readers of the existence and availability of job lists and telling them how to get copies.

The Court also required that the terms of the judgment be posted prominently at places where job applicants were taken and that notices of the terms be delivered to all current city employees and to all job applicants for the next ten years. The notice emphasized that: "HIRING MUST NOT BE BASED UPON OR AFFECTED BY THE PROSPECTIVE EMPLOYEE'S POLITICAL AFFILIATION, POLITICAL SUPPORT OR ACTIVITY, POLITICAL FINANCIAL CONTRIBUTION, PROMISES OF SUCH POLITICAL SUPPORT, ACTIVITY OR FINANCIAL CONTRIBUTION. Nor may hiring be based upon or affected by the prospective employee's political sponsorship recommendations."[44] As a check, the city had to file quarterly affidavits listing the names and positions of all new hires and disclosing the names of any party agent "who had directly or indirectly recommended or sponsored the employee."

In accordance with the U.S. Supreme Court's Elrod and Branti decisions, the order exempted policymaking positions from the ban on political hiring. Although Washington had promised to eliminate the patronage system and expressed his general support of the Shakman decrees during the campaign in the spring of 1983, the newly elected Mayor demanded more than the 250 exempt positions proposed by Judge Bua. He contended that he needed to put more of his own people in key policymaking positions and asked for 1,200 exempt positions. After considerable sparring, Washington settled for 900 jobs, and he also agreed to a provision which allowed the holders of 792 of the exempt jobs to appeal to the Court to reconsider the exempt classification in the event they were fired. This provision was to expire in three years.

While Washington continued to complain that he needed more exempts,[45] the exempt schedule did appear to include enough job titles in each department to give the Mayor control of policymaking. For example, in the Department of Streets and Sanitation, 119 of the 6,000 employees were in exempt positions. These included all 13 Deputy and Assistant Commissioners, the 50 Ward Superintendents who are in charge of service and delivery in each ward, six Assistant General Superintendents, and the Major Supervisors.

Despite his complaints, Washington appeared to keep the promise that he made to city employees not to engage in any "mass" firings. Less than half of the 900 exempts were terminated, and some of those removed from one position were simply shifted to another. Of those terminated, no more than 50 went to court to ask that their jobs be recategorized as nonexempt.[46] The city suffered some initial setbacks in these suits, but ultimately it prevailed in most of them. In one well-publicized case, Judge Bua,[47] whose sympathies were clearly with the fired employees, ruled that the holder of the second highest position in the city's Water Department had to be reinstated. The city put the man back on the payroll,[48] but the U.S. Circuit Court of Appeals reversed Bua. Applying the test it had devised in the Nekolny Case,[49] the Seventh Circuit found that the job of the first Deputy Commissioner was clearly one which "authorizes, either directly or indirectly, meaningful input into government decision-making issues where there is room for principled disagreement on goals or their implementation."[50]

The Plan of Compliance

As is typical in public law litigation, Judge Bua's order left unsettled the precise form that a nonpolitical hiring system would take. He gave the city 120 days to develop and one year to implement a plan of compliance setting forth in detail "a method or methods of hiring to be used for all Government Employment positions (other than exempt positions)," noting that the judgment required only that political considerations be eliminated in hiring and that "it does not impose a civil service system nor does it necessitate that a merit system be utilized."[51]

The city had trouble devising a plan that would satisfy the plaintiffs and Judge Bua. One year after the 1983 judgment, it still had made no real headway. Noting that the numerous Shakman complaints he had received were evidence of the need for a hiring plan,

Judge Bua moved to force the city to act by imposing a hiring freeze. Outraged Washington administration officials, including the Mayor, charged that the freeze was bringing city government to a "grinding halt," but at the same time the administration began to work in earnest to meet the Court's demands, bringing in a leading Chicago law firm for help.

Because the city was daunted by the immensity of its task, C. Richard Johnson and Roger Fross, who headed the Shakman legal team, suggested that it proceed in two steps. First, the city should write a set of guidelines for a plan, and only then should it try to fill in the details of the hiring plan. Accordingly, the city, working with Fross and Johnson, put together a set of guidelines known as the Principles for Plan of Compliance with Shakman Judgment. Satisfied that the city was at last making progress, Judge Bua accepted the Principles and lifted the freeze. After a year of inaction, the freeze had spurred the city to act within two weeks.

The Principles[52] require that the city develop and implement a set of "Detailed Hiring Provisions" which exclude political considerations from hiring, "eliminate the continuing effects of past patronage hiring violations, promote affirmative action, build a high-quality professional workforce, provide for effective management control of employees and allow for experimentation in hiring techniques."

The most important portions of the Principles deal with the development of methods for selecting employees. The Shakman attorneys insisted that Chicago separate the initial screening for applicants from the final decision to hire. First, a screening authority, consisting of either representatives of the Department of Personnel or a joint committee of Department of Personnel people and representatives of the hiring department, would evaluate applicants using objective criteria to be set forth in the Detailed Hiring Provisions. The screening authority would prepare a list of eligibles and then, again using a set list of criteria, would construct a referral list which would be sent to the hiring authority. To prevent "fishing expeditions," the Principles strictly limit the number of names that may be placed on the referral list, generally allowing no more than five applicants for each opening.

In the second phase of hiring, high-level department officials or the department head would choose among the applicants on the referral list. No department member who sat on the joint screening committee could act as the hiring authority.

Because the city has over 3,000 job titles, it was recognized that developing both the overall hiring provisions and the specific screening and hiring criteria for each title would be difficult and time consuming. Consequently, the Principles gave the city 12 months to write and implement the Detailed Hiring Provisions. They also laid down a schedule for submission of individual departmental criteria, and the departments which were expected to be doing the most hiring were given the earliest deadlines.

At the suggestions of the Shakman attorneys, the city hired the professional employment consulting firm of Arthur Young to help it write the Detailed Hiring Provisions. The same firm was later retained to conduct the annual audit of hiring procedures. To facilitate the audit, the Principles require the city to maintain detailed records of the number of applications, the disposal of applications, the criteria used, and so on. In addition, each department must keep a log of all written communications received relating to attempts to exercise political influence over the hiring process.

The Principles also place strict limits on the practice of emergency hiring. Emergency hires can only be made when no eligible list exists for a position, and in a single year a department can hire no more than 0.25 percent of its budgeted workforce on an emergency basis.

By the end of October 1984, the City of Chicago completed formulating the Detailed Hiring Provisions. Within the next year, it developed the qualifying screening criteria, listing the minimum qualifications for each position, the certification screening criteria for use in constructing the referral lists, and the hiring criteria for the making of the actual hiring decision for all 3,000 job titles. These criteria were submitted in batches to the Shakman attorneys for their approval.

The Provisions[53] spell out in great detail the procedures which must be followed and the documentation which must be maintained for all hiring decisions as well as for decisions concerning the transfer, demotion, promotion, and reclassification of city employees. To begin with, departments are required to submit a written request whenever they wish to hire. They must list the criteria they intend to use in filling the position. Any modification of the preestablished criteria must be justified in writing and approved by the Department of Personnel which has the final word in all controversies. Similarly, requests for emergency appointments have to be justified and approved by the Commissioner of Personnel, and the department must submit documentation showing that any individual hired on an emergency basis meets all screening and hiring criteria.

A department may request that the open application procedure be bypassed and the position be filled through promotion, transfer, or demotion or that it be filled by a graduate of a city-approved training program. However, it must justify its request and once again show that the person placed in the position meets the criteria.

When a department first initiates a request to hire, a file is created in which all actions are recorded. At the same time, the data concerning each request for hire and its disposition are supposed to be entered into a special computer file for the independent auditor's use in reviewing city compliance with the decrees. The entire hiring process and the maintenance of the documentation is supervised by a high-level member of the Department of Personnel who is designated as the Shakman Compliance Officer.

Unless a list of eligibles is left over from a previous announcement or a job is to be filled from within or by emergency appointment, the Department of Personnel must make a public announcement of the opening, stating job title, pay grade, minimum qualifications, residency and other requirements, salary range, closing date for acceptance of applications, and the duties of the position. The announcement must also state that any reference to political sponsorship or recommendation must be omitted from any application materials submitted.

Once the applications are received, they must first be screened according to the basic qualifying criteria. The eligible list[54] of applicants who meet these minimum criteria are then judged against the certification screening criteria. For laborer and other jobs which can easily be performed by almost anyone, the Department of Personnel uses a lottery based on social security numbers to develop a sequenced referral list. When a job has more stringent requirements, the referral list is developed through the use of an "examination," generally in the form of a written, oral, or performance test or of some type of credentials evaluation, and/or through the use of a screening panel. Typically, the qualifying and screening criteria for the individual titles include an educational requirement such as a degree in a particular specialty, experience of a specified type and duration, other knowledge, skills, or abilities (such as knowledge of a computer language), and, in many cases, previous satisfactory performance in a specified city position. Except for police and fire and some clerical jobs, no written or performance tests are used in constructing an eligible or referral list or in making the final hiring decision.

Each member of the screening panel independently rates every candidate on the preestablished criteria, weighting the scores for particular items according to the agreement reached by the hiring department and the Department of Personnel. The entire screening panel then holds a "consensus session" to determine which names will be placed on the referral list. In cases where hiring-department members on the panel disagree with the Department of Personnel representative, the Personnel members are supposed to have the last word.

Before the lists are sent to the hiring department, the Shakman Compliance Officer must review all of the application materials in order to strike any politically oriented references. This includes not only references to political sponsorship but all references which "would allow educated guesses concerning political affiliation or political sponsorship."

Although the hiring department alone is responsible for filling positions from the referral list, it must follow set procedures and keep records that document and justify all of its actions. The department must rate each candidate, describe the methods used to evaluate the applicants, and explain why it chose one candidate above the others.

Since most departments use interviews to evaluate applicants, the Detailed Hiring Provisions lay down guidelines for their conduct. Although the hiring departments do the actual interviewing, the design of the interviews is determined by the Department of Personnel. Generally, a Structured Employment Interview format, consisting of questions based on the position's major job duties, is recommended. Frequently, applicants for higher level titles are required to complete a Biographical Employment Evaluation Form (BEEF) delineating "verifiable examples of work experiences regarding a series of major job duties." The BEEF is then used as the basis of interview probes.

Overall, the interviews are supposed to be "strictly and clearly job related" and to focus "on those knowledges, skills, abilities and personal characteristics necessary to perform the job at entry" with questions to be designed to "elicit information on job related behavior." No questions concerning political affiliation are allowed. The interviewer is also warned to avoid politically related topics and to stop a candidate from volunteering "non-work related information about political topics."

Even with the emphasis on structured and job related interviews, the hiring criteria often have a vagueness which allows for a good deal of subjective judgment on the part of the hiring authorities. Many jobs have such criteria as "quality and relevance of previous job experience" or "oral communication skills sufficient to communicate with the public and other city agencies and to relay directives and information to superiors and co-workers."

If, after the hiring department makes its decision, a rejected applicant believes that the requirements of the Shakman judgment were violated, he or she may appeal by filing a complaint with the Shakman Compliance Officer who must investigate the charges and report to the commissioner of Personnel. In turn, the commissioner must act on the Compliance Officer's recommendation within 10 days and must inform the complainant in writing of his or her decisions and of the applicant's right to petition the Court.

In 1986, a few relatively minor changes were made in the Detailed Hiring Provisions with the approval of the Shakman attorneys and the Court. For example, one change allows departments to recruit directly from college campuses (subject to certain restrictions). Another permits departments to recruit for hard-to-fill positions at professional conventions and meetings and through professional association placement services. The Department of Personnel must demonstrate through statistical data that a position qualifies as hard-to-fill, and it must file a list of these positions with the Court. In Spring 1988, about 35 positions were on the list, the majority of them in data processing.

Implementation of Shakman III[55]

The Detailed Hiring Provisions were completed and went into effect in June 1985, almost 16 years after Michael Shakman first filed suit. The impact of the advertising and notice provisions was immediate and dramatic. In 1982, the Department of Personnel posted 90 jobs and accepted a little over 30,000 applications. In 1985, the Department posted more than 1,000 vacancy notices and received almost 191,000 applications.

Although the Department of Personnel was under pressure by the Mayor's Office and the other departments to fill positions quickly, its staff of approximately 170 was not increased. Not surprisingly, the Department was unable to meet all the demands of the Washington administration. The time needed to fill a position rose from less than two weeks to an average of ten weeks. As one official put it: "It used to take a long time; now it takes forever." Because of understaffing, inefficient procedures, and the elementary state of its computerization,[56] the Department of Personnel (DOP) also found itself unable to meet all the recordkeeping requirements of the Detailed Hiring Provisions. The auditors severely criticized the city for failing to provide all of the required documentation and found both the database and programs inadequate. However, the city had clearly increased its documentation of hiring decisions, and the Department of Personnel appeared to be making a good faith effort to adhere to the Detailed Hiring Provisions. The auditors conceded that much of the city's noncompliance with the documentation requirement "occurred as a result of DOP's increased workload during the audit period and the newness of the data requirements." Overall, the auditors found that "with a few significant exceptions, the hiring procedures followed by the City to fill open positions were consistent with the intent of the Detailed Hiring Provisions."[57]

In addition to inadequate recordkeeping, other lapses in implementation were also due at least in part to understaffing. For example, the DOP placed non-career service applications in a holding file, screening the pool of applicants for both qualifying and screening criteria at the time a referral list was needed by a department, even though the Provisions required that these processes be kept separate. Much more serious was the inability of DOP examiners to control the screening panels which composed the referral lists. For a period of two months in 1986, DOP examiners were busy with fire department examinations, and they did not participate in screening panels meetings, thus leaving both screening and hiring entirely to the hiring departments. At other times, screening panels were dominated by hiring department members rather than Personnel examiners. Individual hiring department officials were also permitted to sit on the screening panels and participate in the final interviewing and hiring decisions.

Despite the Department of Personnel's inadequate resources, the Shakman decrees seem to have brought about major changes in the city's personnel system and to have achieved their primary purpose of ending Chicago's old patronage system. The auditors could find no substantial evidence of political considerations influencing hiring decisions. Only three respondents in the survey of newly-hired/promoted city employees and rejected applicants reported that political issues came up during their interviews. In sharp contrast to the past, most of those surveyed said they had learned about job openings through job notices. The single person who found out about a job from a party official was not hired.

In response to an open-ended question asking if the respondent knew or had heard about anything, including political considerations, which gave some applicants an unfair advantage, an overwhelming majority answered no, as summarized in Table 2.1.

Several of those who said they had heard that politics influenced hiring decisions also said that they could offer no evidence that this was the case. Some applicants complained about inefficiencies in the procedures followed by the departments, and several disgruntled applicants simply seemed to be expressing frustration at not being hired.

While politicians may have been "passing the word" on job applicants, they were clearly no longer writing letters of sponsorship. The file of letters from politicians contained less than two dozen items. Moreover, the letters did not appear to have carried much weight. The

Table 2.1
Auditor's Inquiry: Knowledge of Political
Considerations or Other Unfair Advantage

	Hires		Nonhires	
Response	External (N = 34)	Internal (N = 35)	External (N = 53)	Internal (n = 23)
Yes	15%	9%	11%	26%
	(5)	(3)	(6)	(6)
No	85%	89%	83%	61%
	(29)	(31)	(44)	(14)
Not Answered	(0)	(1)	(3)	(3)

Note: Percentages rounded. Number of responses are indicated in parentheses. Percentage differences across groups are nonsignificant when statistically compared.

auditor found that most of the individuals named in the letters did not get city jobs and the few who did were qualified.

In all, the auditors could find only two minor instances of political influence in hiring decisions.

However, the auditors were told by a "high-level city official" that a mayoral liaison was involved in other hiring decisions. The liaison reviewed all proposed hiring decisions in Water, Sewers, Streets and Sanitation, Aviation, and Public Works departments, and he would sometimes delay them for as long as three months. The informant believed that the liaison was interested in hiring skilled people, but that he also wanted "politically well-connected people." The informant indicated that "those with political influence could get hiring decisions through the system faster."[58]

The Commissioner of Personnel dismissed the charges as "frivolous," but the Shakman Compliance Officer did concede that the mayoral aide had final authority over promotions and hiring in the departments that he supervised. The city never admitted wrongdoing, but in response to auditors' complaints, it agreed to stop the practice of having the mayor's liaison sign off on appointments. City officials maintained that the Mayor's Office was concerned only with keeping costs down and with making sure "minorities are getting a fair share." While no one has been able to prove that the Mayor's Office was forcing the departments to approve patronage appointments, the actions of the Mayor's aide was highly suspect.

Most of the infractions of the Detailed Hiring Provisions uncovered by the auditors were relatively minor. For example, the Provisions were violated when some emergency employees were later rehired on a priority basis as regular full-time employees. Although the city bypassed the screening and applications procedures of the Provisions in placing these employees on the payroll, only four persons were involved. In light of the fact that the city was entitled to 197 emergency appointments and made only six, its violations did not seem terribly serious.[59]

There also may have been some violations of the letter and the spirit of Shakman through the abuse of reclassification procedures. In June of 1985 the Department of Personnel adopted Rule 26 which allowed it to reclassify jobs on its own initiative. The Department claimed that the Rule was necessary to combat grade creep whereby departments would get raises for their employees by upgrading positions, even though job duties did not warrant a higher grade. Undoubtedly grade creep was a problem, but Rule 26 had other potential uses. Since a newly classified individual would lose all seniority accumulated in prior grades and would therefore be the first let go in a layoff, city council opponents of Washington charged that Rule 26 was a ploy to get rid of employees hired in previous administrations.

When the Washington administration reclassified 653 employees, the employees filed a class-action suit, and the Mayor's opponents made a tremendous fuss. As a result, the Washington administration was never able to use reclassification to get rid of a large number of employees. The auditors found only that the city had not filed all the forms which were needed to verify that individuals reclassified to higher positions met all the established criteria for their new titles.

The issue raised by Rule 26 is now moot since the union contract adopted at the beginning of 1986 contains provisions dating seniority from the first day the employee is hired by the city rather than from the first day of service in the employee's current title. The contract also forbids a department from automatically filling a new reclassified job with an incumbent of the old title. Reclassification is treated like any other promotion, and the job has to be posted and opened for application by other employees. (Although the incumbent cannot receive priority, the hiring department sometimes gives incumbents the edge by tailoring the criteria to fit the incumbent's qualifications.) Reclassified jobs are open to outsiders only if there are no qualified employees.

Ironically, the most blatant and serious violation of Shakman was committed by the city's Department of Law. Together with the Office of Budget and Management, the Law Department decided that all its employees should be considered exempt. The departments claimed that this was necessary because their work was highly confidential. While that may be the case, the Plan of Compliance clearly requires that any changes in exemptions have to be submitted to the plaintiffs and approved by the Court.

Most of the city departments have also violated Shakman by attempting to influence the screening and hiring process so that jobs go to preselected candidates. The auditors found numerous examples of departments trying to hire favored candidates by pressuring examiners to put names on referral lists, tailoring job criteria, and insisting that eligibility lists be opened or reopened in order to place particular names on them, but they could find no evidence that these efforts were politically motivated. Undoubtedly, there were some cases in which departments were trying to hire individuals with political connections, but (as the audit noted) "alternative explanations are conceivable."[60] The examiners interviewed by the auditors "indicated it was hard to determine if departments are trying to 'sneak someone in' or if it is just because the department needs to fill the vacancy quickly."[61] It should also be kept in mind that it is not uncommon in many organizations for line managers to try to bypass the personnel office in order to hire or promote people they want.

In contrast to some of the line departments, the Department of Personnel appears to welcome the Shakman decrees and to be trying its best to enforce them. This is understandable because the decrees clearly strengthen the hand of the personnel professionals in city government. When line departments try to change the selection criteria or hire favored candidates, Personnel can use the decrees and the specter of court action to enforce its demands that departments adhere to the rules. Experienced personnel officials think that Shakman has forced departments to document and justify their hiring decisions and to adhere more strictly to job-related selection criteria. Because of this and because the notice requirements have greatly increased the pool of applicants, some personnel experts think the quality of new city employees has improved. Some Shakman proponents also argue that the decrees have saved the city money by ridding it of unneeded workers. It is impossible to determine the exact cost of the old patronage system, but there is no question that the city's payroll was padded to meet the needs of the Cook County Democratic Party and that many city workers spent much of their work day doing party work.

Ironically, there is reason to believe that the potential for savings and improvement in the city's workforce has not been realized at least in part *because* of the Shakman decrees. While the decrees, as the second audit covering 1986-89 affirmed, have achieved their "basic purpose" of "restricting political hiring," they have also imposed unwieldly, costly and time consuming procedural requirements on the city which have sometimes kept the city from hiring the best people, particularly for professional positions.[62] The Illinois Commission on the Future of Public Service, which examined Chicago government in 1991, seconded the auditors' view. The Commission, a good government group modeled on the Volcker Commission, concluded that the Detailed Hiring Provisions were "widely misunderstood, misinterpreted and used as an excuse that preempts proactive recruitment processes." It recommended that the city get court permission to simplify the hiring process. It also wanted the city to prepare a handbook explaining the hiring procedures and to train managers in Shakman "interpretation" because it found that people were often paralyzed by the fear that they would somehow violate the decrees and end up in court. Most important, the Commission felt that the city had to take steps to motivate its employees and to change old work habits. This was essential because many of the pre-Shakman workers who got their jobs as a reward for doorbell ringing were still in the city workforce. The Commission believed that Chicago's difficulties in recruiting outstanding individuals were due in part to the general public's perception that all city employees were "patronage loafers."[63]

Unfortunately, the negative image of city workers was perpetuated by periodic scandals such as the one that shook the Department of Streets and Sanitation in May of 1991. The headlines that Chicagoans read while drinking their morning coffee told the story: "City Probe finds 2-hour-a-day jobs"[64] and "Payrollers keep busy; but not on the job."[65] Thirty-seven laborers at the 1st Ward Sanitation headquarters in Chicago's Loop had averaged just two hours a day working although they were paid (at the rate of $13.87 an hour) for seven and a half hours work. According to the City Inspector, "They would show up to sign in and, if they weren't too busy, they would come back and sign out. But that was only if they weren't too busy and didn't have too many errands to run. . . . They didn't do their job cleaning up the city."[66] The men occupied themselves in various ways: one worked at a hotdog stand; another at two flower shops; yet another sold insurance; a supervisor went to the racetrack; and one allegedly used his "free" time to travel to Wisconsin to rob a jewelry store. All of the most egregious offenders were patronage workers hired in the 1950s and 1960s.

Mayor Richard M. Daley sought to identify himself with the forces of reform by denouncing the malingers and taking credit for initiating the investigation. However, he failed to extend the investigation to other wards and did not fire the ward superintendent even though he could easily have done so since the position is Shakman exempt. In general, though, the second Mayor Daley has tried to publicly distance himself from the machine politics of his father. He holds no party post and did not even seek the party's endorsement in his 1989 and 1991 mayoral campaigns. When the Illinois Commission on Public Service recommended changes in the Shakman hiring provisions, he said he agreed with their criticisms of the process, but would not commit himself to asking the court for revisions. He told newsmen, "If I said that, you'd have a big headline: 'Mayor wants to get rid of Shakman.' "[67]

The Sanitation workers scandal made it clear that the corrosive impact of patronage on the work ethic and values of city employees lingered. While there is no necessary connection between patronage and corruption, the machine patronage system was part of a political culture which nourished cheating. Former alderman Dick Simpson, an independent opponent of the machine, asserts that corruption inevitably accompanies patronage:

> Because with the patronage system, if you're going to reward people for working in politics by giving them a job and giving them a salary . . . and if you're going to reward the voters for voting for the party by getting them trees planted and curbs fixed, licenses and permits or whatever, the moral ability to draw the line between payoffs for political purposes and straight-out graft and corruption is just not there. . . . It's conceivable a good precinct captain might somehow be able to draw that line but most of them get pretty fuzzy about it. Therefore, if you're going to have forty thousand patronage workers in the city you're going to end up with a lot of people that can't tell the difference between what's called honest and dishonest graft.[68]

Unquestionably, good machine members were expected above all to be loyal and to back the candidates endorsed by the organization irrespective of ideology or issues. To quote Abner Mikva, a liberal former Congressman (now Chief Judge of the U.S. Court of Appeals for the District of Columbia), the bosses "would deliver services—good, bad, or indifferent, and use them to elect an Adolf Hitler if he was on the Democratic ticket. . . . The patronage party of Illinois stands for nothing except jobs and winning. . . . I've never touched a patronage job . . . because there is a price. There is no free lunch."[69] Part of the price was to obey the leadership and not ask too many questions. The machine was highly centralized and authoritarian in its internal structure. Thomas Guterbock found the members of the ward club he studied had access only to the minimum amount of information they needed to do their jobs. The club leaders concealed much of their activity from the general public and, in many cases, from other members.[70] Even Milt Rakove, an "insider," couldn't get Daley or most of those who knew him to submit to interviews. He reports that Alderman Tom Keane, the number two man in the machine during the Daley years, said when he was approached to write a book about his political life and experiences, "What do they want me to do, put everybody in the penitentiary?"[71]

Chicago After Shakman

For most citizens of Chicago, the path to a job in the city no longer begins in the precinct at the Ward Committeeman's office. Once having got a job, city workers no longer have to work the precincts or buy tickets to the alderman's dinner. While no one would be so naive as to claim that politics has been completely eliminated from the city's personnel operations, the large-scale patronage system of the past seems to be gone. Michael Shakman and the lawyers heading the plaintiff's team have all pronounced themselves generally satisfied with the progress that has been made. They feel that the system has been "opened up;" that compared to "where we were ten years ago, the city's light years ahead; that the man in the street now thinks he can get a job without going to his committeeman; and that most employees are no longer afraid to refuse to do political work or make contributions." As one of the lawyers put it, "Shakman has given them a sword. They know they can go to the courts to vindicate their rights."

Without question, the changes in Chicago's personnel system have, at least in part, been the result of the Shakman decrees. Knowing they could no longer easily be fired, many city workers undoubtedly did, as former Alderman Keane lamented, begin to slack off in their work for the party. While there has been some disguised political firing through the use of such devices as reorganizations, layoffs, and reclassifications, recent mayors have not been able to get away with massive political firings. This has meant that fewer jobs have been available for mayors to use for political purposes. Once the hiring decree went into effect, it became extremely difficult to fill openings on a political basis. Departments such as Streets and Sanitation and Public Works, which had thousands of patronage workers, now have to fill unskilled jobs through the lottery system. Given the numbers of applications filed for such jobs and the public nature of the lottery, it is hard to imagine how one could insure that a particular precinct worker's name would get on the referral list.

As important as Shakman has been in effecting reform, it would be a mistake to attribute all of the changes to the court decrees. For example, recent administrations had fewer jobs to fill not only because of the Shakman prohibitions on political firing, but also because of the increasingly tight city budget. Similarly, the added protections and security experienced by city workers, while due in part to Shakman, must also be attributed to guarantees which were contained in the contracts negotiated with the American Federation of State, County and Municipal Employees (AFSCME) after a new state law guaranteeing collective bargaining rights for public employees (and giving most of them the additional right to strike) went into effect in July 1984. Although in the past Mayor Daley won labor's support by agreeing to pay the prevailing rate—the wages paid in local industries—to city workers belonging to building and craft unions, he refused to sign a formal contract. The unions, in a process that one leader called "collective begging," had to be satisfied with handshake agreements that left workers without formal collective bargaining rights. Mayor Byrne reneged on her promise to support a state collective bargaining law, but Washington kept his promise to do so. With the crucial backing of the Mayor of Chicago, the collective bargaining bill finally got through the state legislature. As a result, AFSCME and other unions began to organize the white collar city workers who had not previously been unionized, and the city sat down to bargain with these unions and with the crafts, police, fire, and other unions which already existed. According to the Commissioner of Personnel, 90 percent of the jobs in the city government are now covered by union contracts. These contracts reinforce Shakman by forcing the city to follow specified procedures and rules in filling jobs, particularly when promotions are involved. Under certain circumstances the city now has to give preference to city employees in making appointments, and it has to award positions within the pool of qualified city workers on the basis of seniority. In short, promotions go to the most senior qualified rather than to the most qualified, consistent with union principles rather than traditional concepts of merit staffing. If the unions are not satisfied that the city has followed posting, bidding, and appointment procedures, they have the right to file a grievance and, eventually, to force the city to submit unsettled disagreements to arbitration.

Finally, the changes in the Chicago personnel system have to be understood in light of the overall changes in the city's politics. Machine Mayors, like the first Daley and Bilandic, struggled to retain their control of city jobs because their power depended on patronage. Shakman threatened this power. Their political base lay in the ward organizations for which jobs were an essential fuel. Harold Washington could support Shakman and cooperate with the Court because he did not need ward organizations to win elections. In fact, support for reform helped him win office because his two victories depended on a coalition made up of nearly 100 percent of the Black voters, and a small (but essential) percentage of the white voters (14.9 percent), nearly all in the anti-machine, anti-patronage "lake-front liberal" wards. The reform image also helped him attract outside support and funds as well as the support of AFSCME.

Washington's support among Blacks was based first and foremost on his race. He appealed to Black voters because he was Black and because he criticized the white organization politicians who, for so long, refused to address the many legitimate grievances of Chicago's Black community. Chicago's Black wards were becoming increasingly disaffected from the machine even before Daley died.[72] The Black community demonstrated its willingness to support a viable candidate before Washington was chosen as that candidate. He did not have to promise jobs to individual Blacks to get them to work for his election. To maintain his support and the extraordinary turnout he needed in the Black community, he did have to demonstrate his solidarity with his race. In this regard, affirmative action served his purposes by demonstrating that he was helping Blacks as a group to get their share of economic and political rewards. Unlike previous mayors, Mayor Washington could help himself politically not so much by giving jobs to individual precinct workers as by giving a greater share of jobs to the Black and Hispanic communities. Since affirmative action—giving more jobs and more of the better jobs to minorities—is blessed by the courts in general and is recognized as a legitimate policy goal by the Shakman Plan of Compliance,[73] the mayor's political needs did not put him on a collision course with the Detailed Hiring Provisions. In 1985, 64.1 percent of the new hires in the city were Black; 10.4 percent were Hispanic. Of the 59 administrators and officials hired, 59.3 percent were Black and 11.8 percent were Hispanic.[74] While Washington's critics saw these figures as proof that affirmative action is the new form of patronage and equated it to patronage under the machine, this characterization is not quite accurate. Washington undoubtedly found affirmative action to his political advantage, but he did not use affirmative action jobs to build a precinct organization. The quid pro quo of the machine—a job in exchange for precinct-based political work—was absent. This does not mean, however, that patronage disappeared in the Washington administration. While the mayor did not try to build a traditional patronage army, he made effective use of other forms of patronage, including some jobs. In addition to the Shakman-exempt positions he awarded to his supporters, he found jobs to use for patronage purposes in such agencies as the Chicago Housing Authority (CHA) and Chicago Transit Authority

(CTA), which were not party to the Shakman suit. Not only did Washington fill the top jobs at these agencies with campaign aides and other political allies, he also used low level CHA jobs to recruit election workers.

Although the mayor vehemently denied any political motive, nearly 240 CHA residents were hired as janitors just before the 1987 election. The CHA executive who hired them once was a top Washington political operative and used his vacation time in 1987 to spend the last three weeks of the campaign working full-time for the mayor's reelection. The *Tribune* reported that many of the residents hired "actively supported Mayor Washington's reelection effort and worked to register voters, canvass neighborhoods and serve as election judges."[75] There have also been accusations that CHA funds were used to buy tickets to the mayor's fundraisers, that CHA employees were coerced into making contributions to the mayor's campaign and that contractors with the CHA and other agencies were pressured into making political contributions.

In 1987 Washington announced that he was beginning a new jobs program. Under this "Chicago First" program, the Mayor's Office of Employment and Training would refer job applicants to private companies doing business with or receiving loans from the city. The city originally planned to require that businesses with city contracts or subsidies participate in the program, but it backed off and made participation voluntary after the initial announcement led to a storm of protest. Again the Mayor denied that this program had anything to do with politics or patronage, but some of his supporters believed it did. One black alderman told the *Tribune*, "I don't care what Washington says to the liberals on the lake front, the fact is that people out here want patronage. And if it came to me through my organization, then we'd know where they are when it comes time to ring doorbells for the mayor."[76]

Since the Chicago First program had just gotten started when Washington died, its form of job patronage never played an important role in building the mayor's power. Because of Shakman, Rutan, and the restraints imposed by union contracts and shrinking city resources, it is unlikely that the patronage army of the machine's heyday will ever be resurrected. To be sure, future mayors will always control some jobs. They will be able to appoint their people to high level policymaking posts and to various boards and commissions, but they are unlikely to depend on the distribution of jobs to keep them in power. Instead, it can be expected that they will rely primarily on preferments or, if you will, other forms of patronage to build and maintain their power. Unless a change is made in the law,[77] future mayors will probably follow Washington's lead in making extensive use of city contracts for patronage purposes.

There is, of course, nothing new in using city contracts for political advantage. The first Mayor Daley made masterful use of contracts to solidify his support in business and labor circles. When he first came into office, Daley followed the traditional strategy of the Irish bosses and raised taxes in order to expand the public sector and provide more government jobs for his supporters. Within a few years however, white homeowners in the neighborhoods revolted against the higher taxes needed to pay for bigger government and Daley changed his tactics.

Using "federal urban renewal funds, eminent domain and zoning," Daley launched an ambitious redevelopment program focusing on the downtown center and on massive public works projects such as the expansion of O'Hare Airport and the building of the McCormick Place Exhibition Center.[78] The mayor appeased white ethnic voters with lower taxes and city services for homeowners and with policies that kept the growing black population segregated in the ghetto "plantations." At the same time, his pro-growth policy brought him the backing of developers, downtown merchants and businessmen, bankers, lawyers and the politically connected unions. As a bonus, "the building and the contracts also greatly increased the patronage— via private jobs—available to the machine."[79]

During his first term in office, Harold Washington, the man who defeated the machine, rejected the "builder" tradition which was associated with his old antagonists and shifted the city's focus from downtown development to small scale "people projects" in the neighborhoods.[80] But Chicago's first African-American mayor was a shrewd politician who understood the advantages that could be milked from using the city's multibillion dollar budget. By judiciously parcelling out city spending (much of it through awarding the no-bid contracts allowed by city law), Washington could reward his supporters in the black community *and* "encourage" the businessmen and professionals, both black and white, who got city business to fill his campaign coffers.

Shortly after taking office, Washington issued an executive order directing that at least 25 percent of the city's business go to Blacks, Hispanics, Asian-Americans, and other minorities and that 5 percent go to women. By 1987, the mayor was able to report that in the previous year $70 million in city business had gone to female and minority businesses. This represented 34 percent of all city contracts, a significant increase from the 4 percent of city contracts that had gone to minorities and women in 1983.[81] The city also required that airlines renovating O'Hare Airport and commercial developers using city land or bond money set aside 25 percent to 30 percent of their contracts for minorities and women. The city also awarded lucrative legal work for the sale of municipal bonds to black lawyers who supported the mayor; other legal work also went to favored law firms. In this way Washington channeled city business to the minority community that put him in office in 1983 and to the movers and shakers whose support and money he sought. Unlike Daley, Washington could not rely on precinct workers to win elections or on assessing a patronage army for the funds he needed. In the days of expensive pollsters, consultants and most of all, television commercials, politicians have to amass a large war chest. Before he was elected, Washington accused Jane Byrne of raising "obscene amounts of money." She did, in fact, raise over $12 million after she took office, but Washington raised even more and the second Mayor Daley had topped his predecessors' totals by the end of his second year in City Hall. Significantly, Daley not only used the funds for his own campaign, but also employed his war chest as a substitute for his father's patronage foot soldiers. In 26 wards he helped aldermanic candidates by paying for posters, mailings, campaign phone banks and other services.[82]

Clearly, the dynamics of Chicago politics have changed since Michael Shakman first began his battle against the legions of the Cook County Democratic organization. In all likelihood the machine would eventually have lost its hold on Chicago anyway, but Shakman's victory in the federal courts almost certainly contributed to its decline. It was left however, for the Black voters of Chicago to finally oust the machine from the mayor's office. There is an element of poetic justice in this, for it was the Black voters of the city who provided the crucial votes that first put Richard J. Daley into that office in 1955. In that election African-Americans, under the leadership of William Dawson who was then the preeminent Black politician, had voted for Daley in order to defeat Martin H. Kennelly. Daley welcomed Black votes, but would not abide independent Black leaders. He set about to systematically undermine Dawson, primarily by denying him control of patronage jobs. By the mid-1960s, Daley had eliminated Dawson as a threat and created a cadre of new Black ward leaders who were "dependent on him and forced to deal . . . with him from positions of subservience and weakness."[83] The six Black aldermen in the City Council became known as the "Silent Six" and didn't "open their mouths unless they got a signal from either Tom Keane, Daley's floor leader, or Daley himself."[84]

While Daley "took care" of the Black leaders he had co-opted, providing jobs for them and their precinct workers, and used federal welfare-state programs to "buy-off" middle class Blacks with social-service jobs and those at the bottom of the social scale with welfare payments[85] and public housing, he did nothing to integrate Blacks or to meet their demands for better education, higher level jobs, or for other government services and benefits. In particular, the machine remained adamantly opposed to desegregation in housing or in the schools or to pouring resources into Black neighborhoods. As a result, Black middle-class voters withdrew from the political arena and over-all turnout in the Black wards went sharply down. This suited Daley who, in his last years as the mayor and chairman of the party organization, depended more and more on the solid backing of the city's outlying white ethnic areas rather than on the inner city ghettos.

Gradually, however, Black voters, outraged by a series of blatantly racist acts such as Daley's order to "shoot to kill" rioters in 1968 and the 1969 police murder of Black Panther leaders Fred Hampton and Mark Clark, began to mobilize against the machine. At the same time the Cook County organization was weakened by the success of the Shakman suit and of a number of other lawsuits which challenged racial discrimination in the police, fire and personnel departments; by several embarrassing scandals, especially one involving a gang of burglars who were all policemen; by the prosecution and conviction of some of its prominent members, most notably former governor Otto Kerner; and by its decreasing clout and resources as the city lost population and tax revenues to the thriving suburbs. After Daley's death in late December of 1976, no one was able to hold the machine together and "the organization entered a period of contention, regression and precipitous decline."[86] The decline was exacerbated by the loss of state and federal funding as Republicans captured the Illinois governorship and the presidency and proceeded to cut the funds going to urban areas, particularly to poor Black inner-city residents. In 1983 the black community, galvanized by the impact of the Reagan administration's policies, rallied behind Harold Washington. The Congressman was the beneficiary of a highly effective registration drive which brought in 100,000 new Black voters and of a record turnout in the Black wards of the city. In contrast to 1979, when 35% of the eligible Black voters had gone to the polls, in 1983 over 73% voted—virtually all of them giving their vote to Washington.[87]

Whether Washington, who had just vanquished the organization regulars and gained control of the City Council following a court ordered ward remap and special election in 1986, would have been able to bring together Chicago's Blacks and whites as he was attempting to do or to establish a strong organization of his own will never be known. When he died, he left no obvious successor and the "movement" that had put him into office split into bitterly opposed factions. With two African-American candidates dividing much of the Black vote, Richard M. Daley was able to win the 1989 special election to fill the remainder of Washington's term. Daley waged a low-key campaign promising to "calm the troubled waters of Chicago politics" and bring racial peace to the city.[88] Following two years of relative peace, good press and generally competent government, Daley breezed to victory in the 1991 primary and general election, winning an overwhelming majority of white ethnic, lakefront and Hispanic as well as approximately a fifth of the African-American votes. The election, which took place during the Persian Gulf War, was remarkably low-key for Chicago and drew a low turnout of 48 percent of the registered voters in the primary and 45 percent in the general election.[89]

How successful the second Mayor Daley ultimately will be remains to be seen. However, it is already clear that he does not intend to base his power on a revival of his father's patronage army. As a modern politician, he has tried to project a nonpolitical image, disassociating himself from the Cook County Democratic organization, while focusing on being a good manager of the city's government.[90] In an *Illinois Issues* interview, he said he was "convinced now in the 1990s people don't look at elephants and donkeys; they look at candidates and philosophy . . . the political system is changing rapidly in this country."[91] Although he didn't say so, Daley also clearly recognizes that the politics of the 1990s requires big money and that money can buy the services patronage workers used to provide and many, such as computerized mailings, that they could not. Rather than trying to increase the number of city workers, Daley has reduced them by privatizing some city services, contracting with private firms to do custodial work and other jobs that were once done by public employees. Some of the mayor's opponents have suggested that Daley is pushing privatization in order to get around the Shakman decrees and have raised the specter of workers again being required to get a letter from an alderman or committeeman and to do political work in order to get and keep jobs with the private contractors. Some of this may, of course, occur but it's more likely that Daley sees privatizing as he says he does, as a way of improving city services by getting around the time-honored city worker tradition of sloth, bloat and inefficiency.[92] It's also likely that he values privatization as a way of strengthening his ties to the business community which can provide him with hefty contributions. Certainly, he has shown every sign of understanding the political uses of contracts, including the variety that has come to be known as "pinstripe patronage" and involves "no-bid consulting contracts, legal work, bond business, office leases

and low-interest loans."[93] In this respect, he is following in the footsteps of former Illinois Governor Jim Thompson who was such a
master of pinstripe patronage that he is sometimes credited with
inventing it. For his part there is evidence that Daley is funneling
much of the city's legal business to favored law firms, including one
which employs his brother. Over half of the $1 million in city legal
business awarded in the year after the 1989 election went to a firm
which had raised more money for Daley during the campaign than
any other city law firm. Other businesses which contributed to Daley
have also been rewarded with city contracts.[94]

In the Chicago of the 1990s, mayoral candidates woo lawyers,
developers and businessmen and the airwaves are littered with campaign commercials. All the while the machine dwindles into irrele-
vance. The Cook County Democratic organization hasn't even
endorsed a mayoral contender since 1983 and the candidates they
have endorsed in other elections have often lost in landslides. By 1992
less than 10 of the 50 wards had organizations which could even begin
to get out the vote, the chairman of the county party was an almost
unknown former state senator and once powerful aldermen were
reduced to waxing nostalgic over the good old days. Said one, "It used
to be a great job. . . . You had clout, you had jobs, you had power.
Now, if you're an alderman, you've got to be a committeeman just to
protect your flank. . . . Pretty depressing, huh?"[95]

CHAPTER 3
THE STATE OF PATRONAGE:
INDIANA, WISCONSIN AND ILLINOIS

There's an old *New Yorker* cartoon that shows the United States as seen by a diehard Manhattanite. Once past the Hudson River everything quickly dissolves into an amorphous landscape, boring in its sameness. That is probably the way most New Yorkers (and Californians) still think of the Midwest, but when it comes to politics they couldn't be more wrong. The Midwest states may be similarly situated geographically, but politically they inhabit different worlds. The sharpest divide has been between a group of states which are "issue-oriented" and another group which are "job-oriented."

Michigan, Wisconsin, Minnesota

When John Fenton, a political scientist, studied the politics of the Midwest in the mid-1960s, he found six states which all had "intensely competitive two-party politics, but otherwise differed. In Ohio, Indiana and Illinois politics were "fastened to the traditional job-oriented mold." People participated on a day-to-day basis because they wanted jobs or contracts rather than because they were concerned with issues or public policy. Elections took the form of battles between the "ins" and the "outs" in which:

> The "ins" are the people who have the jobs and want to keep them. The "outs" are the lean and hungry individuals who want the jobs and contracts. The interest groups operate outside the

71

parties for they are concerned with issues rather than jobs. In the political campaigns, the job-oriented politician uses the issues as a means of securing the support of interest groups and through them the votes to win the jobs and contracts.[1]

While the parties in Michigan, Wisconsin and Minnesota were as competitive as those in Illinois, Indiana and Ohio, they were more concerned with influencing public policy than with obtaining jobs and contracts. In each of these issue-oriented states the Democratic party had been transformed after World War II by groups of nontraditional political leaders. The dynamics of the transition to programmatic politics were similar in the three states:

> First, the Democratic party was an empty shell. Many of the traditionally Democratic but relatively conservative German and Irish Catholic voters had deserted the Democratic party in the 1930's and early 1940's . . . (in addition) job-oriented politicians in the three states lost interest in political activity because of the adoption of strict civil service laws and the outbreak of World War II, which dimmed the luster of political jobs and appointments by providing better-paying employment opportunities elsewhere.[2]

In the second place there were "astute political and interest group leaders" such as the United Auto Worker's Walter Reuther who were able to move into the Democratic party to fill the leadership vacuum left by the withdrawal of the traditional job-oriented politicians. The "professors, women, labor leaders, Socialists and liberals who captured the three state Democratic parties" were ideologically committed to "policies and programs which would alter the status quo by providing a larger share of goods and opportunities for the less privileged members of the society." Those who were relatively satisfied with the status quo—"the more successful farmers, professional people and businessmen"—became the leaders of the Republican party, where they replaced the job-oriented politicians who had lost interest in the wake of civil service reform. As a result of these shifts, the two parties developed distinctive identities and related to each other very differently from the way in which Republicans and Democrats related in the job-oriented states. According to Fenton:

> There was none of the mutual esteem that Republican and Democratic "pros" professed for one another in Ohio, Indiana and Illinois. After all, the Democratic and Republican "pros" in the traditional two-party states wanted the same thing—jobs! But in Minnesota, Wisconsin and Michigan the political leaders sought

different ends and the result was meaningful competition at every level of government and an absence of bipartisan collusion that characterized the politics in other states. After election, no urging was needed to persuade the issue-oriented politicians of Minnesota, Wisconsin and Michigan to earnestly attempt to translate their programs into public policy. Their only reason for participation in politics was commitment to issues. The businessmen left good-paying jobs with American Motors or General Motors. . . . Similarly wealthy liberals . . . or university professors, such as Hubert Humphrey, were not attracted to government by patronage jobs but rather by a commitment to certain ideals and a desire to see them incorporated into day-to-day activities of government.[3]

The differences between the job-oriented and issue-oriented states seem to be a function of the kinds of people who settled in them and the cleavages produced by the Civil War. There were few Southern settlers in Michigan, Wisconsin or Minnesota; consequently, there was nearly unanimous support for the Union forces during the Civil War. Following the War Between the States, the Republican party dominated the political stage in each of these states until the hold of the traditional politicians in the party was loosened at the time of the Great Depression and World War II. However, in Ohio, Indiana and Illinois there were settlers from both the South and the North and the populace was split by the Civil War. Two-party competition was thus established from the time of the War. The parties were deeply rooted in these states and the traditional job-oriented professionals who controlled them were able to maintain themselves in power. They were strong enough to waylay civil service reform *and* to keep issues out of campaigns. In contrast to states like California where the Progressive movement under Hiram Johnson succeeded in wiping out patronage, Indiana, Ohio and Illinois produced politicians of both parties who worked together to prevent reformers from eliminating patronage. Progressivism tended to take hold where the parties were already weak and then to perpetuate that weakness. Where the parties were strong and the leaders of both parties benefitted from patronage, they were able to fend off civil service reform.[4] In general, once a particular form of party politics becomes established, whatever the initial cause or causes, it tends to have staying power. There is "considerable place-specific continuity in forms of local party structure over the last century or . . . century and a half."[5]

Such Midwest states as Wisconsin, Indiana and Illinois illustrate this continuity. In Wisconsin, for example, the great Progressive leader Robert La Follette who served as governor from 1900 to 1906, still casts a giant shadow over the state's political life. Although La Follette initially built his own power by using machine-type tactics including jobs for his supporters, once he was firmly in control he abolished virtually all patronage. Wisconsin passed a strong civil service act in 1905 along with anti-lobbying and corrupt practices legislation.[6] Almost 80 years later, Neal R. Peirce and Jerry Hagstrom found that:

> Wisconsin's strain of Progressive politics—born when the people revolted against hard times around 1900 and ousted the corporate magnates and corrupt political bosses they blamed for their misfortunes—runs exceedingly deep, reflected both in an activist government and extraordinarily clean politics. While other states expect (and thus often get) bribery and corruption from their public officials, the people of Wisconsin will make a major issue of incidents customarily shrugged off elsewhere.[7]

In recent years some governors have tried to increase the number of appointments under their control and to restructure the civil service to make it more responsive to the popularly elected executive. Given the Wisconsin tradition, such moves always meet with great suspicion and are greeted with cries that the governor is politicizing the civil service.[8] The current governor, Tommy Thompson, a conservative Republican first elected in 1986, has drawn fire from the guardians of the Progressive tradition for his attempts to make more state appointments. Until 1977, a new governor was able to appoint only a handful of people (20). On the recommendation of a commission, about 43 administrative jobs were shifted out of civil service so that a new governor could place his people in them. However, Thompson's Democratic predecessor replaced fewer than half of the holders of exempt jobs, while Thompson replaced about 85 percent of them. At present the governor is allowed to make a little over 100 appointments. While this would be considered an exceedingly modest number in a state like Illinois, many Wisconsinites are appalled by it. Thompson has also been accused of giving some of these jobs to campaign contributors who were not qualified to hold them and of "quashing the morale of state workers" by his actions. One state worker told the *Capital Times* (anonymously) that Thompson had "destroyed what was once the best civil service system in the country" and the newspaper editorialized that the governor's "favoritism weakens good government."[9] A group of government employees, the Association of Career Employees, filed a lawsuit charging the governor with violating the state civil service law (and evading his own hiring freeze) by creating a number of special temporary "project" positions and filling them with his political friends. The Association also reminded the governor that "in Wisconsin, we do not follow the principle that 'to the victor belong the spoils'."[10] Its head, a former bureau director, said he had been driven from government and choose to retire early because he "was just fed up with the whole political atmosphere under which [his] agency operated." Other employees have also said that there is a general feeling of distrust and fear among state workers and that many good people are leaving the government.[11]

Governor Thompson is unrepentant. He maintains the electorate wants him to put his "people in place;" that they wanted him to bring in "people who are more cooperative, more willing to listen" in order to change the attitude of the entrenched bureaucrats.[12] While this may be true, it does seem that Thompson has gone further than previous governors in stretching civil service rules and extending his tentacles deeper into the lower levels of the civil service. Clearly, there is also a climate of fear within the ranks of the civil service; no one, not even professors at the University of Wisconsin, was willing to go on record in talking to me about the governor's actions. The governor has also opened himself to criticism by making some notably unfortunate appointments such as an old crony from the legislature who Thompson put in charge of the state office of tourism. This man "proceeded to sexually harass female employees and offend just about everyone, while promoting himself and Thompson through tourism ads and brochures and helping friends get lucrative state contracts." Still, he was able to stay in his job until he decided to run an ad promoting Wisconsin—complete with the governor's picture—in a Japanese skin magazine![13]

Patronage in Indiana

It was Tommy Thompson's misfortune to be the governor of a state with a moralistic, reformist, issue-oriented political tradition. His use of patronage would undoubtedly have raised fewer eyebrows in a job-oriented state like Indiana where politics has been described as a "business conducted by men who devote their lives to it and make their living at it."[14] Historically the Indiana parties have not allowed themselves to be distracted by issues from their singleminded pursuit of the jobs and money needed to keep them in office. In fact, political victory has seemed to be a means to an end, the end being material advantages for the party and its adherents. In such an atmosphere it has been easy to lose sight of the line separating one's private interests and the public interest. John Fenton was led to comment that the "unique quality of Indiana politics" is "the extent to which 'corrupt practices'" are "institutionalized and accepted as a normal part of their political game by the press and citizenry of the state."[15]

Nothing illustrates the character of Indiana politics better than the state's distinctive manner of handling the issuing of driver's licenses and automobile license plates. In a system begun by a Democratic governor in the 1930s, the governor appointed the Commissioner of the Bureau of Motor Vehicles. This official then awarded "concessions" or franchises to private firms to operate license branches in each of the state's 92 counties. This may seem like an early version of the "privatization" which is currently trendy, but it was really just old-fashioned machine politics since the firms were run by either the county chairman or another leading party official of the governor's political party. When a citizen went to one of the local bureaus to register a car or get a driver's license or license plate, he would pay two fees. One fee would go to the state; the other fee would be kept by the local firm. After paying its expenses and taking its "profits," the firm would hand over a portion of its fee to the party committee and to various campaign committees. In turn the county committees were required to pass along some of their booty to the state committee. According to the Republican state chairman, the State Central Committee realized more than a half million dollars—about one fourth of the total funds it collected that year—from the license branches in 1983.

Needless to say, the party which controlled the bureaus gained a stock of jobs to give its supporters. The county chairmen also gave themselves another advantage by devising a scheme for rewarding their big contributors with prestigious low numbered license plates. In Marion County (Indianapolis) contributors of $1,000 or more would get a number "1" license plate; $300 bought a number "2"; $150 a number "3" and so on.

Since the Democrats did not elect a governor between 1968 and 1988, by the late 1970s they were becoming quite unhappy seeing the Republicans reap the license bureau bonanza. With lawsuits looming on the horizon, the Republicans cut the Democrats in for a share of the kitty. The license bureaus were authorized to sell personalized or vanity plates for $40. Of that amount $30 would be divided between the Democratic and Republican state central committees which would each give half of their share to the county central committees in the county where the plate was bought. In 1983 each party received almost $200,000 from the sale of the vanity plates.[16]

Although lawsuits were filed challenging the system, including one brought by the Indiana Civil Liberties Union, the state Libertarian party and the Democratic mayor of Fort Wayne (the state Democratic party refused to join in the suit), it remained intact until 1988. The license bureau arrangement had been an issue in the 1984 gubernatorial election which the Republicans barely won, and they feared they might lose the governorship in 1988 (as they did). They decided to seize the initiative and turned the operation of the license bureaus over to the state. However, some Indiana political observers maintain that the Democrats, now that they are in the State House, have replaced Republican employees with Democrats in the lower level jobs in the bureaus. Ironically, many of the Republican managers have been kept in their jobs, often operating in the same office space as before, primarily because they alone had experience in running the license operation.[17]

The fate of the vanity plate fee is as yet unresolved. In December of 1989 the Republican party announced it would not take the state party's share and asked the county parties to renounce their share. The Democrats said they'd follow the Republican example. There were bills introduced in the state legislature in 1990 and 1991, but they didn't get anywhere. Some Republican county chairs had second thoughts and began pressuring the state chairman to change his policy and take the money. The chairman resigned; his successor was willing to take the license fee share, but the money which was collected had been given to the state auditor and he refused to hand it over to the party, saying it had to be refunded instead to the people who had paid the fee when they purchased plates. In the meantime, several citizens who just happened to be Democrats filed a suit designed to insure that the money would go to the purchasers rather than to the Republican party. This suit is slowly working its way through the courts. For their part, the Democrats (whom some say can afford to be magnanimous now that they control the governorship) have been turning their share of the fee back to the Motor Vehicle Bureau to help pay the costs of the state takeover of the license bureaus.

As one would expect, patronage has played a central role in Indiana's politics since the days of the pioneers. In 1988 almost 18 percent of the state's 40,000 employees held patronage appointments in nonmerit agencies. By official admission, patronage employees constituted 63 percent of the total number in the Highway Department; 57 percent in the Department of Revenue; 54 percent in the Department of Natural Resources; and 100 percent in the Bureau of Motor Vehicles. A watchdog group called the Highway Users Federation for Safety and Mobility charged that Indiana was the only state which checked political affiliation before hiring. Often, in the Highway and some other departments, this would be done through the use of a "clearance card." The Republican state committee issued 4×6 cards bearing the title "Political Endorsement." The card had blanks for the prospective job holder to provide basic information about himself or herself, including whether or not he or she had voted in the last primary and for which party he or she had voted. This information made it easier to check the applicant's party affiliation since by law Indiana primary voters have to publicly declare which party's ballot they want. In the middle section the card had space for seven signatures of endorsement from various party officials. The purpose of the card could not possibly be mistaken; at the bottom the applicant was informed:

> Political endorsement is required for most non-merit government employment and appointments. The elected office-holder who is responsible for filling such positions is dependent upon political party organization for campaign assistance. For this reason, the office-holder asks party officials to endorse all persons who are hired for non-merit jobs. Political endorsement will be valid for either one calendar year or the length of time the applicant remains in continuous state employment.
>
> If you are not now registered to vote, please do so in the county of your residence before requesting political endorsement. You can obtain the name and address of the required signatories by contacting your Republican County Chairman. Start the endorsement procedure by first contacting your precinct vice-committeeman and secure all endorsements 1 through 6. Return the completed card to the state agency or county chairman who furnished you the card. They will forward the card to State Headquarters for the State Chairman's endorsement.

The use of clearance cards was challenged in a federal lawsuit brought in the mid-1980s and when Evan Bayh came into office in 1989, he unilaterally abolished the clearance card system, but there are accusations that prospective employees (especially in the Highway Department) still have to be cleared politically.[18]

Indiana law actually requires that applicants for jobs in the State Police and for some jobs in other departments, including conservation officers in the Department of Natural Resources, auditors in the Department of Revenue and bank examiners in the Department of Financial Institutions, declare their party affiliation. This is necessary because legislation passed in the late 1930s and early 1940s dictates that no more than half of the employees in the agency or the unit can belong to one political party; promotions also have to be divided equally between the two parties. Both rules were supposed to be reforms designed to insure that neither party could control sensitive investigations.

Following the Rutan decision, the Bayh administration proposed dropping the bipartisan requirement for the state police, on the grounds that Supreme Court rulings made the mandated political declaration unconstitutional. For the same reason, the governor said he had instructed state hiring authorities to ignore the bipartisan split law. Evidently, however, someone in the administration had second thoughts because the proposal "got lost" and was never presented to the legislature. The governor's office also refused to release the governor's directive to the press even though state law required that he do so.

There were also some other curious developments. For the first time in Indiana history, the superintendent of the state police allowed employees to "redeclare" their party affiliation. Soon after, two employees who switched their allegiance were given promotions. Then there was the matter of Senate Enrolled Act 108, which was crafted to fill a gap in the state's laws that did not indicate how party affiliation would be determined for gubernatorial appointees. Although Governor Bayh denied that he had appointed people who were really Democrats to positions that by law were supposed to go to Republicans in order to maintain the required political balance, he chose to veto the Act which would have made it harder for Democrats to masquerade as Republicans (and vice versa). Under the Act an individual's party affiliation would be determined by the ballot chosen in the most recent primary or, if the person hadn't voted in the last primary, the chairman of the party with which the person claimed to be affiliated would have to approve the nomination. In his veto message the governor said the law wasn't needed and that it would unfairly require "the governor to share appointment powers with party officials."[19]

Once they were on the payroll, employees weren't allowed to forget their party obligations. If they should, they were likely to be rudely reminded. Former Gary mayor Richard Hatcher tells of his experience working in the Lake County prosecutor's office just after he had finished law school. He says he was "naive" and didn't know he was expected to contribute part of his salary to his boss's campaign fund. When he went to pick up his third or fourth paycheck, the secretary told him she was under orders not to give him the check until he had a talk with the boss. Naturally, he went to see the prosecutor who immediately demanded to know why Hatcher hadn't given anything to the "Flower Fund." Hatcher said he hadn't heard about the Fund and asked what it was. He was told it was used to buy flowers and birthday cards for the office workers and was also used for "political purposes." When Hatcher asked what would happen if he didn't start contributing, he was told that they'd keep his paycheck. Instead of contributing to the Flower Fund, Hatcher resigned.[20] Years later, when he became mayor, Hatcher refused to play ball with the county party and would not give it jobs in exchange for support; nor would he assess city workers for his campaign fund or otherwise take steps to build a traditional machine.[21]

In Indiana assessments have been the norm for both parties. The state is famous for the 2 Percent Club which was first established on a formal basis by a Democratic governor who held office in the 1930s. The club takes its name from the fact that state employees were expected to give 2 percent of their gross salaries to the party which controlled the State House. Elsewhere in Indiana there were other clubs—sometimes 2 percent, sometimes 1 percent—for county and local employees. In 1976 a disgruntled state employee filed a lawsuit against the practice in federal district court. Although the employee agreed to an out-of-court settlement which left the system intact, the system was faced with a threat from another quarter. A federal law, sponsored by an Indiana Democratic congressman and named in his honor, was passed in 1976 which was clearly aimed at the Indiana Republican party. This law, the Roush Act, forbids the solicitation of political contributions from state employees whose jobs are funded by federal money. In response to this threat the Republican state administration devised a "voluntary" payroll deduction plan which was put into effect in 1979. This "reform" was a brilliant stroke; in contrast to the days when the party had to remind workers to send in their checks (sometimes even accompanying them to the bank to make sure the party got its money), the money went directly from the state to the party, which deducted it every month from the paychecks of the workers who had volunteered to donate. In 1987 the Republicans got $356,285 from this source while the Democrats received a paltry $927.[22]

When Evan Bayh became governor, he issued an executive order doing away with the withholding system. But, in the absence of a statute, other elected state office holders continued to take the 2 percent, as did many county and local officials. Even where payroll deductions were abolished, employees were still expected to make voluntary contributions, to buy and sell tickets to party fundraising events and to do volunteer work for the party. In general, employees have continued to go along with the parties even though the Elrod and Branti decisions should have protected them from being fired if they refused the parties' demands. Some employees are unaware of their rights; others know about the Supreme Court decisions forbidding political firings, but fear there would still be retaliation. While a worker might be able to win in court, filing a lawsuit is not a realistic option for many of them because most lawyers will not take these cases on a contingency basis and few workers can pay attorney fees upfront. Nor is a worker likely to get much help from his union since public employee unions have been weak in Indiana and have only recently begun to make inroads into the state.[23]

In his gubernatorial campaign Evan Bayh promised to eliminate patronage. Although, as the preceding discussion indicates, his record is far from spotless, by Indiana standards he has lived up to his pledge not to do "business as usual." The governor says there are county chairmen who won't even speak to him because they feel he hasn't given them the jobs they deserve. Some of them, not understanding why he can't fire all of the Republicans working for the state, grumble that Republican governors did a lot more for their party than Bayh is doing for his. To mollify them, Bayh set up a job-referral service whereby lists of job openings in the state would be mailed to the county chairman. Since Bayh did not promise that the people recommended by the chairmen would get the jobs, this was perfectly legal. In fact, many Democrats, including a number of big contributors and relatives of prominent party members, did get jobs in the Bayh administration. While many of these people were placed in policymaking and non-merit jobs outside civil service, some were put into merit positions. The governor's press officer admitted that prior to Rutan "if two job candidates had similar qualifications, the Democratic supporter won out."[24] While the press officer didn't say so, it also appears that contracts have been going to Bayh supporters. The governor's former law firm has been so favored that insiders have nicknamed it the "State House East." Other contracts have gone to big contributors, but in all fairness it should be noted that virtually all businesses that deal with the state cover their bases by giving money to both parties. Allegedly, any who haven't already given or haven't given enough are contacted by the state Democratic committee on the day they file their bids for state work.

Some complaints against the Bayh administration's hiring and firing have surfaced in a handful of lawsuits that have been filed in federal court. In at least two of these cases, the Bayh administration appeared to be justified in firing the workers as their jobs could reasonably be classified as policymaking positions. One plaintiff, for example, was the general counsel for the Indiana Utility Regulatory Commission; another was a subdistrict highway manager supervising

68 clerical and maintenance employees who were responsible for keeping 800 miles of roads in repair. When the highway superintendent's case went to trial, the governor's executive assistant in charge of transportation argued both that the position was a policymaking one and that the firing of all 37 subdistrict superintendents (all Republicans) was part of an overall management change made to cut waste and inefficiency. However, he undercut his own testimony when he conceded that the Bayh administration felt there were too many Republicans in the Highway Department and that he "considered that one strike against them." Moreover, the aide admitted that political recommendations had been one factor in appointing replacements for the fired workers and that county Democratic officials had been asked to make recommendations for the jobs. He insisted, though, that political recommendations were not the "overriding factor" in hiring even though the plaintiff's job had gone to someone nominated by a county chairman.[25]

Bayh administration spokesmen claim that any preference shown Democrats ended with the Rutan decision. Department of Natural Resources officials say, for example, that summer jobs in the parks are no longer patronage jobs and are filled on a first-come, first-served basis. The head of personnel added that "If they absolutely can't walk and talk and chew gum, they can't do the job. But for some of these jobs, you don't need a brain surgeon."[26] And the governor asks that his administration be judged in light of Indiana's political tradition. He is fond of pointing out that "there's an old adage that says a dark speck shows up on a white hat. It's not even seen on a black hat. To a certain extent, that's what we're seeing here. . . . to say we've been perfect—no. But we are trying, and to a greater extent (are) meeting a higher standard."[27]

However one feels about Governor Bayh, it is unlikely that over a hundred years of Indiana history will easily be reversed. Patronage has been a way of life in Indiana and many people see nothing wrong with it. Many Indianans wouldn't even consider applying for a government job if their party weren't in power and they take it as a given that once one is hired for a job, the party has a rightful claim on the employee. And one southern Indiana politico probably spoke for many when he told the *Indianapolis Star*, "If we can't have fun by getting our side in, we shouldn't be a party to begin with. . . . I don't need the hassle of politics if I can't get my friends and children jobs."[28]

The Illinois Political Tradition

Illinois, like Indiana, epitomizes job-oriented politics. Its leading city has, of course, been home to one of the country's strongest and most long-lasting machines, but patronage politics is hardly the sole province of Chicago Democrats. Patronage has flourished in both parties; downstate and in the populous north; in the rural hinterland and in the cities and even in the expanding high tech corridor in DuPage County, one of the so-called collar counties surrounding Cook County. As in Indiana, politics in Illinois is a game played by professionals who care a great deal about getting their share of clout, jobs and money and are quite happy to work with each other, irrespective of party, to carve up the spoils. Again, as in Indiana, corruption has flourished within the state's materialistic, cynical political culture.[29] In the 1930s William Allen White wrote that, "Under primary, under convention, under despotism or under a pure democracy, Illinois would be corrupt and crooked. . . . It is in the blood of the people."[30]

It is certainly in the blood of some of the most prominent Illinois politicians. Orville Hodge, the Republican State Auditor in the mid-1950s, went to jail for embezzling over two and a half million dollars; in 1980 the Attorney General went to jail for income tax evasion; and two post-war governors—Otto Kerner and Daniel Walker—also served time, as have a significant number of Chicago City Council members along with Cook County judges caught taking bribes in the federal sting operation called Greylord. The number of jailed politicians would undoubtedly have been even greater if it weren't for the fact that "relatively few Illinois politicians actually go to jail for corrupt practices simply because prosecutors' offices and the courts are so often compromised."[31]

Although Illinois was one of the first states to adopt a civil service system,[32] merit reform did not exactly flourish in so hostile an environment. Only a portion of jobs under the Governor's jurisdiction were covered by the Civil Service Act. Jobs administered by other elected officials such as the Secretary of State and the Attorney General, as well as those in a number of other separate state employment systems (although not all of the jobs in these systems were available for patronage) were excluded. Even in the governor's jurisdiction, some jobs were specifically exempted from civil service and others which were ostensibly under civil service were used for patronage purposes. As Thomas Page explains in his study of the Illinois personnel system:

> by a kind of tacit understanding, examinations were not given regularly enough to maintain usable registers for certain classes of positions under the Civil Service Act. These were invariably staffed by provisional appointees who only rarely acquired protected status as a result of an examination at a later date. The Civil Service Commission recognized that if it did attempt to conduct

examinations and maintain registers for all these positions, it could expect to face retaliation at the hands of the General Assembly, possibly with the consent of the governor, when appropriations were considered for the next biennium.[33]

By the late 1940s, it was becoming clear that the Illinois civil service system was not meeting the needs of the state's growing government. The Civil Service Commission was too weak to enforce the protective features of the law. Its effectiveness and efficiency were also hampered by the overly rigid procedures the law prescribed for classifying positions, determining pay and examining and certifying employees. The situation was ripe for change, but it took a coal mine disaster to get it started. In 1947 111 men were needlessly killed in the explosion of Centralia Mine No. 5. The deaths could have been avoided if the Illinois Department of Mines and Minerals had heeded the dozens of warnings given by its inspectors and shut down the mine. But the Department was a political agency staffed by patronage appointees; its officials owed their jobs to the Governor and were expected to contribute to his campaign fund and work for him at election time. In fact the mine inspectors, all political appointees, were even being pressured to solicit money from the owners they were supposed to be policing.[34]

The blast at Centralia gave the Democrats an opportunity to wrest the governorship from the Republicans. At the behest of Jacob Arvey, its chairman, the Cook County Democratic Central Committee slated two blue-ribbon, reform candidates, Paul Douglas and Adlai E. Stevenson II, to head the ticket. Stevenson would have preferred the United States Senate and Arvey had to use all his persuasive powers to convince him to run for governor. Arvey also had to sell the committee on running two Democrats who were not part of the machine and might not serve its interests. Arvey later told Milton Rakove that he thought the machine politicians only went along with the slating because Harry Truman's troubles in the national arena had convinced them it was a "losing year" for Democrats.[35] The pros were wrong and Truman, Douglas and Stevenson all won.

In his inaugural address, the aristocratic Stevenson signaled that he would be a different kind of Illinois governor. He asked for a number of reform measures including revision of the civil service law; legislation which would force disclosure of state payroll information in order to discourage patronage abuses; expansion of the merit system; and placing the state police under its own merit system so that new governors could no longer terminate police employees and replace them with their own partisan supporters.[36] Stevenson also appointed Maude

Myers, a career employee who had risen by virtue of her ability to be the executive director of the Civil Service Commission. Its members chose her to be the Commission President and in that position she worked with outside groups of business and civic leaders to promote a thorough overhaul of the civil service system. Before he left Springfield for the national stage in 1952, Stevenson succeeded in reorganizing the state police and placing it under a merit system and in getting the legislature to adopt a number of measures proposed by a "little Hoover Commission" he had created to recommend changes in state government administration. He also brought some exceptional people into the state government. His leading biographer, John Barlow Martin, wrote that Stevenson's greatest achievement as governor may have been the improvement he wrought in the "tone, or spirit of state government by bringing in good men." Martin adds that "in a state as big and corrupt as Illinois" this is "no small accomplishment."[37]

The patrician, idealistic, cerebral Stevenson was definitely not a wild-eyed radical trying to bring down the machine. Stevenson had gotten the message when Arvey told him, "As far as your major appointments go, I wouldn't even make a suggestion if you asked me to. As to the rank and file, you'll have to get help somewhere—you won't know enough people to fill all the jobs—and if you need help I'll give it to you." When reporters asked the new governor what would happen to the 30,000 state employees, Stevenson replied that his "disposition will be to appoint Democrats where qualifications are equal." Stevenson personally interviewed prospective Cabinet members and appointed Republicans when he thought they were the best candidates, but for low level jobs he generally was willing to work with the Democratic organization. He even had Maude Myers at the Civil Service Commission prepare monthly reports for him so that he could show the machine just how accommodating he was. One of his aides said that Stevenson "felt good when he got 500 Republicans fired and 500 Democrats hired. He had Maude make a table comparing the speed with which Democrats replaced Republicans under him and under Governor Horner (the last Democratic governor). If a politician complained to him about patronage he'd pull out this list."[38]

Stevenson worked out a system for dealing with the patronage pressures on him. Job descriptions would be sent to screening committees in Chicago and Springfield. These committees would then ask the county chairmen to make recommendations for the positions. The committees would screen the applications and forward the best one to the department directors who would decide who to hire—subject to the governor's veto. When he thought it was necessary, Stevenson was willing to buck the machine and back his department heads. In one case his Director of Public Welfare had given him a "list of jobs that needed professionals—doctors, psychiatrists and others and told him those jobs could not be filled by political patronage." According to the director, Stevenson agreed even though it hurt him politically. He explained: "Lots of those jobs had been filled on a patronage basis in the past. He had to resist all sorts of pressure. And he had to fight the battle over and over—these political fellows never give up. I found forty or fifty payrollers in that department. I fired a Democratic state central committeeman. You can imagine the heat that put on the Governor. But he made it stick. I fired a Chicago precinct captain and there was all kinds of hell to pay. The man was a slave to his political sponsor. His sponsor had got him into a job he wasn't able to do."[39]

Stevenson was realist enough to accept the organization's help when he needed it. Without the deal negotiated by state Senator Botchy Connors he would never have gotten the legislature to approve state police reform. Under Governor Green the state police was an all-Republican force. The Democratic legislators in Springfield were not about to give all of these Republicans permanent tenure under a merit system. So, in a compromise devised by the regular organization Democrats, Stevenson fired half the Republicans and replaced them with Democrats. Thus, when civil service went into effect on January 1, 1951, 250 Democrats and 250 Republicans were locked into position. After that, new appointments to the force were to be made on the basis of merit.[40]

Because Stevenson became the Democratic candidate for president in 1952 rather than running for reelection, he was not able to see the civil service reform process he had started through to the finish. Instead, it was left to his successor, Republican Governor William Stratton to act on the recommendations of the legislative study commission that had been appointed. Stratton understood the realities of the Civil Service system in Illinois. Well before he had become governor he had written a friend that "jobs with the State Civil Service have been more or less (in) name only. . . . Civil Service . . . has been abused so that I would not know of any branch of it where it could be considered really permanent."[41]

The new governor, who considered himself a progressive Republican, was a hands-on administrator with considerable knowledge, experience and interest in the details of government administration.[42] With his support a Personnel Code, formulated along the general lines recommended by the National Civil Service League in its Model Law, was adopted in 1955. This was the same model that was later used by Mayor Richard J. Daley in his personnel reform. Both

Stratton and Daley, as strong executives, were attracted to the model because it incorporated the views of President Roosevelt's Committee on Administrative Management which advocated strengthening executive control of personnel matters. The Illinois law, which went into effect in 1957 replaced the Independent Civil Service Commission with a Department of Personnel headed by a Director, who would be appointed by the governor and "serve at his pleasure." A three-person bipartisan Civil Service Commission remained as a watchdog, but it was no longer to be responsible for day-to-day personnel administration. That would be the job of the Department of Personnel which would have jurisdiction over classification and pay, conditions of employment, and merit and fitness. To eliminate the rigidity that had marked the old system, the 1955 Code gave the Director discretionary powers to change and interpret rules and to institute new procedures. In addition flexibility was also supposed to be fostered by replacing lists of numerically ranked candidates (and the usual requirement that the hiring authority choose from the top three on the list) with much longer lists of individuals ranked in categories so that a manager could choose any one of a dozen or so candidates in the A or superior category. The law did, however, reduce flexibility in one respect in an attempt to eliminate past patronage abuses. Emergency appointments were limited to 60 days; temporary appointments were to last no more than six months; and provisional appointments were to be for a maximum of three months in any one year.

The law specified that certain positions, such as those of the private secretaries of department directors would be excluded from the merit system. It left it up to the director, and therefore the governor who appointed him, to determine which policymaking positions at the top (this did require the approval of the Civil Service Commission) and unskilled positions at the bottom would be exempted from civil service, thereby making them available for patronage. The reformers intended that the Director of Personnel would be a professional rather than a politician and they were able to have language inserted in the law which required that the director must have "practical working experience in the field of personnel administration." Following the recommendation that the newly created personnel Advisory Board had made, Stratton appointed a General Motors personnel executive to be the first head of the Department of Personnel. However, the Governor, the legislators and the county chairmen were not willing to allow the director to pursue civil service principles too avidly. There was a prolonged struggle and when the dust settled over 200 policymaking positions and 6,000 unskilled jobs had been exempted from the merit system.[43]

The general consensus among experts on Illinois politics is that William Stratton was one of the state's better governors with some impressive achievements to his credit. A hard working, dedicated man he built the Illinois toll road system, pushed through the first legislative reappointment since 1901, sponsored major building programs for the state's universities and mental hospitals and fought for judicial reform and civil rights.[44] By Illinois standards Stratton was a man of integrity. He would not allow 2 percent funds and early in his tenure he issued a directive to agency heads telling them that he was "unalterably opposed to political assessment . . . from employees. . . . (They) are entitled to every penny they earn. If anyone approaches an employee in your department . . . seeking an assessment, I want that person to report immediately to you."[45] He also insisted that patronage employees do an honest day's work and would not tolerate ghost payrollers. During the 1956 primary campaign, he took the highly unusual step of actually firing two Republican county chairmen from their state jobs because they were not working.[46] For all that, Stratton was the son of a prominent downstate Republican who had risen to be Illinois Secretary of State; he had spent all his life in politics and saw patronage as a normal and accepted part of the political game. He was not about to let the personnel professionals and do-good reformers deny him any of the patronage Illinois governors considered their due. When Donald McAmis returned to his General Motors job, Stratton rejected the recommendation of the Advisory Board and appointed one of his staff to be director of the Department of Personnel. At the same time, the new director continued to handle patronage matters for the governor. With his man in charge, Stratton was able to keep on using "most state positions for patronage purposes. . . . it was everywhere in state government—wherever a job, a board or commission appointment, a contract, a fee or any other favor could be provided."[47] Department heads understood that the governor's office was to be informed of any openings. Departments would get "directives" from the governor's office "asking that a specific person be interviewed, or in some cases, appointed, retained, or terminated. . . . If no name could be referred to the department, it would ask for a 'release' to recruit on its own initiative."[48]

Although Stratton professed to believe in civil service, he jumped at the chance to add to his stock of patronage. When the Illinois Toll Highway Commission was established, its jobs were all exempted from civil service and the governor played a role in filling all of them. State Racing Board jobs at the tracks were also kept out of civil service as were many summer jobs, including more than 1,200 at the annual State Fair held in Springfield. Stratton was personally involved in handing out these plums. His staff would solicit recommendations for jobs from the state chairman and, in the case of the State Fair, kept careful track on a county outline map of how the appointments were distributed. David Kenney wryly notes that the "system sometimes had odd results. . . . in 1955, the two 'Curry boys' were properly recommended by their county chairman, approved, and assigned to the swine department as assistant superintendents. When they reported for 'work' the 'boys' turned out to be seventy-six and eighty years old."[49]

Stratton seemed to consider Maude Myers a bit overzealous in her dedication to reform and tried to oust her from the chair of the Civil Service Commission. Although she managed to hang on to her post, Stratton was able to thwart any attempt of the Commission to forcefully police the personnel system. As a watchdog, the Commission had no bite. For example, it had no power to take legal action on its own. The Attorney General was supposed to act as its legal arm, but the politician elected to this job was not likely to take a state agency to court on behalf of the Civil Service Commission. Stratton and the legislature also saw to it that a Hatch-Act type provision in the Personnel Code, which would have restricted the political activities of state employees, was a paper tiger; no agency or official was given the power to enforce the provision.[50]

Stratton's biographer, David Kenney, believes that in the final analysis, the patronage system the governor built so assiduously may have played a role in his downfall. The old adage has it that for every job a politician gives away, he creates nine enemies and one ingrate. It seems that all the ingrates and enemies ganged up to defeat Stratton when he ran for a third term in 1960. Even though 3/4 of the Republican county chairmen and over a thousand precinct committeemen got government jobs under Stratton, it was never enough. Stratton found himself "suffering from the 'what have you done for me lately' syndrome. . . . a position once filled could not soon be filled again. . . . so that as time went on there was a steadily decreasing number of jobs to be distributed. . . . the longer Stratton was in office, the more difficult it was for him to maintain strong local units in a patronage system."[51] Although he tried, Stratton never again won elective office after his 1960 loss. He moved to Chicago and began a successful career in business. In 1990 when he was in his mid-seventies, Stratton was appointed by Governor Thompson to one of the three seats on the Civil Service Commission.

Under the governors who succeeded Stratton, the patronage train continued to roll merrily along. Otto Kerner, the Democratic winner in 1960, was Richard J. Daley's man in Springfield and was not inclined to question the system that nourished the machine which nourished him. Even Richard Ogilvie, a Republican elected in 1972, who is revered today for his skillful management, excellent nonpartisan cabinet appointments, and his courage in pushing through an income tax which he felt was needed urgently by the state, quipped to a Peoria reporter that "the only trouble with patronage is there's not enough of it."[52] On balance, Ogilvie did nothing to disturb the personnel and patronage system shaped by Stratton, with one important exception. Together with the Attorney General, the Chairman of the Cook County Republican Central Committee, a number of Republican officials in northern Illinois counties and, of course, the Democratic defendants, Ogilvie signed the 1972 Shakman consent decrees which prohibited the state from firing its employees for partisan reasons. State employees could choose voluntarily to do political work but "compulsory or coerced" contributions or political activity were barred. If Illinois were to violate the decree, any registered voter could take the state to federal court. The 1972 Shakman decree did not eliminate patronage in the state any more than it did in the city of Chicago, but it did end the mass firing of state workers by new governors and it did put some limits on party manipulation of state employees.

The citizens of Illinois rewarded Ogilvie's courage and competence by voting him out of office. He was beaten by Dan Walker, an anti-Daley Democrat who talked reform but didn't deliver reform, or, for that matter, much of anything else. By the end of his single, troubled term, Walker had broken his promise not to solicit state employees for campaign contributions and was being accused by some state workers of forcing them to work for him and the candidates he backed in state elections.[53] (This was after the federal court had turned down Walker's request to have the state exempted from the Shakman decree.)

The 14-Year Governor: Big Jim Thompson

In 1976 Illinois elected the man who would be its governor for the next 14 years. Because of his extraordinary tenure—the longest in Illinois history—James R. Thompson had an unprecedented opportunity to put his mark on Illinois government and politics. However, Thompson, an unquestionably able and intelligent man, chose the path of compromise and accommodation rather than innovation and change. He appeared to revel in the frenzy of campaigning and the perquisites of gubernatorial life—he was especially fond of leading trade missions to foreign capitals—but he was a hands-off manager who left the details to others, hated living in Springfield and never seemed to be deeply involved in the work of governing. As the *Chicago Tribune* once editorialized, "No one has seen anyone less interested in state government since the Queen of Romania passed through in the 1920s."[54] But he did like to play the game of politics and he became very good at it. From a beginning as a political outsider, a crusading prosecutor who had put former governor Otto Kerner and the powerful Alderman Tom Keane as well as dozens of other officials (mostly Democratic) in jail, Thompson became a master of political manipulation. He developed an effective working alliance with the Democratic leadership in the legislature and (at times) with Chicago's Democratic mayors at the same time that he strengthened the state Republican party and his own organization. Thompson raised the art of patronage to new heights, unabashedly practicing the "new" pinstripe patronage while perfecting the old-fashioned "blue collar" trafficking in jobs. Under his tutelage, every job in the state became grist for the patronage mill; the entire civil service system was subverted by the governor.

Although "Big Jim" (so named because he stands at 6 feet 6 inches) says he decided to be a politician when he was 9 or 10 and signed a high school friend's yearbook "Jim Thompson, President of the United States, 1984–92," he did not take the traditional political route to the state house. After getting his law degree, he worked for the Cook County State's Attorney where he made something of a reputation arguing appeals, including several before the Supreme Court. His argument supporting police methods of eliciting confessions in the landmark Escobedo case was noteworthy. Even though it failed to convince the Court which ruled that a person being interrogated by the police has the right to have an attorney present, it made him an "instant hero" to police and prosecutors across the nation.[55] Ironically, Thompson did so well at the State's Attorney's office that he managed to survive the purge which followed the defeat of the Republican who had hired him and was kept on by the newly elected Democrat. After a few years, Thompson left to write and teach law at Northwestern University, where he and his mentor, Fred Inbau, also founded the Americans for Effective Law Enforcement to promote "law and order." He moved from Northwestern to the office of the Illinois Attorney General and then to the federal prosecutor's. In 1971 at the age of 35 he became the United States Attorney for the Northern District of Illinois where he aggressively pursued corrupt politicians and policemen, winning convictions in almost every case.

With his flair for publicity and his skill at establishing personal relationships with reporters, Thompson soon became the best known Republican in Illinois. Although he had never been active in party politics, had no experience as a campaigner and had never held elective office, Republican party professionals correctly saw him as a winning candidate. Thompson resigned his position as U.S. Attorney to join the prestigious firm of Winston and Strawn which paid him at the yearly rate of $50,000 during the time he campaigned for governor. One of the firm's partners also served as head of Thompson's campaign organization. Not surprisingly, Winston and Strawn, to which Thompson returned on leaving office in 1992, was a prime beneficiary of pinstripe patronage in the form of state legal business during the Thompson term.

But the "no-bid consulting contracts, legal work, bond business, office leases and low-interest loans channeled to insiders" which are the stuff of pinstripe patronage[56] were far in the future in 1976. In that first campaign Thompson fought as "Mr. Clean" waging war against "Mr. Machine." The Cook County Democratic machine had succeeded in defeating the hated Dan Walker in the primary, but its candidate was overwhelmed by Thompson in the general election. Because of the adoption of a new state Constitution, Thompson had to run again in 1978. With his campaign skills finely honed and a photogenic wife and newborn daughter at his side on the campaign trail, he again won in a landslide, albeit his margin of victory was somewhat smaller than it had been in 1976. By 1982 the negatives had begun to pile up and he beat Adlai Stevenson III by a mere 5,000 votes. Most of the Illinois political cognoscenti thought Thompson won only because Stevenson, who has been described as a man who has "charisma in reverse,"[57] waged a singularly uninspiring campaign. In 1986 Stevenson, the son of the late governor and presidential candidate, promised to do better and bets were on him to win, but Thompson got lucky again. In the primary Lyndon LaRouche disciples won places on the Democratic ticket as candidates for lieutenant governor and secretary of state. The inept post-Daley Democratic leadership had failed to publicize the party slate and voters blindly chose the extremist LaRouchites, largely, it seems because the citizens of Illinois preferred the All-American names of the LaRouchies to the ethnic names of the endorsed candidates. Since the governor and lieutenant governor are elected as a unit, Stevenson decided to resign from the Democratic ticket and run as the candidate of a hastily formed new party. Thompson was the beneficiary of this Democratic comedy of errors and was elected to a fourth term.

At the start when Thompson first took the oath of office on January 10, 1977, he gave a lofty, high-minded inaugural address in which he promised, among other things, that "there will be no jobs bought; there will be no favors sold."[58] The next day, at his first press conference, he expanded on this theme. He pledged that his would "not be a political administration;" that he would not fire people in "non-policy making positions . . . simply because they belong to a different political party" or didn't support his candidacy. He even said that he wouldn't use any subterfuges such as eliminating job titles in order to oust the occupants and then creating similar titles to be filled with his supporters. At the same press conference, the newly appointed head of the Department of Personnel said he would work to "re-establish the credibility of the Department" and would begin by getting rid of "political operatives" holding civil service jobs.[59]

During the transition period and the first year or so of Thompson's administration, the governor gave the appearance of acting in the spirit of that pledge. There was a nationwide talent search to find the best people for cabinet posts and the governor made a number of excellent appointments. Although most of the people he put in the top jobs were Republicans from Illinois, there were some notable exceptions and he put both out-of-state people and Democrats in some key posts. For this Thompson won praise from editorial writers, but not from Republican party officials who were furious with him for neglecting their interests. There hadn't been a Republican in the statehouse since Ogilvie left Springfield in 1972 and the county chairmen were hungry for jobs. They didn't seem to understand that Thompson's hands were tied by a combination of civil service protections, the 1972 Shakman decree, and the 1976 Supreme Court decision in the Elrod case which made it impossible for the governor to remove en masse the Democrats who were in state jobs. To be sure, some Democrats could be "persuaded" to leave, but the fact remains that Thompson did not have thousands of jobs to give away.

Unhappily for him, the governor made a bad situation worse by putting the wrong people in charge of his patronage operations. In a single year he went through four different patronage chiefs, each of whom managed to irritate the veteran politicians. At one point the county chairmen were so angry with Thompson that they pointedly did not issue an invitation to him to speak to their Association meeting in Springfield.[60]

Clearly, things changed between 1977 and 1990. As Thompson himself remarked to a reporter in 1990, "It came as some irony that at the end of my administration, after all this, the Supreme Court of the United States certifies what these Republican chairmen refused to believe all along—that I had the best patronage machine in the nation and that it was a Republican machine."[61] What is not so clear is what brought about the change. Thompson's presidential aspirations may have been an important factor, making him more sensitive to the wishes of the county chairman who influence the selection of delegates to the Republican national convention. One party leader had actually threatened to "work to elect an independent slate of delegates to the (1980) convention and use that as leverage with the governor on patronage."[62] Perhaps Thompson simply recognized that "Republican county chairmen have always been an important force in party affairs"[63] and decided it was best to have them on his side. He did seem to have a growing appreciation of the chairmen's power. When after five tries, he finally found an effective patronage chief in 1980, he sent the man on a tour of the state to visit more than 90 county chairmen. His gesture was interpreted as a signal of a "more sympathetic attitude and the promise of additional patronage."[64] It is also possible that he had begun to see how useful patronage could be in making deals with legislators, Chicago Democrats and other political influentials. Or, it may be as David Kenney has suggested, that Thompson had been "careful to give county chairmen what patronage he could from the beginning," and it was only the unreasonable expectations of the party regulars that prevented them from seeing that Thompson, even though he was not one of them, was trying to help the party.[65]

The Thompson "patronage machine" that drew the Supreme Court's censure most likely was not planned, but rather, evolved over the many years of the governor's tenure. In part its development may have reflected Thompson's penchant for "institutionalizing" the Office of Governor. It was natural for Thompson to put patronage operations on a more systematic footing, just as he had systematized the rest of his office. He expanded the staff; created distinct groups for scheduling, budgeting, patronage and other functions; and introduced a more centralized, hierarchical and bureaucratized organization. At one and the same time he tried to centralize and increase his own control *and* lighten his own workload by delegating much of the authority to conduct day-to-day operations.[66] His need for a large staff was such that he broke his campaign promise to get rid of so-called "ghost payrollers," which in this case referred to people who worked out of the governor's office but were carried on the payrolls of other departments. A few weeks after taking office, Thompson was forced to publicly admit that he had put some of his campaign workers on the payrolls of various agencies. Six months later, he again broke a promise to stop using ghost payrollers by the end of the fiscal year. The *Tribune* reported that Thompson was using money from the Department of Transportation budget to pay secretaries who were listed on the payroll as being engineering asistants and patronage dispensers who were being paid as "technical advisers."[67]

In some respects Thompson needed both a big staff and patronage to help him gain control of the burgeoning state government. Like Reagan and other bureaucrat-bashers, Thompson and the people closest to him never trusted career public servants. Consequently, the governor moved to make top-level bureaucrats more responsive and accountable to him by stripping them of civil service protection. By coincidence, Thompson signed the bill which limited the tenure of approximately 1,000 senior civil servants to a four-year (renewable) term, just a few days after Judge Bua's ruling in the Shakman hiring case. In signing the bill, which was sponsored by a former member of the governor's staff who had been elected to the legislature, Thompson maintained that it was not a ploy to increase patronage, but an "experiment" that was designed to "return to the original purpose of the personnel code, which recognized the objective that principal policymakers and administrators serve at the pleasure of the governor or their director." As he later explained to a newsman, he believed that high-level employees "should be monitored . . . a governor should be able to get rid of them if they are not performing, the same way the voters can get rid of a governor they feel is not performing. . . . this is all about getting accountability into state government."[68]

Since there has never been an in-depth study of term appointees, it's impossible to know how the loss of tenure may have affected their attitudes. Although only 53 employees out of a total of 1,117 whose appointments were up for renewal were terminated between 1979 and 1989, the law may still have had a chilling effect, making administrators more cautious and less willing to question the governor's policies and actions. There's also reason to believe that the law makes it difficult to recruit out-of-state administrators, who, according to a "highly regarded career executive," see term limitation "as a blatant patronage ploy that offers no job security to creative managers."[69]

Whatever the true motives behind the term appointment law, at best it yielded only a handful of jobs. No one could build a "patronage machine" on such a slender reed. The real foundation of the Thompson employment system was the governor's executive order of November 12, 1980. The order stated categorically that "no agency, department, bureau, board or commission subject to the control or direction of the Governor shall hire any employee, fill any vacancy, create any new position or take any other action which result in increases, or the maintenance of present levels in State employment, including personal service contracts. All hiring is frozen."[70]

As such, there was nothing new in a hiring freeze. Governors Kerner, Ogilvie and Walker had all dealt with tight budgets by freezing hiring. Thompson himself had imposed his first hiring freeze when he took office in January of 1977. But this second hiring freeze turned out to be different from previous ones. For one thing, it lasted over ten years, even though the governor had said when he announced it, that the freeze was to be in effect for only 60 days. Of much greater importance, this freeze was to serve as a mechanism for establishing systematic control by the governor's office of all the more than 70,000 employees under the governor's jurisdiction.[71] The governor's order directed that there were to be "no exceptions" to the freeze without his "express permission" after the appropriate requests were submitted to his office. At a press conference, Thompson emphasized that there were to be no "automatic exemptions" for agencies such as the Department of Mental Health as there had been in past freezes. In practice this meant that no one could be hired (or, as it turned out, transferred, recalled from layoff, or promoted) for any job under the governor, be it a civil service position covered by the code or a job exempted from the code, without the express approval of the governor. Whether or not this was the governor's original intent, the system made it possible for him to use any, and all, jobs for patronage. We will probably never know if Thompson forsaw all the possibilities of the freeze back in 1980. We do know that the head of the Civil Service Commission, a Thompson supporter who had helped his campaign, wrote a letter protesting the freeze order; there was no answer. And, there are knowledgable people in Springfield who say that the freeze always had a political, as well as a fiscal, purpose. On the other hand, Professor David Kenney insists that the governor was not so Machiavellian. He writes that the system was mainly a "response to hard times that made a freeze on hiring necessary. Once in place, it proved useful for patronage purposes (some in the administration may have had that objective from the start) and was retained primarily for patronage uses once the recession of 1980–81 was over." He continued that "it would be crediting him (Thompson) with more guile than he possessed to state that he was trying to build a personal organization."[72]

Be that as it may, the governor did greatly strengthen his own position with the freeze and the system that developed out of it. Aside from the freeze order itself, the system did not rest on any formal executive orders or legislation. The Personnel Code was not changed. Civil service rules were left in place. The governor's staff simply worked around the Code's rather loosely formulated provisions. No one interfered because the governor was careful to put his own people in place in the state personnel agency. The Department of Central Management Services (DCMS), which absorbed the old Department of Personnel in a 1982 reorganization, has had a series of highly partisan directors who could be trusted not to rock the patronage boat. For example, the head of DCMS at the end of the Thompson administration, was a thirtyish man, Gene Reineke, who had no training whatsoever in personel administration. His experience was exclusively as a political operative. In his early twenties he went to work for the Lieutenant Governor. By 1981 he had graduated to the Governor's office. Eventually he was put in charge of patronage, with the euphemistic title of the governor's Director of Personnel. Before going to DCMS he served as the director of Thompson's mammoth pork barrel project, a long-term capital development program called "Build Illinois" which, as the *Chicago Tribune* put it, "helped coin the phrase 'pinstripe patronage.'"[73] When Thompson left office, Governor Edgar made Reineke the executive director of the Republican State Central Committee and of Citizens for Edgar, the governor's fund-raising organization.

Under directors like Reineke, DCMS offered no resistance to Thompson's subversion of the civil service system. The agency contined to give civil service examinations (although it discontinued the entry-level examinations which had been introduced under previous governors).[74] Other than typing and dictation tests, DCMS never developed any performance exams; it did not use assessment centers or otherwise adopt any of the more recent and more highly regarded methods of testing. For many positions it used "unassembled exams" which are not exams at all in the ordinary sense of the word. In an unassembled exam an applicant's education, experience and other credentials are evaluated by a DCMS employee who assigns each item a value using an established scale in order to arrive at a total numerical score. On the basis of these exams—both assembled and unassembled—DCMS dutifully constructed eligible lists for the various agencies which were hiring. After the hiring decision was made, DCMS would process the necessary paper to put the new employees on the payroll. It did not monitor the agencies nor train the hiring authorities. It never challenged any of the abuses of the system, including those associated with the use of category rankings. In eligible lists, applicants would be grouped in broad categories rather than ranked individually according to their scores. Agencies could hire anyone in the "A" category; no distinctions were made among the individual candidates even though their scores might differ considerably.

Technically, the Thompson administration abided by the civil service rules and could truthfully state that every one of the approximately 5,000 persons hired each year was qualified. In reality the rules were stretched and manipulated. There was a lot of leeway in the evaluation of credentials and in the initial establishment of the criteria to be used in judging applicants for particular positions. The written tests were more difficult to fudge, but it didn't take a rocket scientist to pass most of them. If a person failed, he or she could retake the exam. In the event that the patronage candidate could only get on the "B" list, there were several tactics that could be used to "work through" the "A" list. As Nowlan, Hanley and Udstuen explain, "one tactic is to convince candidates in their job interviews that the job is not really what they want, or is otherwise unattractive. The "A" list is shortened by each candidate who signs a form saying he or she is no longer interested. Agencies consider candidates for a position from a pool of at least three eligible persons. Thus if the "A" list is shortened to only two candidates, the pool is automatically enlarged to include all persons on the "B" list."[75]

None of this bothered DCMS. Nor did it interfere when the governor's patronage office would direct an agency to hold off in asking for an eligible list until a patronage candidate could be examined and get on the list or until it could find a patronage candidate with the appropriate qualifications for the job. If all else failed and the governor's patronage office deemed it vital to place the sponsored person immediately, the rules would be bent by giving the job seeker an emergency, temporary or provisional appointment. Although there were time limits on these appointments, the limits were not always strictly observed, and, even when they were, the appointment gave the patronage director a chance to find another job for the person, or alternatively, it gave the person time to take (and retake) the examination in order to get on the eligibility list.[76]

Sometimes, a new position might be created for a person whom the patronage office wanted in a job. While any changes in the classification plan (as well as changes in the exempt status of a job) have to be approved by the Civil Service Commission, this has never been much of an obstacle to the Thompson patronage machine. The Civil Service Commission has been a watchdog in name only. It has neither the will nor the resources to effectively monitor DCMS or the governor's office. Because the law requires that the commission be bipartisan, all three members can't be from the governor's party, but that has not hampered Illinois' governors any more than a similar requirement for appointments to the independent regulatory commissions has hobbled American presidents. It's always possible to find someone, nominally of the opposition party, who will not make trouble for the person doing the appointing. The everyday work of the Commission is carried out by the professional staff, but they have no clout and few resources. The legislature and the governor have not seen fit to give the Commission a decent budget. In recent years it has had a total of ten employees, including clerks and secretaries, to run its operations in Springfield and Chicago. It has been unable to conduct investigations of complaints or perform regular audits of the departments to determine if they are complying with the Personnel Code. Nor can the staff easily use the courts, even when there are very suspicious goings-on such as the instances in which a person is shuffled from an emergency to a temporary to a provisional appointment or moved several times from one classification to another. The State Attorney General would have to represent the Commission before the courts in any request for a restraining order and that official has generally been reluctant to take one state agency to court on behalf of another agency. For all these reasons, the Commission has busied itself primarily with hearing individual appeals relating to discharges and the like, rather than aggressively policing the personnel system.

So, the way was clear for the Thompson patronage machine to develop. Some time after the freeze order was issued, a committee consisting of the head of the Bureau of the Budget, the Director of DCMS and the head of Policy and Planning in the governor's office, was formed to enforce it. Whenever an agency wanted to fill a vacancy, it had to get permission from the committee. Other personnel actions such as promotions, transfers and the creation of new positions also had to be approved by the governor's office.[77] In time even temporary clerk hires and summer internships for outstanding college students were subject to the approval of the governor's Office of Personnel, i.e. the patronage office. Although by law the director of an agency is in charge of its personnel department and has the final authority over such matters as hiring and promotion, under the Thompson system the director had to work through an employee known as the liason or "key person." This individual was placed in the department, often as an administrative assistant to the director, by the governor's patronage office to act as its liason. The key person would monitor personnel actions, relay information on vacancies, and provide the governor's office with weekly updates on anticipated openings and plans to create new job classifications.[78] It was also the liason's job to deal with the freeze committee to arrange the unfreezing of positions.[79]

Once an agency had the go-ahead to hire, it could begin the process of finding someone to fill the job. There were times when it had no choice as the patronage office would tell the agency to give a particular person the position. In all cases the agency had to get the approval of the patronage office before it could put someone on the payroll. Sometimes the patronage office insisted that the agency search until either it or the agency could find a suitable Republican candidate for the job. Whenever there was a choice between a Republican and a Democrat who both met the minimum qualifications, the governor's office insisted that the Republican be hired.

Not surprisingly, there were frequent clashes between the agency directors and the patronage office. Particularly for higher level jobs, the directors wanted to hire the most qualified people whom they felt would be best for the agency. While in theory the governor's office wanted to hire good people, its more immediate concern was in maintaining the governor's political position. It would base its decision to approve or disapprove a particular candidate on political criteria. With the help of the county party organizations, it would check out the applicant's primary voting record, the support that the person gave to Republican candidates, especially his or her financial contributions to the party and its candidates; sometimes it would even check the voting records of the person's relatives and their financial contributions to and support of Republican candidates.[80] Many referrals to the patronage office came from the county chairmen and other prominent Republicans, but referrals were also accepted from other people who were in a position to help the governor, including Democratic legislators and other office-holders and private persons who contributed large sums to the party or were otherwise important to the administration.

Because of the difference in their interests, agency directors were often forced to bargain with the patronage office. There was a certain amount of "give" in the system which agency heads could exploit. Sometimes a director would agree to hire a few low-level patronage employees in exchange for permission to put the director's choice in a more crucial high-level post. At other times the director might find a political sponsor for the person he or she wanted to hire, but this had the disadvantage of obligating the director to eventually return the favor to the sponsor. As a last resort the agency head might, if appeals to the patronage chief failed, go over his head to the governor to make an appeal, but this was a tactic that could only be used on a rare occasion.[81] A director's success with the patronage office depended on a number of factors including the type of agency and the position in dispute and his or her own abilities and political standing with the governor. David Kenney, who headed the small specialized Department of Conservation, reports that his "hiring was constrained by the patronage system, but in many cases the system couldn't provide an acceptable person, so I could look elsewhere." In an agency like the Department of Transportation (IDOT), which had always been a patronage stronghold, the director probably had much less freedom to maneuver, especially with respect to road crew jobs which county chairmen expected to be able to distribute. Since the Thompson patronage operation functioned in part to satisfy the demands of the chairmen and other Republican party officials, the head of IDOT was always under pressure from the patronage office.

In addition to keeping the party leadership happy, the governor's patronage machine served other purposes. Because of Shakman, the Elrod and Branti decisions and the Hatch Act (for employees in programs receiving federal dollars), the Republicans could not force state employees to work for and contribute to the party. But, all the same, many employees did help the party at election times. Some simply believed in the party; many felt obligated to the job-givers; others, aware that there were a number of ways of making an employee's life miserable short of firing, were afraid to say no. The end result was that Thompson's patronage helped the party; not incidentally, it also helped Thompson himself by building a "network of political operatives and supporters useful in re-election bids."[82] The governor also helped himself considerably in his dealings with the state legislature. As he gained political experience, Thompson learned to play the Illinois political game, giving legislators control of jobs in return for favorable committee action and votes. Even more than previous governors, Thompson had to make deals in order to get anywhere with the members of the General Assembly. Because the Democrats were in the majority in both houses for nearly all of his tenure, he could not depend on party loyalties for votes. (Actually, he couldn't always depend on the Republicans either, since many of them had their own agendas and didn't feel they owed him anything—even in return for jobs that they considered their due.) Moreover, the Illinois legislature, like Congress, has become more splintered with each member focusing on his or her own career and local interests. Increasingly, the legislators want something for their district or for the interests they back in return for their support so that each vote requires the assembling of a new coalition on the basis of hard bargaining.[83] In this bargaining the governor can trade "pork," such as public works projects and other spending in the legislator's districts, and patronage, both in the form of paid state jobs and appointments to the many boards and commissions, which though generally unpaid, bestow prestige and (sometimes) power. Naturally, given their control of the legislature, Democrats were frequently on the receiving end of the governor's deals. Reportedly some of the Democrats were not at all shy about letting the governor know what they wanted. one powerful Democratic senator was known to bring a long list of patronage demands to Thompson's staff at the beginning of each legislative session.[84] But Thompson avowed that he didn't mind "sharing patronage with the Democratic leaders." As he saw it, "they're entitled to something by virtue of being leaders. I respect their office." And, he added, "Maybe that makes me an old-fashioned politician."[85]

What Thompson Wrought

For years the most important people in Illinois state government—the governor and his staff and the leaders of the legislature—have viewed the state's personnel system through a distorted lens. Instead of focusing on improving the system so it could better serve the public, Illinois movers and shakers have been concerned primarily with milking it for patronage that would further their own partisan and personal interests. It appears that when the governor and his people thought at all about the state's administrative agencies, they thought about how they could keep the bureaucracy from harming the governor's interests. As Paula Wolff, who directed the policy and planning staff for the entire Thompson term, told a conference of public administrators, it was necessary for the governor to control the selection of *all* state employees to insure that they had the "right attitude." She argued that every worker—even the one who operates the highway snowplow—represents the governor's policies and should be chosen by him. If a governor couldn't pick people who believe in his policies, he might end up with employees who could hurt him by performing poorly or, even by sabotaging his programs. So in this somewhat paranoid view the governor, rather than mid-level bureaucrats pursuing their own agendas, has to have the final say in staffing decisions.[86]

Is it any wonder that a nonpartisan blue ribbon commission of business, academic, labor and government figures which studied the Illinois personnel system in 1990 issued a scathing report describing the state's personnel code as "antiquated;" its "hierarchical work structure" as "rigid, inefficient and non-productive;" and its managers as "inadequately prepared" and "ill-equipped" for their jobs? Instead of actively recruiting the best and the brightest, Illinois waits for applicants to come to it and then discourages all but the very persistent. It is impossible for an ordinary citizen to even find out what jobs are available since "no member of the general public ever has access to a complete listing of all the openings in state government at any given time." Without knowing if there are any vacancies, individuals have to go to the trouble of filling out separate applications for each job that interests them, and then they face a wait of three to six months to hear from the state (if they hear at all). As one University of Chicago graduate student told the Commission, "It's like government is a wall of glue, a place where you send your application and then it just sticks like glue." If all this weren't bad enough, the state's negative image further tends to scare away many potential employees.[87] As Samuel Gove, the dean of the academic experts on Illinois politics, told the Commission, "At the University of Illinois the best students do not even consider state government as a career. . . . One of the major reasons is that political credentials have been prerequisite for employment. . . . credentials have even been necessary for entry into internship programs that were designed to be nonpolitical."[88]

The Thompson administration's proud claim that it has only hired qualified people is clearly a misleading and hollow boast. Through its actions, the state has sharply limited the pool from which it chooses its employees. The Commission found that even people who had chosen the public sector over the private and were enrolled in graduate training programs in public policy and administration steered clear of the state. Moreover, the state does not necessarily choose the best from among those people who do decide to apply for its jobs. The construction of eligibility lists by categories lumps the best applicants together with those who barely manage to squeak by. Once an applicant gets into the "A" category, even though he or she may be the worst of 100 people on the eligibility list, the person is considered qualified although certainly everyone in the "A" category is not, as the Thompson administration maintained, equally qualified.

Miraculously, the state actually does have dedicated, hardworking and competent individuals among its employees. Unfortunately, many of the best of these employees have been demoralized by the patronage system. Conscientious employees find it very upsetting to have to work with some of the people that system has foisted upon their agencies. Managers have also complained about having to waste time interviewing applicants when the patronage office has already decided who will get the job. Some are bitter about having to negotiate with the patronage office over hires and of having to sacrifice some positions to the governor's patronage needs. Almost everyone resents the fact that the public so often sees them as lazy and unqualified patronage jobholders. There are people who don't even admit publicly that they work for the state. And, needless to say, many employees have experienced frustration and anger at seeing jobs and promotions repeatedly go to the politically connected.

Because of the patronage system, countless citizens have opted not to work for the state or have left state jobs in disgust. In a large metropolitan area like Chicago, the state is only one of thousands of employers and individuals have many career options. However, in Springfield, where government is the main employer, or in many of the state's small towns where a state prison or a mental hospital is the chief, and best paying, employer, there are fewer choices. Even so, most employees and would-be employees have put up with the system. Patronage has, after all, always been part of Illinois political life; Thompson was simply more thorough than his predecessors.

Despite the risks, a few brave souls decided they had to fight for the jobs and promotions they felt were rightfully theirs. Separately, five of these people made their way late in 1984 and early in 1985 to the small Springfield law firm that had been founded in 1977 by Andrew and Mary Lee Leahy. Most lawyers wouldn't touch a case challenging the governor's patronage machine. Taking such a case in a town that lives on state business certainly wasn't the prudent thing to do. But, Mary Lee Leahy had not spent her life being prudent. As a young woman, she first became actively involved in politics in 1968 when she worked Chicago bail bond hearings defending people who had been arrested in the riots that took place during the Democratic National Convention and after the assassination of Martin Luther King. By the next year, she—like her University of Chicago Law School classmate Michael Shakman—was running as an independent candidate for the Illinois Constitutional Convention. Unlike Shakman, she beat the Democratic machine's candidate and went to the convention. She was on the winning side against the machine again in 1972 when she was one of a team of lawyers who helped unseat Mayor Richard J. Daley's slate of delegates to the Democratic convention. Much to Daley's chagrin, his group was replaced by a delegation headed by Jesse Jackson and an independent Chicago alderman named William Singer. Thinking back on this victory, Leahy told political writer Lynn Sweet that, "Once you've taken on the Daley machine in Chicago, to take on other things after that wasn't difficult."[89]

After serving as the director of the Illinois Environmental Protection Agency for a year and the Department of Children and Family Services for three years in the administration of the maverick Democrat, Dan Walker, she stayed in Springfield rather than moving back to her native Chicago. For a time she was the only woman in private practice arguing before the Springfield court. In time much of her practice came to be devoted to sexual harrassment and employment and sex discrimination cases. Because of that and because she had always been concerned with First Amendment issues, having worked in her law school days on the briefs in the landmark Pickering case which established a public employee's right to free speech, she was a natural choice for the Rutan plaintiffs. At first however, she hesitated to take the case. It was a bad time in her life. Her daughters were in college, her husband was dying of cancer, and she was singlehandedly trying to hold their practice together. She knew what she'd be up against and it just seemed "overwhelming," but she says her husband laid an "Irish guilt trip on her" by asking "If you don't file the case, who else will?"[90]

So she took the case, combining the complaints of four people who were either working for or had worked for the state and one who was trying to get hired by the state. Each had acted independently in deciding to sue and in fact they did not all meet each other until 1991 when Leahy brought them together to discuss a possible settlement with the state. There was no outside group pushing the five into being part of a test case. Although Mary Lee Leahy is a Democrat, the Democratic party did not have any role in her decision to go ahead with the suit.

The suit Leahy filed is known as the Rutan case because Cynthia Rutan's name was listed first in the pleadings. Rutan, who lives in Springfield with her husband and two sons, believed she had been denied a promotion for political reasons. In 1974, before Thompson became governor, she had gone to work for the state's Department of Rehabilitation Services as a Disability Claim Specialist. Although she had a good work record, had done well on the promotion interview and was, in all respects, qualified to be a supervisor, she was repeatedly passed over in favor of less qualified candidates. When she asked why she didn't get a promotion, she was told that her voting record had been checked and that her name didn't "clear" the governor's office.[91] Since Illinois law requires that a voter publicly declare which party's primary—Democratic or Republican—he or she wants to vote in and this declaration is recorded, Thompson's office was able to find out that she had voted in the Democratic primary. Rutan was also told that people who got promotions were those who actively suported the Republican party. So she went to the Sangamon County Republican Central Committee, where she was given a promotion form to fill out.[92] (See Figure 3.1.) Although no one ever spelled it out, it was clear that Rutan could improve her chances of being promoted by joining the Republican county political club, contributing to the party and working for its candidates. Instead of doing that, an incensed Rutan went to Leahy.

Outrage also drove James Moore to the Leahy law offices. In 1978 Moore, a veteran, moved back to his native southern Illinois. He applied for a job with the Illinois Department of Corrections believing his chances to be good because state law gives veterans preference in hiring. As he now says, he was "naive enough" to believe the signs posted in state offices which affirmed the state's commitment to veterans and to equal opportunity policies. Although Moore was qualified

Figure 3.1

SANGAMON COUNTY REPUBLICAN CENTRAL COMMITTEE
200 SOUTH SECOND STREET, SPRINGFIELD, IL 62701

Print or Type
Name_____ Date_____

Address_____ Precinct_____ Township_____

Telephone_____

Voting address if different_____ Precinct_____

Age_____ Date of Birth_____ Social Security #_____

Present position_____ Dep't_____

Desired position_____ Dep't_____

How long in present position_____

Reason for change_____ Are you qualified?_____

Give name of test taken_____ Grade_____ Date_____

For which party did you vote in primary elections?

1984____ 1982____ 1980____ 1978____
NOTE: (if under age, question applies to parents.)

Enter name here:_____
Do you hold a membership in the Lincoln Club of Sangamon County?___
Would you be willing to become an active Sangamon County Republican
Foundation Member? _____ (The foundation is a voluntary, financial
assistance organization)
Would you be willing to canvass and work your precinct or neighborhood
for candidates the Central Committee recommends as qualified for local,
state, and national offices? _____
I affirm that the information given on this application has been answered
honestly to the best of my ability.

_____
Signature of Applicant

I recommend the above applicant because _____

_____

_____
Signature of Precinct Committeeman

(R.A., pp. 14, 24).

and there were openings at the state prison in Vienna where he wanted to work, he wasn't hired. By 1980 Moore realized that he needed political sponsorship and he went to see the Republican Chairman of Pope County who told him he had to get two signatures on his "card" if he wanted to work for the state. He also told Moore that being a veteran didn't matter.[93] Since Moore couldn't get a job without the support of the district's state representative, he wrote to the legislator in question. Representative Robert Winchester sent Moore a letter telling him that "there are over 1,100 applications on file at the Vienna Correctional Center. Of those, 450 have been strongly recommended by the precinct committeemen within the Republican organization." He suggested that Moore "make contact with your precinct committeeman and your Republican County Chairman. . . . you will have to have the endorsement of the Republican Party in Pope County before I can refer your name to the Governor's office."

Moore, who had voted in a Democratic primary, couldn't get the county chairman's signature and was not hired. When he saw jobs that he was qualified for go to party officials and their relatives, Moore decided to take action against what he calls "discrimination of the basest sort." He later told Mary Lee Leahy that he couldn't understand how the First Amendment could safeguard the right of a protestor to burn the flag, but not the right of someone who had served his country to support the political party he believed in without being denied state employment.

Moore was the only one of the plaintiffs who did not work for the state. It was his treatment therefore that raised the hiring question: Could a government exclude qualified individuals from holding a nonpolicymaking job solely because the person did not support the "right" political party? Rutan's treatment posed the same question with respect to promotions. The other three plaintiffs' situations raised similar questions about the proper grounds for laying off a worker or denying a transfer or a recall from a layoff.

Ricky Standefer was laid off from his temporary job at the Illinois State Garage. Eventually, five other garage employees who were laid off at the same time were offered other jobs with the state. Only Ricky Standefer did not get another job. The five others had Republican sponsors. Standefer, who had voted in a Democratic primary, had no sponsor and did not get a new job.

Franklin Taylor, another plaintiff, was a double loser. He didn't get a promotion even though he had more seniority than the person who got the job *and* he was refused the transfer he requested from Fulton County to Schuyler County where he lived. He lost out in both cases because he didn't have a party sponsor. Taylor, who had worked as an equipment operator for the Illinois Department of Transportation since 1969, could not get the required approval of the Republican chairman of both counties.

The fifth plaintiff, Dan O'Brien, had worked for the Lincoln Development Center of the Department of Mental Health and Developmental Disabilities from 1971 until April 1983 when he was laid off from his job as a dietary manager. According to the personnel rules,

O'Brien would retain his seniority and all his benefits as long as he was recalled within two years. In December 1984 the business administrator of Lincoln Center told him he was scheduled for recall. However, there was a hitch. His recall had to be approved by the Governor's Office of Personnel. When that office would not give its approval because O'Brien had voted in a Democratic primary election, he was not recalled. Since he needed a job, he switched his party affiliation in order to get the backing of Joe Sapp, the Logan County Republican chairman. With Sapp's support, O'Brien was hired by the Department of Corrections. However his salary was not as high as it would have been in his old job, and he lost all his seniority because more than two years had passed since his layoff. That, according to Mary Lee Leahy, made O'Brien, like Rutan, Moore, Taylor and Standefer, a "victim" of the governor's employment system. On their behalf Leahy filed a suit against Governor Thompson, the Republican Party of Illinois, two Republican party officials and several current and former state officials.[94]

The Rutan case went first to Harold Baker, the Chief Judge of the United States District Court in Danville, Illinois. In July of 1986 Judge Baker dismissed all of the complaints. The plaintiffs appealed to the United States Court of Appeals for the Seventh Circuit. Initially a three-judge panel heard the appeal. Their decision, which was subsequently affirmed by all of the judges of the court sitting together (en banc), partially overruled and partially upheld Judge Baker's dismissal. Working on the premise that patronage is constitutional except in the case of a discharge or an action which is the "substantial equivalent of a dismissal," the appeals court held that Judge Baker was correct in rejecting Moore's claim. The court reasoned that Elrod and Branti dealt only with firing and that hiring on the basis of political affiliation had not been found unconstitutional by the Supreme Court, so Moore had no case. The other four defendants might have a case if they could show that the state's actions towards them amounted to the same thing as a dismissal. Therefore, the appeals court overruled Judge Baker and sent the four cases back to the district court.[95] However, neither the plaintiffs nor the defendants were willing to accept the verdict of the Seventh Circuit and they both appealed to the Supreme Court, which decided it would hear the case.

Consequently, on January 16, 1990 Mary Lee Leahy found herself, for the first time in her career, arguing before the nine justices of the nation's highest court. Most lawyers consider oral argument a nerve-wracking experience. Rarely does a lawyer get to speak for more than a few minutes of the thirty alloted to each side before one of the justices cuts in. Leahy had prepared herself by attending several of the oral arguments which took place in the week before Rutan was scheduled. She says that made her "feel very comfortable" in the courtroom and that, knowing what to expect, she actually "had a wonderful time."[96] That may be because she handled the justices' queries easily while the opposing lawyer, former U.S. Attorney Thomas Sullivan, seemed confused by the questioning. For example, Sullivan first argued that the Thompson personnel system was not a "strict" partisan one, but a "loose" one of "friendships and political considerations" since it did not require a loyalty oath to the Republican party. He then conceded that Moore was not hired, Rutan was not promoted, and Taylor didn't get his transfer because they "lacked adequate sponsorship." He defended these acts of the state in part by arguing that they served the state's interest in maintaining the party system by "increasing participation" and providing an incentive to employees "who have supported the party." This led to the following dialogue:

> JUSTICE KENNEDY: Do you want us then to decide the case on the assumption that the Illinois system does coerce political activities and political beliefs?
> MR. SULLIVAN: No, Your Honor, and it is not—
> JUSTICE KENNEDY: Well, I thought that—that the opposite was your point. You are justifying it by saying that it encourages party activity in those that are partisanship—
> MR. SULLIVAN: It does in some. It does in some.
> JUSTICE KENNEDY: Well, how—you can't have it both ways. It either coerces party membership and party activity or it doesn't. Which is it?
> MR. SULLIVAN: Well, Your Honor, in—this system will benefit—both Democrats and Republicans—
> JUSTICE KENNEDY: I am not talking about who is benefitted and who is hurt. I am asking about the proposition whether or not this is coercive of a person's political beliefs and political expression and political participation?
> MR. SULLIVAN: I—I do not think it is.
> JUSTICE KENNEDY: Well then, I don't see how it serves the interest that you have been claiming in the first half of the argument that it does, that it promotes party—
> JUSTICE SCALIA: You ought to tighten it up a little.
> MR. SULLIVAN: Pardon me?
> JUSTICE SCALIA: You ought to tighten it up a little; it's too loose. It's not doing the job you want it to do.[97]

Even with Justice Scalia's helpful suggestion, Sullivan could not convince a majority of the justices to back the Illinois position. Scalia, of course, not only accepted the state's argument that patronage hiring is constitutional, but went further than the state dared, to contend that patronage firing should also be permitted and that the Court should therefore reverse Elrod and Branti. Chief Justice Rehnquist, Justice Kennedy and (in part) Justice O'Connor joined Scalia's dissent. On the other side, Justices Brennan, White, Marshall, Blackmun and Stevens accepted Leahy's basic argument that the Illinois system was unconstitutional because there was no compelling state interest which would balance the harm done by depriving individuals of their First Amendment rights of freedom of speech and association.[98] The majority agreed with Leahy that under the Thompson patronage system the plaintiffs (and all those in a similar position) not only had to "reject or abandon their beliefs," but, in addition, had to "support that which they do not believe in order to obtain a promotion, transfer, recall from layoff or employment. They must vote in the favored party's primary, not by choice. They must work for the election of candidates whose views they do not accept. They must contribute money to support a party with whom they do not wish to associate."[99]

The Court decided that victory at the polls did not entitle the winner to control all the jobs in a government. A governor like James Thompson could appoint anyone he wanted to policy-making jobs. Beyond that, the state's jobs were not his personal property to dispose of as he wished. As a victor, the governor could only lay claim, as Justice Brennan put it, to "those spoils that may be constitutionally obtained."

Clearly, the majority decision was a victory for Leahy and her five clients, as well as for the forces of reform. But the decision did not end the battle against patronage for the plaintiffs or for the people of Illinois. The Rutan case had gone all the way to the Supreme Court on a motion to dismiss; there had never been a trial in the lower courts to determine if the plaintiffs' claims were valid. The Supreme Court decision meant that the state had no right to base its hiring and promotion (and other hiring decisions) on political considerations, but in order to win damages, Rutan and the other four plaintiffs would have to show that *their* treatment was in fact due to political considerations. If the state, for example, could show that Cynthia Rutan wasn't promoted because her work was not up to standard, the state would not have to compensate or promote her. This meant that after more than four years the case was back where it began in the courtroom of Harold Baker of the United States District Court in Danville, Illinois.

By its very nature, a Supreme Court decision has an impact far beyond the immediate parties to a case. The Court's decisions are the law of the land. In Rutan the decision meant that, no matter what the outcome of the proceedings in Danville, patronage hiring was against the law. Any government which continued to base hiring and other employment decisions for nonpolicy-making positions on political considerations was liable to find itself on the losing side in a federal court suit. The decision applied to all governments, not just that of Illinois. In its wake many governments throughout the nation began to reexamine and revise their personnel practices. However, the spotlight was definitely on Illinois and the state was forced to cope with the implications of the Rutan case. If it wanted to avoid having a court-appointed receiver take over the direction of its personnel system, complete with court-supervised compliance plans and audits a la Shakman, Illinois was going to have to respond to the Rutan imperative of eliminating its patronage from its civil service system.

The Implementation of Rutan in Illinois

Governor Thompson, his lawyers, and his staff were confident that they would win in Rutan. When the decision went against him, the governor appeared stunned by the defeat. He seemed, at first, unable to imagine how the state could make hiring decisions without the guidance of patronage. Plaintively, he asked reporters: "What other basis are we going to use? Because one is tall and one is short? Because one is old and one is young? Do we hire by lottery? What does this all mean?"[100]

Since Thompson had already announced that he wouldn't seek reelection in November of 1990, he evidently decided to leave it to his successor to sort out the meaning of the court's decision and to devise a response to it. Lawyer that he is, he did move immediately to protect himself legally by issuing an executive order directing all administrators under him to "conform their personnel practices to the principles of *Rutan*." The order added that "under this ruling, no one may be denied State employment, promotion, transfer or recall to a position based on political party affiliation or support."[101]

At the same time, he began a series of legal maneuvers designed to blunt the decision's impact (and possibly reverse it) and to keep the whole question of patronage buried until after the election. First, he asked the Supreme Court, which was already recessed for the summer, to rehear the case although he almost surely knew that it was highly unlikely that five justices (including at least one who had been in the Rutan majority) would agree to his request. As expected, the Supreme Court turned the governor down, but the petition had served its purpose of delaying any further action in the case. In the fall there were further legal moves in the Seventh Circuit so that, in the end, the case did not get back to Judge Baker in Danville until the election was over and the Republican candidate, Jim Edgar, had won the governorship.

While all this was going on, Thompson's patronage people were trying to figure out how they could salvage as much patronage as possible without actually violating the Rutan decision. Some of them harbored the hope that the patronage operation could be continued on a decentralized basis through the agency liasons.[102] Perhaps because of this, the freeze was not lifted. However, the Thompson administration did take some tentative steps toward implementation partly because the agencies needed some guidance. Thompson and his staff were also anxious about what the courts might do and wanted the agencies to produce documentation of personnel decisions which could be used to "defend against any claims that may arise."[103]

Thompson's administrative order of July 17th set out some general guidelines for the state's agencies to follow. Basically, the order warns the agencies that they will have to be able to document and justify (in job-related terms) their personnel decisions, especially their decisions to interview particular individuals on the eligible lists and to hire one person rather than another. The order also cautions the agencies that they aren't allowed to investigate or give any consideration to an applicant's political affiliation. Most tellingly however, the order does allow agencies to "consider recommendations and referrals from any source, including elected officials or representatives of any political party." Although the order states that the agencies should consider these recommendations and referrals "only if they relate to the job qualifications of the particular candidate" and "that no consideration should be given to the political affiliation of the person making the recommendation or referral," this provision does seem to leave the door open to political influence.[104] It's hard to imagine a savvy Illinois agency head ignoring a recommendation from the governor or a powerful legislator.

In October Thompson's office issued a second administrative order with more detailed instructions for interviewing candidates and documenting their hiring decisions. The most striking thing about this order is that it had to be written at all. No government with a decent personnel system would have to issue such elementary instructions. Capable administrators should already known that they should develop hiring criteria based on the nature of the job *before* they begin to interview and evaluate candidates; that they should conduct structured interviews using a standardized set of questions that will enable them to "gather pertinent information about the candidate's knowledge, skill, abilities and personal characteristics;" that they should systematically evaluate the candidates' interviews and credentials; and that a record should be kept of what they have done.[105]

Thompson's orders did not begin to answer all of the agencies' questions. For example, the agencies were never told which positions were to be exempt from Rutan. The second order promised that a preliminary list of policy-making and confidential positions would be published within two weeks, but a list of exempts was not published until March 1992. Under the circumstances, there was considerable confusion and uncertainty. The old system had broken down, but there was no new one to replace it. In the absence of direction from the governor's office, the agencies did not know what to do. For a time there was almost no hiring. Everyone was afraid of running afoul either of the courts or of the new governor so people just hunkered down and adopted a "wait and see" posture.

Rutan and the New Governor

In January of 1991 Illinois had a new governor for the first time in fourteen years. Like Thompson, Jim Edgar is a Republican who decided as a boy that he was going to be in politics, but there the resemblance ends. In contrast to the sophisticated, outgoing, luxury loving Thompson, Edgar is a somewhat reserved and low key teetotaler whose idea of a good time is a weekend with his family in their country log cabin outside of Springfield. He was born and raised and went to college in the small downstate town of Charleston. At college he met and married a pretty girl from another one of Illinois' small towns. When he graduated, he decided against law school and accepted an internship with the president of the state Senate. Except for a brief stint as a salesman after he lost his first election (for state representative), he stayed in state government. He was elected to the state legislature on his second try and later served as the governor's lobbyist. In 1981 Thompson appointed him to fill the vacancy left when Alan Dixon moved from the office of the Illinois Secretary of State to the United States Senate. Once in office Edgar cultivated local Republican leaders and won plaudits for his programs, particularly his aggressive pursuit of drunk drivers. He was elected on his own in 1982 and reelected in 1986 by the largest plurality ever recorded by a candidate for state office in the history of Illinois. Party workers helped him in that election and again in 1990 in the much closer gubernatorial contest; in fact he attributed his 1990 win in part to the get-out-the-vote effort mounted by his organization.[106]

Not withstanding his clean cut, gentlemanly image, Edgar is a tough shrewd partisan who knows how to play the Illinois brand of hardball politics. As Secretary of State he made no bones about preferring to hire Republicans for the 4,000 jobs under his control. Since his opponent in the governor's race was the Illinois Attorney General, himself a career politician who had filled many of his jobs on a partisan basis, patronage never became much of an issue in the campaign. Still, because of Rutan, the subject did come up occasionally and Edgar solemnly promised that he would abide by the court's decision.

Within days of his inauguration, the new governor issued an Administrative Order reaffirming the Thompson orders concerning Rutan, but revoking the 1980 order which had originally set the patronage machine in motion by declaring a hiring freeze. This first brief order was followed by a longer "clarification," a partial list of positions which were determined to be covered by Rutan (i.e. nonpolicy-making), and by the distribution of a manual laying out the procedures to be followed in interviewing and selection. The Thompson administration had contracted with the firm of Ernst and Young to prepare the manual and to develop a list of exempts and Edgar simply signed on to this arrangement.

Edgar's orders made the Department of Central Management Services responsible for implementing the new procedures. These were spelled out in greater detail, but were otherwise similar to those put in place by Thompson.

As a first step in filling a vacancy, an agency is required to check with the DCMS on the Rutan status of the position involved. If DCMS determines that a job is not a Rutan exempt policy-making one, the agency can then go ahead with the hiring process.[107] Except for the fact that the agencies no longer have to go through the governor's office to fill nonpolicy-making jobs, the hiring process does not differ drastically from previous practices. The agencies do have to proceed more carefully and provide more documentation of their actions than was the case in the past. Interview questions and hiring criteria have to be developed *before* interviewing begins. When the agency has made a decision, it has to submit Employment Decision and Candidate Evaluation Forms. The first asks the agency to "explain the reasons for hiring the selected candidate" and to compare the person chosen to the other candidates who were interviewed. The latter form asks the agency to list the hiring criteria and to provide the winning candidate's numerical score on each criteria together with written comments on the candidate's experience and qualifications in relation to each of the criteria. Both the interviewer(s) and the director of the agency also have to sign an affadavit certifying that the questions and criteria were devised before interviews began and that "political party affiliation, support or lack thereof" played no role in the hiring decision.

The Edgar administration has tentative plans to establish special panels to interview and rank candidates for some jobs which have high turnover. Many supervisors have expressed their unhappiness about the prospect of being left out of the selection process and it is unlikely that this change will be made soon. The administration also wants to appoint a number of State Employment Advisors to "accept candidate referrals and advise candidates on state job opportunities." The advisors will enter information about the candidates into an automated counseling system and it will then be transferred to DCMS for "eligibility list generation." This sounds suspiciously like a way to reintroduce political influence even though DCMS has said that the advisors' counseling and recruiting "will be kept completely separate from interview and selection activities."[108]

There will probably be more changes in the state's personnel system in the next few years. In September of 1991 Governor Edgar followed the recommendation of the Illinois Commission on the Future of Public Service and appointed a twenty-three member Human Resources Advisory Council. He gave the blue ribbon panel of business leaders, political figures, labor unionists and academics two years to prepare a "comprehensive report on how to revise and restructure" the Illinois personnel system. The report is supposed to "focus on developing a civil service system" which among other things "retains safeguards and checks for career employees against political abuses or arbitrary actions."[109] The governor also authorized the Council to supervise and evaluate three pilot programs that were being established (as recommended by the Commission) to test personnel innovations.

All of Edgar's actions were designed with an eye toward the federal court. The state hoped to avoid extensive and prolonged court supervision of its personnel operations by demonstrating that it was complying in good faith with the Rutan decision. Before his first month in office was finished, Edgar's lawyers were in court asking Judge Baker to limit the impact of Rutan. The Illinois attorneys argued that a court-appointed receiver wasn't needed because Thompson and Edgar had already acted. They told the Judge that "there is no basis (or need) to enjoin practices which do not exist, and indeed, have been expressly prohibited by two governors of the State of Illinois." The state also wanted Judge Baker to dismiss the plaintiffs' claim for $1.2 million in damages and to severely reduce the scope of the lawsuit by refusing to grant it class-action status.[110]

Behind the scenes lawyers for both sides were trying to negotiate a settlement that would eliminate the need for a trial. After one tentative settlement fell apart, the lawyers managed to hammer out an agreement to submit to Judge Baker who found it acceptable. According to the terms of the settlement, which went into effect in June 1992, Cynthia Rutan will get her promotion[111] and the other plaintiffs will get the jobs they sought. The state will also pay attorney's fees and costs and give each of the five $6,000 "in recognition of the costs they have incurred, the risks they undertook in filing the litigation, the contributions they have made to the prosecution of the last six years, and the benefits they have provided to the various class members."

Although Cynthia Rutan said she was "pleased" with the settlement,[112] the five plaintiffs seem to have been shortchanged. Because of its claims to sovereign and qualified immunity, the state got out of having to give the plaintiffs back pay. The "token"[113] $6,000 payment hardly compensates for their losses. If Cynthia Rutan had been promoted in the early 1980s, the salary increases she would have earned each year would have added up to more than $6,000. To be sure the five do have the satisfaction of knowing that they took on the state and won in the Supreme Court of the United States. Cynthia Rutan has said that the pleasure she got on the day the decision was announced would sustain her for the rest of her life,[114] and there is no question that the case which bears her name has landmark status and may well have delivered the knockout punch to the patronage armies of American politics.

The plaintiffs did succeed in getting the state to acknowledge Rutan as a class-action suit and to concede that the Supreme Court's decision meant that "hiring, promotion and transfer, and recall decisions into nonexempt positions are to be based on factors other than political affiliation and support." The state also agreed to give another chance to job applicants who, sometime between February 1981 and June 1990, had received an "A" grade on an eligibility test for a nonexempt position, but had not been hired. Their names would be put back on the eligibility list and kept there until July 1, 1997.

The state of Illinois also agreed to post public notices in every agency under the governor's control informing workers of the Rutan ruling and instructing them that they have the option of contacting a designated representative in their agency or an outside attorney if they "believe a personnel decision has been made in violation of the Rutan decision." Although the notice doesn't discuss damages, any employee who manages to win a Rutan case in federal court in the future will be able to get both compensatory and punitive damages. However, as long as the state doesn't revert to the blatant patronage practices of the Thompson era, it is unlikely that it will be paying out large sums of money. Hiring and promotion cases are very difficult to win. Both hiring and promotion criteria necessarily have to have some "give." This is essential for good management, but it also means that the employer can usually make a reasonable argument for not hiring or promoting a particular person. Since lawyers are aware of the difficulties such cases pose, most won't take them on a contingency basis[115] so employees brave enough to come forward and challenge the state also have to have a sizeable sum of money to spend before they can file a lawsuit and have their day in court.

In negotiating the most crucial terms of the settlement, Governor Edgar's attorneys did an effective job of containing the "damage" done by Rutan. The state achieved its primary objective of avoiding a court-appointed receiver. The involvement of the federal court ended in June 1992 (although, of course, a new lawsuit could be filed in the future if someone believes the state is in violation of the Constitution). Illinois did say that it intended to continue "to comply with the Supreme Court's decision . . . as long as it is the law," but it did not legally commit itself to instituting or maintaining any specific personnel practices. State officials, in the words of the settlement, "retain the discretion to modify existing personnel practices and procedures and to implement new ones, with their sole obligation being to ensure that any personnel practices and procedures comply with applicable Supreme Court decisions."

Finally, the state said it would publish a list of Rutan-exempt positions and that any future revisions would also be made public, although once again Illinois did not make a legal commitment to do this. The state did, however, release a list of 2,800 Rutan-exempt positions in March.

It's hard to see this settlement as anything but a victory for the state, especially when its terms are compared to Shakman. The state did not commit itself to advertise jobs; it is still permitted to accept political referrals and recommendations; it has not adopted an impartial hiring device such as a lottery for unskilled jobs; and it is not obligated to observe any specific rules or keep any specified records. Most important of all, the state is being allowed to police itself. There is no court or other disinterested neutral third party to act as a watch dog. Relying on DCMS to audit the state's personnel practices and insure compliance with Rutan is comparable to letting the fox watch the chicken coop. If Governor Edgar had appointed a respected personnel professional to head DCMS, one might have more confidence in the department's integrity. But, Governor Edgar appointed a college friend who served him faithfully in the Secretary of State's office. With this man at the helm, the Governor need not worry that DCMS will cause him any problems by asking nasty, probing questions about patronage. DCMS will also probably be quite sympathetic to the governor's point of view when revisions to the exempt list are considered in the future. Certainly, he already has reason to be pleased with the first list that DCMS compiled with the help of Ernst and Young. That list gave Edgar 2,800 jobs, nearly 5 percent of the total number of employees under the governor's office. The President of the United States appoints fewer than 5,000 employees out of three million. Under Shakman, the mayor of Chicago gets to appoint about 900 people out of a total of 40,000, while in Wisconsin the governor directly appoints fewer than 200 people.

Since so much of the implementation of Rutan depends on the governor, it's legitimate to ask whether he can be expected to work diligently to eliminate patronage. So far he has given off mixed signals in his appointments and other actions. He has appointed a number of his trusted political lieutenants to key jobs in his administration. For example, the sister of an influential Republican fundraiser who was in charge of Edgar's patronage operation in the Secretary of State's office, now heads the governor's Office of Personnel. Edgar has also kept many of Thompson's appointees, sometimes in the same job, sometimes in a different one. These people generally believe in patronage and are used to working in a patronage system; it would be naive to expect them all to try to eradicate patronage in the new administration. On the other hand Edgar appointed a civil engineer who had worked in the Department of Transportation for 22 years to be its head. In the past this patronage haven had been run by political operatives.

It's still too early for a definitive evaluation of the state's response to Rutan. There are supervisors who say they are still getting referrals, but that there isn't much follow-up and they aren't being pressured to hire the people who are referred to them.[116] Some insiders say it's still "business as usual" in many agencies and that everyone is just being more careful not to leave any paper trails. Also because the cash-starved state has few job openings and is laying off workers, legislators and other political movers and shakers are concentrating on protecting the people they have already placed in state jobs. Bargaining revolves around keeping employees in their jobs rather than getting new jobs. Legislative trade-offs also focus on getting pet projects off the list of those frozen because of budget shortfalls. And, reportedly, now that it is more difficult to use low-level jobs for patronage, interest has shifted to the Rutan exempt positions and it is harder to get high quality, professional people in those jobs.[117]

The Edgar administration has already been embarrassed several times by revelations of questionable personnel practices, although some of these have involved transgressions that occurred when Thompson was governor. For example, a southwestern Illinois Republican county chairman and his "bagman" were indicted for selling state jobs over a period of fourteen years. The scheme was uncovered when the bagman unwisely complained to the state Attorney General that he had been laid off from a state job which he had paid to get.[118] There was also an Associated Press investigation of post-Rutan hiring at a new state prison in Taylorville which indicated that nearly 80% of the new hires who had declared a party affiliation were Republicans even though the correctional center is located in Christian County where Democratic primary voters outnumber Republicans five to one. Of 91 people put on the payroll following Rutan, only ten were Democrats, while 38 were Republicans and 43 had either not registered to vote or had not voted in a recent primary. Before Rutan 47 people were hired— 35 Republicans, five Democrats and seven with no declared preference. The director of the Corrections Department insisted that "political influence is irrelevant" in filling jobs though he admitted that corrections officials may still talk to party leaders and state legislators about applicants' qualifications. The area's Republican state senator said he continued to send copies of job applicants tests to Corrections but no longer made an "extra effort" on behalf of Republican applicants. A Democratic Senator whose district includes Taylorville said she wrote letters of recommendation for many people who wanted jobs at the prison, but that her "success story was not terrific."[119]

Another episode involving the Sangamon County Republican Party showed just how hard it is to change deep-seated attitudes and practices. The *State Journal Register* revealed that when it sent reporters to the party headquarters in Springfield to ask for state job applications, they were given forms which asked questions about the political and financial help they'd given to the Republican party in the last four years and also asked the applicant to join the county Republican party. Furthermore, the receptionist reminded the reporters to have the applications signed by their precinct committeemen before returning them. The heads of the local Republican party and the county Democratic party, which had also given out "applications for employment" (although these did not ask for specific political information), contended that they were only "counseling" people who wanted jobs.[120]

There were also protestations of innocence from Nicki Zollar, one of Edgar's appointees who used an old ploy to give a job to the man who had dispensed patronage in Edgar's Chicago Secretary of State's office for six years. Because the man did not have the required legal experience, he could not be made chief legal administrator in Zollar's Department of Professional Regulation. So Zollar got permission from DCMS to abolish the existing administrative post and create a new position which would not require any legal experience. When questioned by newsmen, Ms. Zollar claimed she couldn't remember if the man's resume had come to her from the governor's office, but confessed she did feel "comfortable" with him because "he had worked for the governor in the past."[121]

When Edgar was running for governor, he promised he would do more than simply abide by the Rutan decision. He said he believed it was "important that we tighten up disclosure laws, that we do have guidelines on how we hand out contracts in state government, to reassure the public that it's not just going to our friends." Therefore, he said, he'd propose a package of reforms including curbs on political fundraising, strengthening of disclosure requirements, tougher conflict of interest rules and better control of no-bid contracts and other forms of pinstripe patronage. He even went so far as to say he would ask that the election laws be changed so that voters would no longer have to declare their party preference in primaries. Candidate Edgar argued that this change should increase voter turnout because a lot of people were staying "out of the primary process because they don't want to have their name on a list that anyone can go look at saying they're a Republican or a Democrat."[122]

Once he was governor Edgar pledged in his first State of the State speech to rein in the Department of Commerce and Community Affairs, which had been widely condemned as a patronage dumping ground presiding over expensive pork-barrel projects. He also repeated his promise to rein in pinstripe patronage, saying he would soon "announce a procedure for awarding contracts for legal service, bond counsel, investment advice and underwriting on a rotation basis to qualified professionals because of what they know and not whom they know." Further, he pledged that the "same no-nonsense business experts who develop that procedure also will determine a means for evaluating the work of those contractors to see if taxpayers got their money's worth."[123]

Edgar did cut DCCA's jobs and funding and after a delay of almost one year he reorganized the agency, but he never did anything to promote the general reforms he had promised. He did not introduce any proposals of his own, nor did he back proposals offered by others. The Executive Director of the Illinois Common Cause said the group, which lobbies for governmental reform, could "see no action whatsoever from the governor's office."[124] Instead of leading the way on campaign reform, the governor's people were caught playing fast and loose with the existing rules. In April 1992 Edgar held his annual Springfield fundraiser. The event brought in $650,000, much of it from the sale of tickets at $50 a piece to thousands of state employees. Tickets are not supposed to be sold on state premises or on state time, but a reporter was able to buy them at the offices of Public Aid. When the reporter identified himself to the official doing the selling, the official quickly avowed that he normally sold them "only on break" and pointed to a cup of coffee on his desk as evidence that he really was on break. When he was told of the incident, Edgar said that it "shouldn't have happened," but there were reports from all over Springfield of "workers being called into an office on their breaks and told about the fund-raiser." Employees of the Department of Revenue also received letters at their homes from the agency's Deputy Director urging them to buy tickets.

It appears that the governor's staff tried to stay within the letter of the law while violating its spirit. Before the fund-raiser, Cabinet members were called to an after-work conference held at the headquarters of the Republican State Central Committee which, according to those who were there, was designed "to make sure they knew about the fund-raiser and the legal ways tickets could be sold." Later, there was a second meeting of managers who were told specifically how they could distribute tickets legally. The fund-raiser brought the governor's total campaign fund for the 1994 election to over $2 million. He was well on his way to topping the $8.8 million he had for his first race when he outspent his Democratic opponent by nearly $1 per vote. Edgar spent $5.33 for each vote, while the Democratic candidate spent only $4.37.[125]

Edgar's approach to contracts was somewhat similar to his handling of fundraising. There were some feeble passes at reform, but the overall thrust seemed to be on continuing to garner the rewards of pinstripe patronage while staying within the law and maintaining as clean an image as possible. As Secretary of State, Edgar had already shown that he understood how useful contracts could be. Indeed, it is possible that he might not have made it to the governor's office if he hadn't used contracts to win the support of black leaders who helped him get the votes that were the key to his narrow victory. Before the election he saw that black groups got Department of Transportation Contracts and he personally awarded more than 60% of the money appropriated to a literacy program his office directed to African-American groups. A number of respected black leaders who headed groups which received contracts deserted the Democratic camp to endorse and campaign for Jim Edgar.[126]

Presumably, Edgar had learned how to use contracts from watching his former boss, Governor James Thompson who was a master of the art. Some Illinoisans even credit Thompson with having invented pinstripe patronage, but that is provincial hyperbole. There is no doubt though that Thompson was the first Illinois governor to realize the full potential of the pinstripe variety of contract patronage. This is partly because Thompson had more opportunities than the governors who came before him. In the 1980s more insurance companies failed so there was more liquidation work for lawyers; the state issued more revenue bonds so there was more work for investment bankers and lawyers; the state government was growing and needed office space so there were more rental payments for building owners; and the state began to play a direct role in economic development so there were low-interest loans for old and new businesses. [127]

Like Plunkitt of Tammany Hall, Thompson "seen his opportunities and took 'em." In one of his last interviews as governor, he told the *Sun-Times* that pinstripe patronage is "no myth. It's a shorthand way of describing how legal business and related business is done on a non-bid basis in Illinois." He went on to say that his use of patronage, both "regular" and pinstripe, was a "deliberate policy." He explained that he oversaw the state's hiring of investment bankers and lawyers because, "If I don't somebody else will, and I'll be held responsible. And if I do, then I'm assured that it's being rotated among the firms and among the bond houses." The governor denied that he had ever abused the process and insisted that the taxpayers had benefitted from his actions because the state got "first-class service" from its lawyers and bond houses. [128]

The relationship between Thompson and his friends was definitely not one-sided. With their help he was able to raise almost $24 million. Some of the help, it should be noted, came from the state's labor unions which liked Thompson for the jobs his programs provided for their members. Thompson's business friends, both the beneficiaries of pinstripe patronage and those who received the more "traditional" state contracts for such things as road building and the purchase of office equipment, also helped him out in other ways. For example, firms which got state business sometimes found between-election jobs for members of the governor's campaign staff. If you examine the careers of the people who handle campaign publicity, scheduling and the like, you will find a number who drift in and out of government and private sector jobs. Friendly firms can provide a place for an elected official to "park" his staff between elections or provide a berth for an up-and-coming young politician. They also can, and do, provide jobs for assorted relatives, supporters and hangers-on. [129]

Just because Thompson set the overall policy, it shouldn't be assumed that he personally made every decision that helped one of his political supporters or campaign contributors. Thompson put people who could be trusted to know what to do without being told in key spots like the Illinois Department of Transportation with its valuable jobs and contracts. David Kenney, who served in Thompson's cabinet, asserts that it "would have been out of character" for Thompson to put pressure on agency directors. He says that "some of them were politically sensitive and acted on their own intuition to make such awards in the directions that they thought the governor might approve. Some may even have inquired of the governor's staff as to where certain patronage of that sort might go. That staff had some to confer at its own discretion, and doubtless the governor conveyed his wishes to them directly or indirectly." Some state officials struck off on their own. As Professor Kenney explains, "A lot of what could be called pinstripe patronage might better be called 'contemporary patronage.' It went to the contemporaries of the . . . employees of state government. In many cases it was their patronage, not the governor's or the party's."[130]

Undoubtedly some state officials today are acting on their own in awarding contracts to their supporters (and, in some cases, relatives), but the practice is too pervasive for the governor's office not to know what is happening. When the *State Journal-Register* confronted Edgar's spokesman with evidence from public records that well-connected firms were continuing to get lucrative contracts, he backed away from an earlier assertion that Edgar was "sending a message that the contract game is over." On second thought, the spokesman said Edgar never intended to eliminate pinstripe patronage, but that under Edgar "the contract game is over as it existed."[131]

Edgar did cut some of the pinstripe contracts and the state's overall spending may have been reduced somewhat, but in several cases the administration appeared to be playing games with the numbers. For example, the Illinois Department of Public Aid publicly announced that it was reducing the consulting contract of a former Thompson aide by $3,000. The Department then turned around and quietly gave the man an identically worded new contract for $16,000. In the same month the Department of Transportation announced it was decreasing the maximum payments in the contracts of two firms, headed respectively by a former Republican legislator and a Thompson cabinet member. But IDOT neglected to say that the dollar decreases were reductions in planned increases and that the firms actually ended up receiving an additional $50,000. The Edgar administration subsequently renewed the contracts for the next fiscal year even though the need for the firms' services seemed questionable. The former legislator was paid to "develop and maintain liaison with local agencies and municipalities" which deal with IDOT, while the former Cabinet member was hired to study ways to "help minority and female enterprises get financing."[132]

While there are surely some grantees who perform necessary and useful work, a lot of them seem to be getting paid for nebulous and dubious services. One has to wonder about an administration which can't find money for mental health, public aid and education, but somehow finds $226,000 for a consultant to formulate a mission statement and survey the attitudes of employees and day-care providers for the Department of Children and Family Services. It's no doubt a sheer coincidence that DCFS, which has functioned so inadequately that it is under federal court orders to reform, gave such no-bid contracts—worth over $2 million—to firms that were major contributors to the agency director's failed bid for elective office. Even members of the DCFS Advisory Council, who are appointed by the governor, thought that the agency didn't need to survey day-care providers, who had been very forceful in expressing their views. As one Council member said, "If they had paid attention to the 10 public hearings we had, they'd know what the providers think. . . . this is a waste of money that could have been used to provide services to children in Illinois."[133]

DCFS could also have done a good deal for the children of the state with the money it spent for the lawyers it hired to defend itself in court. Although the agency employs 20 in-house lawyers and can call on the Illinois Attorney General, who is the state's official litigator, it paid out over $1.6 million in fiscal 1991 to private law firms. The biggest chunk went to the giant Chicago firm of Skadden, Arps (whose managing partner is the husband of Thompson advisor Paula Wolff) for representing DCFS in a class-action suit brought by the American Civil Liberties Union. DCFS, like many other state agencies, turns to private litigators in part because it doesn't trust the Democratic Attorney General. Even if it did, the Attorney General's office is underfunded and couldn't at present handle all of the state's litigation with the staff it has. While some specialized legal help will always be needed, Edgar could save Illinois millions of dollars by giving the Attorney General enough money to hire more Assistant Attorneys General who get paid less than one-fifth of the going rate the state pays for private lawyers.[134]

In fiscal 1991 the state's business was worth $12.2 million to private law firms (this figure doesn't include court-ordered fees and expenses). The following year state agencies had contracted for more than $15 million of legal services before the year was half over. The greatest sums went to a handful of large firms who have close ties to the administration and gave considerable sums to the Edgar campaign (and before that, to Thompson's campaigns). Besides Skadden, Arps which topped the list at $1,289,548, Winston and Strawn (the firm with which Jim Thompson is associated) received over $1 million in fees from the state and Jenner and Block ended up with $660,530 in legal work in fiscal 1991. Jenner and Block's biggest plum has been the Rutan case. Illinois has already paid the firm more than $1 million for its unsuccessful defense of the state and can expect to pay more for the firm's work in negotiating the settlement and for providing advice on the implementation of Rutan.[135]

In a muckraking series that appeared at the end of Edgar's first two years in office, the *Chicago Tribune* proclaimed that a "new age of patronage" had dawned in Illinois as state contracts reached the $4.6 billion a year mark.[136] The *Tribune's* examination of thousands of documents, including 224,903 computer records of state contracts, indicated that the political use of contracts had not slowed since Thompson left office. Edgar has continued Thompson's practice of waiving state laws which would prevent officials and state workers and their families from doing business with the state. Nor has the new governor done anything to stop the revolving door between contractors and state government from continuing to spin. Edgar's chief legal counsel left after two years to become vice president of a health maintenance organization. Although his responsibilities at the HMO include seeing that the state renews the organization's $9.7 million-a-month state Medicaid contract, Edgar has kept the man on the Governor's Health Care Reform Task force which is charged with finding ways to fund Medicaid.[137]

Other elected state officials such as the Secretary of State and the Attorney General also use no-bid consulting contracts and the other instruments of pinstripe patronage to reward their political allies and financial supporters. Together the various Illinois officials spent $204 million on no-bid contracts for professional services in 1991.

Illinois law places no limits on campaign contributions from firms or individuals doing business with the state. Since the law also does not require competitive bids or specify the procedures to be used in renting or buying property, state officials have been free to buy property and rent space for their agencies from their political friends. In one case a contributor completed a deal to lease a building to the Department of Children and Family Services before he had even bought the property involved. With the state paying premium rates, the contributor stood to make a million dollars on the five-year lease.[138]

It should be emphasized that there is nothing unconstitutional or illegal in awarding contracts on a political basis. The Supreme Court decisions limiting patronage apply only to jobs. Moreover, the United States Court of Appeals for the 7th Circuit, which includes Illinois, has specifically ruled that the Supreme Court decisions cannot be extended to contracts. Judge Richard Posner, writing for the court in that case, argued that a "decision upholding a First Amendment right to have one's bid considered without regard to political considerations would invite every disappointed bidder for a public contract to bring a federal suit against the government purchaser." The Judge also felt that it would be nearly impossible to separate politics and business because the "pervasive role of government in modern American life has made it important for business firms to be on good terms with the major political groupings in the society. It seems unlikely that the cautious neutrality that characterizes the political activities of American business would be altered even by an iron-clad constitutional rule against allowing politics to influence the contracting process."[139] Ironically, the loser in the contract case—a Springfield businessman whose bid on a contract to install and maintain benches along the city's streets was rejected—was represented by Mary Lee Leahy.

While not illegal, Edgar's political use of contracts is important as a sign that the basic political culture of Illinois has not been fundamentally changed by Rutan. Because patronage is so much a part of that culture, Nowlan, Hanley and Udstuen are probably right in predicting that after a lull "over time patronage considerations will again become important in state government personnel practices."[140]

If they are in fact right, this is not good news for Illinois. Job-oriented politics has not served the people of the state well. When Peirce and Keefe surveyed the Great Lakes states in the early 1980s, they wrote (as Fenton had before them) that the "inevitable result of patronage and payoff is a low level of service for the people." In 1977 per capita income in Illinois was the eighth highest in the U.S. but the state "spent less than the national per capital average for higher education, for the local government aid, for public welfare, and for health and hospitals." By the 1990s Illinois' ranking on most indices for spending on education, welfare, mental health and other services had fallen even lower. The judgment that Peirce and Keefe pronounced in 1980 remained valid: "Over most of its history Illinois has been a rich state that chose not to do more for its people."[141]

126

CHAPTER 4
THE LAST POLITICAL MACHINE

Nassau County, Long Island—November, 1991

Lewis Yevoli didn't really expect to win. After all, a Democrat hadn't been elected town supervisor—roughly the equivalent of a mayor—in Oyster Bay for over 20 years, and Yevoli was running against an incumbent who had won by 20,000 votes—45,681 to 25,825 in 1989. Moreover, the Democrats had been steadily falling further behind the Republicans in the number of registered voters they could claim. Because New York state requires prospective voters to fill out a party enrollment form when they register, each party has an exact count of the number of voters who are willing to indicate that, as the form states, they are "in general sympathy" with its principles. If a voter doesn't want to commit himself to a particular party, he can return the form signed, but blank. In 1981 there were 44,992 registered Democrats, 70,391 registered Republicans and 27,152 "blanks" or independents in the town of Oyster Bay. By 1991 the number of Democrats registered had fallen to 42,111 while there were 74,736 Republicans and 30,846 uncommitted voters.

Actually, Yevoli's situation was even worse than the registration figures would lead one to believe. In running against Angelo Delligati, Yevoli wasn't just battling a single man; he was also taking on the organization which backed the candidate. That organization—the Nassau County Republican party—was a formidable foe which no Long Island Democrat would ever make the mistake of underestimating. The organization, which has been called the "last political machine,"[1] has been regularly clobbering the county's local Democrats for most of the twentieth century. The Democrats have not been a real power in county politics since 1917. They experienced some success in the tumultuous 1960s when they managed three times to win the race for county executive. Under the form of government adopted by Nassau County in 1938 the county government is the preeminent government, providing "health, welfare, judicial, major public works and police functions." The County Executive, who is elected to a four-year term, acts as the chief administrator and executive. He is responsible for planning and preparing a budget, represents the county in dealing with other governmental units, and appoints, with the approval of the legislative body called the Board of Supervisors, the heads of the various county agencies, who all report directly to him. The County Executive also presides over the meetings of the Board of Supervisors, but can only vote in case of a tie.[2]

A Democrat, Eugene Nickerson served as the Nassau County Executive from 1961 to 1970 when the office reverted to the Republicans who had held it from 1938 to 1960. After 1970 the Democrats were unable to win the office back. Although the County Executive is the single most important official in Nassau County, the Executive doesn't completely control the government. Even when Nickerson was in the executive chair, the Democrats had to reach an accommodation with the Republicans who dominated the Board of Supervisors.

For electoral purposes Nassau county is divided into three towns and two cities. The "towns" are not towns in the usual sense; each of them contains many villages and unincorporated areas. The villages have their own local governing officials while the unincorporated areas do not. The two cities are located within the larger area of the towns, but have their own governments which are responsible for city finances and administration. Although in most of the United States, cities are larger than towns, this is not necessarily the case in New York state. Both the cities and the towns vary greatly in population size.[3] In Nassau County the town of Hempstead, with over 800,000 people is far bigger than the two cities of Long Beach and Glen Cove. At election time the two cities and the three towns of Hempstead, North Hempstead and Oyster Bay chose a total of six supervisors. Because of its larger population, Hempstead elects two supervisors while each of the other four units elects one. The supervisors, with the exception of the one from Glen Cove who is only an advisor in the city-manager-run city, are both officials of the local town or city government and members of the Board of Supervisors. However, the six are not equal in their voting power. Following the Supreme Court's one-man, one-vote decisions of the 1960s, each supervisor's vote was weighted to reflect the number of constituents each represents. Thus the Presiding Supervisor (i.e. mayor) and the supervisor (town councilman) from the town of Hempstead together have 58 votes while the supervisor from Glen Cove has only six. It takes 65 votes out of a total of 108 to pass resolutions (which deal only with minor matters) but 72 votes are needed to pass major measures, including all budgetary proposals. The Democrats have not controlled the Board of Supervisors since the First World War. In recent years the only Democrat on the board has been Bruce Nyman, the supervisor from Long Beach, a small Democratic enclave on the Atlantic Ocean. With seven votes, Nyman has had no clout. In 1989 the Democrats managed to elect a second person to the Board when Ben Zwirn, defeated the North Hempstead Supervisor. Together Nyman and Zwirn could make more noise on the Board, but Zwirn's 15 votes were not enough to stop the Republicans. Zwirn was also stymied within North Hempstead where the Republican controlled town board could block his initiatives. He hoped to improve his position in 1991 by winning reelection and helping to elect two other Democrats; this would give the Democrats a 3 to 2 majority on the town board.

The Republicans were determined to stop any Democratic advance. They marshalled all of their considerable resources, outmanning and outspending the Democrats. In Oyster Bay, for example, Delligati had over $113,000 to Yevoli's $23,000, and was expecting more money from the county organization. Like other Republican candidates, he could also call on the machine's army of patronage workers. People were being sent from the machine's stronghold in Hempstead to work against Zwirn and Yevoli. While their workers were ringing doorbells and distributing campaign literature, the party was also reaching out to voters with direct mail, posters, newspaper ads and even, radio and TV commercials. Usually Long Island candidates don't employ TV and radio because it is too expensive and wasteful to buy time on the New York metropolitan area stations which serve the Island.

In contrast to the Republican candidates, the Democrats were largely on their own. They could expect almost no help from their impoverished, fractured party. Bruce Nyman was not exaggerating much when he said, "There is no Democratic Party in Nassau County."[4] In the midst of the campaign a group within the party, including Yevoli and Zwirn, tried to dump John Matthews, the party chairman. After the election Yevoli said, "If John had any common sense, he would tender his resignation. He didn't do anything. I haven't heard from him."[5] But Matthews didn't resign and before the year was out, one group of Democrats was taking another to court.

Despite all of this, the Democrats thought they had a chance in 1991 of making inroads against the Republicans. Zwirn's victory in 1989—the first for a Democrat in the North Hempstead Supervisor's race since 1917—had given them hope. They believed there was a good possibility that Zwirn might repeat his win. Although the Republicans were waging all-out war, their candidate—Robert Previdi—was weak. Previdi, a low-key, conservative, banking executive who had never won an election and had once pronounced the Clean Air Act a "cockamamie bill,"[6] seemed out of touch with an angry electorate. In Oyster Bay, the Democrats were hoping to lay the basis for a victory in 1993. With Yevoli, a popular State Assemblyman, they thought they had a chance, as the town's Democratic chairman put it, to "come close this time and then win in two years."[7]

On election night about 100 of Yevoli's campaign workers and supporters gathered with him at his headquarters to monitor the returns. By 10 P.M. the crowd was nearly delirious and a stunned Yevoli decided he'd better call his wife Carole. "Come down," he told her, "It looks pretty good."[8] Before the evening was out, Yevoli knew that he'd be trading his $29,000 a year Assemblyman's job for the $96,624 job of town supervisor and member of the county Board of Supervisors. After more than two decades, the Democrats had finally elected one of their own to the town's chief administrative post.

Over in North Hempstead another miracle was in the making. Not only was Ben Zwirn trouncing Robert Previdi 34,160 votes to 20,273, but the Democrats were also taking control of the town government, winning the three open seats on the town board and ousting the Republican Town Clerk and Receiver of Taxes. It's hard to say if the Democrats or Republicans were more surprised by the Democrats' clean sweep. The victory meant that Zwirn would now have a majority on the town board and could begin to change policies and personnel. As Zwirn happily told commuters at the train station on the morning after the election, his hands were finally "untied" and he could act.[9]

With the victories of Yevoli and Zwirn, the election signalled a sea change in county politics. Together the three Democrats on the Nassau County Board of Supervisors—Nyman, Zwirn and Yevoli—would have a total of 44 votes which would put them in a position to veto almost any Republican initiative. For years the Republicans had treated the Democrats with scorn; now Thomas Gulotta, the County Executive, and the Republicans on the Board would have to learn to work with the Democrats. If they didn't, then, as one Democrat remarked, "Theoretically all business could grind to a halt if both sides refuse to move. . . . This may be the only government in the United

States of America without a majority. There's no tie-breaker."[10]
Already investors were getting nervous and Moody's was threatening
to lower the county's bond rating.

Neither the jubilant Democrats nor the downcast Republicans
could know exactly what the election meant for them in the long run.
The once invincible Republican machine was definitely hurt, but it
was too early to pronounce it dead. Without question there would be
changes in the towns and the county. About the future only one thing
was certain: to quote that sage Yogi Berra, "It ain't what it used to be."

The Machine that Wasn't Supposed to be

To Americans the phrase "political machine" brings to mind images of
Boss Tweed and the New York City courthouse or of a jowly Richard J.
Daley murdering the English language. Machines are supposed to
take root in big cities. They are for immigrants and fat, cigar smoking
men in smoky back rooms who take advantage of the ignorant
masses. Machines are supposed to thrive on people who trade their
votes for a job or a buck or a basket of food at Christmas. They are not
supposed to be for the home-owning, solid citizen, split-ticket voters
of suburbia who like to think of themselves as political independents
who vote for the man or the issue rather than the party. Yet, the reality
is that one of the most long-lived and powerful of all America's
machines did take root in the supposedly infertile soil of suburban
Nassau County.

Nassau County sits uneasily wedged between the New York
City boroughs of Queens and Brooklyn—which occupy the western
tip of Long Island—and Suffolk County, which still has working
farms, on the eastern end of the Island. Together they fill the long,
narrow island that extends from Manhattan out into the Atlantic
Ocean. Until the Second World War, much of Nassau County was
covered by potato fields. There was a trickle of migration from the
crowded city before the war. After the war, the trickle turned into the
proverbial flood as more and more people poured into Nassau
County, buying the houses which were being put up by the
thousands. In 1947 the first Levittown was built on one of the potato
fields. Monthly payments for the small, single family houses which
sold for $6,990 were $60; if you were a veteran, you didn't have to put
any money down. With these prices growth was so frenetic during the
1950s "that the number of people moving into Nassau County in a single year often surpassed the entire population of 55,448 in 1900." In
the booming 1950s and 1960s, Nassau grew faster than any other
county in the United States. By the 1970s the county had almost 1.5

million people. Although the population has since declined to 1.3 million, in the late 1980s Nassau could still boast that it was the "nation's most populous suburban county—with more people than 15 of the 50 states. If it were a city instead of a county, it would be the nation's sixth largest."[11]

Unlike many of the nation's cities, Nassau County's population is largely white, well-educated and affluent. While there has been some growth in the numbers of minorities, in 1990 they accounted for only 17% of the county's population.[12] Houses in Levittown now sell for more than $100,000 and in 1989 the median family income in the county was $46,475.[13] Nassau had the "highest number of home owner households among the nation's top standard metropolitan statistical areas" and it was among the leaders in "effective buying income, the number of households with income over $50,000 and the percentage of households over $50,000."[14] The county, where millionaires built their Gold Coast estates on the North Shore at the turn of the century, also has its share of the wealthy, although many of the most fashionable have moved on. Despite the departure of the society rich, one-fifth of the wealthiest zip codes in the nation are located in the county.

From the time it was separated from Queens and made an independent county in 1898, Nassau has been home to many Republicans. The Democratic branch of the Roosevelt family lived up the Hudson in Hyde Park, but the Republican Roosevelts had their family estate on Long Island where Teddy's home at Sagamore Hill on Oyster Bay still stands. From 1898 until 1916 the Democrats were able to give Nassau's Republicans some competition. They were helped by the Republican split in 1912 when many Long Islanders bolted the party to support Theodore Roosevelt's bid for president under the banner of the Bull Moose party. However, the Republicans regrouped under their new leader, G. Wilbur Doughty, and succeeded in winning all of the county offices in the election of 1916.[15] With the exception of the brief Democratic resurgence in the 1960s, the Republicans have maintained their political supremacy in the county. The Democrats were able to win votes for their national and state candidates, but fared poorly in local contests. There were Democrats among the wealthy of the county, but many of them would not contribute to Democrats running for the town and county offices though they would give to presidential campaigns.[16]

Although the Republicans have profited through the years by implying that a vote for the local Democrats is a vote for the big city bosses of Tammany Hall scheming to "annex Republican Nassau to Democratic Queens," in the 1920s the true boss on Long Island was the Republican leader, Doughty. Leonard Hall, the son of Theodore Roosevelt's coachman at Sagamore Hill, who rose through the ranks of Nassau's Republicans to become national chairman of the Republican party in the Eisenhower years, once commented that, "Doughty was a real boss. When he spoke, the discussion was over. He always kept his word; he was known for that. But cross him and you were finished. There's no one like him today. We used to call him the 'Last of the Mohicans'."[17] Doughty was genuinely interested in seeing Long Island develop, but he saw no reason why he and other Republicans shouldn't profit from the growth they promoted. Accordingly, many of the county's contracts went to a firm run by Doughty's brother-in-law and, as one observer put it, "zoning was bought and sold like potatoes." The Morgans, Vanderbilts, Whitneys and others of their class who lived in the county also gave their money to keep the machine running. There were so many super-rich Republicans in Nassau County in the 1920s that the Republican National Finance Committee had 49 members—one from each of the states plus one from Nassau.[18]

Doughty died in 1930. In 1935 his nephew J. Russel Sprague, gained control of the county's Republicans. It was Sprague, as county chairman from 1936 until 1959, who built the modern Republican machine. He saw that he would have to do something to win over the new people moving into Nassau and that he would need disciplined party workers to be effective. He was also determined that he, not the Gold Coast rich, would control the party and that meant he had to have another source of money. The solution turned out to be simple. Patronage was the key to the new party. The money would come largely from within the party. The party foot soldiers and their generals, from the committeemen in the election districts to the executive committee members at the top, would be given jobs, contracts, legal fees and other preferments. In return they would work for the party and contribute to its coffers. Patronage job-holders were expected to give 1 percent of their salaries to the party. Members of the executive committees were expected to raise a certain amount (in recent years it's been a minimum of $400) for each of the 18 or so election districts in their areas. They were also required to sell tickets to the party's annual dinner and from time to time they were asked to support other fundraisers and contribute to special funds. The party was happy to sell dinner tickets and accept contributions from outsiders, but it didn't go after big donations of thousands and tens of thousands for fear that the givers might try to dictate policy.

The party chairman, a position created by Sprague, rides herd over the organization's members and insures that they meet their obligations. Sprague saw to it that the duties of the chairman included having the final say on all patronage and on the management of the party's campaigns. With this power, the chairman could reward and punish the party legions and control the direction of the organization. Other than Sprague (who retired in 1959), the most effective of the five men who have served as chairman has been Joseph Margiotta who was in the post from 1968 to 1983. Together, Margiotta and Sprague gave the Nassau County Republican Organization the shape and character it has had into the early 1990s.

Fittingly, for a Republican enterprise, the Nassau County party is organized and run like a corporation. The party committeemen are at the bottom of a tightly structured hierarchy. There are two of them in each of the county's approximately 1,000 election districts. In New York state the election district is the smallest political unit. The committeemen are elected in the primaries every two years by the party's enrolled voters. In turn the committeemen choose both the party's candidates (at the annual conventions) and the area or zone leaders who serve on the executive committee. However, in reality, power flows down from the top of the organization rather than up from the bottom with the committeemen generally rubber-stamping the choices made by the higher-ups. Within the leadership ranks final power rests in the hands of an inner circle consisting of an informal "board of directors" composed of the county chairman and the top five or six town and city leaders who advise him.

The local committeemen and their block captains do the organization's grunt work of getting out the vote at election time, enrolling new party members and selling tickets to party functions. Like the precinct captains, aldermen, and ward committeemen in the old Chicago machine, the Nassau committeemen help the party win support at the grassroots level by doing favors for their neighbors. As Congressman Raymond McGrath, who continues to serve as a committeeman, says, "When people have a complaint about the garbage not being picked up or the streets not being swept, they come to me."[19] Usually the committeemen have deep roots in the community and know most of the seven or eight hundred voters in their neighborhood so they can appeal personally to voters in their districts.[20]

The party is always looking for new talent. Once in the organization, an able, hardworking recruit can work up to a higher post on the executive committee or perhaps into the first of a series of elective positions. The organization has been compared to a baseball team which starts its rookies out on the farm team and gradually brings them up through the minor leagues and finally into the majors. One Long Island political scientist has commented that the "party seems to have something like a well-worked-out career ladder along which politicians get promoted. It seems every Republican congressman was once a state senator, before that a state assemblyman and before that a town supervisor."[21] Congressman McGrath, who started out as a teacher, served as a deputy parks commissioner and was in the New York State Assembly for four years.[22]

At every step on the ladder, the organization has exacting performance standards. The 69 or 70 members of the executive committee, for example, are not allowed to rest on their laurels. Every year the party puts out an Executive Performance Rating which ranks the executive committeemen on their fund raising and their area's vote in key races. The leaders are also awarded bonus points for getting a certain number of signatures on candidate petitions and for sending someone from their zone to the national Young Republican convention. All along the line, leaders are encouraged to compete with one another. As McGrath says, "We pride ourselves on the fact that we had a petition drive for county executive and got something like 78,000 signatures. We set those kinds of goals for ourselves, and we reward those election districts, and committeemen who exceed those goals."[23]

If a member of the executive committee doesn't measure up, he or she might be called in for a heart-to-heart talk with the county chairman. If the executive committeeman hasn't paid for his dinner tickets, he might get a letter from headquarters. According to Joseph Mondello, the man who succeeded Margiotta as chairman, "It is not a dunning letter. . . . we are reminding them what to do. 'You have eaten of my food and drunk of my drink and now you must pay of my bill.' "[24]

When the chairman is unhappy with someone below him, he can penalize that person in a number of ways. Patronage is probably his most potent weapon. He can see to it that a person gets fired from a patronage job (although this is very rare), or more likely, he will simply cut off any further patronage. An executive committee member who was in the doghouse would no longer be able to get jobs or promotions for his people and would no longer have an influence over nominations. The party chairman has also been known to redistrict a local leader's area making it more likely that the underling would be ousted from his leadership post.

Although the chairman can use his power to discipline party leaders, he does not rule by fear alone. He has carrots aplenty, in the forms of jobs, contracts, insurance business and the like, to supplement his stick. As will be seen in the next section, both the local committeemen and the members of the executive committee, receive ample material rewards for their efforts. But the leaders are held together by more than the cash nexus. They are also tied to one another by ethnic, neighborhood, friendship and family relationships.

In its early years the Republican organization attracted many of the Italian and Irish Catholics who were moving to the Island and wanted to leave the big city and its liberal Democratic politics (not to mention its minority population) behind them. At the top the party still has a strong ethnic, particularly Italian, flavor although over the decades it has drawn others, including a few women and blacks, into its ranks. When Margiotta became chairman, he worked at deepening the social bonds among the committeemen. Every year he would host a number of parties and outings, both in Nassau County and in Albany, for the party's workers and leaders. While outsiders were invited to some of the party functions, the affairs were designed primarily to foster solidarity within the party. Margiotta believed that the dinners, receptions, boat rides and golf outings improved esprit de corps and minimized in-fighting among the party's members (although there were always feuds, enmities, and backstabbings within the party's ranks).

The leaders of the Nassau County Republican Organization have taken very good care of themselves but, like any good "businessmen," they have also plowed most of their "profits" back into the business. While the impoverished Democrats work out of a dingy crowded office above a closed auto showroom located in a seedy industrial area, the Republicans own an impressive three-story building—fittingly, a former bank—on a main street in Westbury. They also have their own printshop which is housed in a separate building. For the most part the Democrats of Nassau County rely on volunteers—their spokesman (part-time) is a retired newspaperman who works for minimal wages; the Republicans have more than twenty staff members who get good pay and benefits, including medical and dental insurance and pensions. The Republicans have also used some of the millions collected every year to buy the latest election technology. They have their own polling operations and a full complement of computers. These resources are all brought to bear at election time. The greatest part of the party's money is spent on campaigning with the county organization coordinating the campaigns of all the Republicans running for office in a particular year and allocating money where it thinks the funds will do the most good.

Margiotta prided himself on running things in a chairman-of-the-board style which he felt was well suited to a Republican organization operating in an affluent suburban environment. He liked to say that Nassau was too sophisticated for dictatorial tactics and boasted

THE LAST POLITICAL MACHINE

that he ran the party by "dialogue and conference." He told Alan Eysen, "I have more meetings than most business executives before I take action. They've seen me change my viewpoint when enough of the fellows in the room want to go a different way." It is true that Margiotta consulted a wide circle of advisers and sometimes backed away from a decision, but many Republicans considered him to be arrogant and dictatorial and Eysen suggests that Margiotta may have encouraged "surface displays of differences among the county's powerful Republicans" because it helped him to fight charges of bossism. In some ways his handpicked successor, Joseph Mondello, has been more open, but he has also lacked Margiotta's deft touch and businessman's demeanor. Mondello's associates say he has such an uncontrollable temper that they have nicknamed him—behind his back—"Mad Dog." He will "lapse into a tantrum for little reason. . . . He turns purple and veins pop out in his neck, and half-hour lectures are not uncommon. . . . the net effect is to stifle opposition and to guarantee that he hears what he wants to hear."[25]

Unquestionably, the Nassau County Republican Organization's institutionalized structure has enabled it to survive with less than perfect leaders at the top. It made it through a period of inept leadership and internal dissension in the interval between Sprague's retirement and Margiotta's ascension. And, despite the battering it took in 1991, it is still functioning with Mondello at the helm although most politicos agree that Mondello is less able than Margiotta. In all likelihood it was probably Mondello's mediocrity that led Margiotta to choose him in the spring of 1983. Margiotta was not ready to give up the chairmanship, but he had no choice. He had been convicted of mail fraud and extortion in 1981 and by 1983 all of his attempts to avoid prison, including appeals all the way up to the Supreme Court and a plea to President Reagan for a pardon, had failed and he was finally forced to begin serving his sentence. Most people believe that Margiotta wanted someone who was loyal and would not perform impressively as chairman so that he could take over again when he got out of jail. Mondello, who started out as Margiotta's "go-fer"—picking up laundry and take-out food and driving the boss from place to place—had risen to the inner circle and was given a place on the Hempstead Town council by dint of his being (in his own words) the "most loyal of the loyal." When Margiotta first went to prison, Mondello faithfully made the 130-mile trip every month to visit him. But gradually Mondello's loyalty faded as he became used to the powers and perks that came with the chairman's job. With the support of such Margiotta enemies as United States Senator Alfonse D'Amato, the machine's most highly placed member, and the majority of the party's leadership, Mondello was able to hold on to the chairmanship. There was a feeling that Margiotta, as a convicted felon, should be kept at arm's length. However, since he had taken the rap for the party as a whole, he was helped economically. With the party's blessing, he now works as a political consultant for Hofstra University and other clients and lobbies for a number of developers. As he says, "I know the Island; I know the state. I can advise people what to do."[26]

Sprague designed the Republican organization so that it could run itself. Today, it is carrying on, but the engine is sputtering. According to Newsday's Nicholas Goldberg, Mondello is a poor political strategist who is uninformed, quirky, impulsive, unpredictable, suspicious and inarticulate. Mondello himself admits that he has problems communicating and sometimes sounds more like Yogi Berra than a modern executive. When he was asked if he spoke a foreign language, Mondello replied: "I have trouble with English, as we all know." Goldberg writes that Mondello's

> [C]ritics say he has no attention span. . . . if a staff member comes in with a memo, or if an executive leader poses a political problem, Mondello will generally listen for only three or four minutes before losing interest. After that, he begins writing personal checks, or picks his teeth with a long, thin, gold, toothbrush-size device recommended by his periodontist. Sometimes he knocks off work at 4 p.m. He doesn't have the patience to read newspapers, but has them read and interpreted by those around him. The result, according to his detractors, is that the chairman has only the sketchiest knowledge of local issues and political problems—and that many important decisions must be delegated to underlings.[27]

Part of Mondello's difficulties arise from his decision to become the presiding supervisor of Hempstead. This means he has to perform all of his party duties plus the duties of the presiding supervisor, which include being chief administrator of the town and head of the county Board of Supervisors. The two posts together simply appear to be too much for him to handle.

Although the Nassau organization is limping, it continues to be the strongest party organization in the state of New York. In addition to Senator D'Amato, the majority leader of the state Senate is a product of the organization. It also remains a force in the national Republican party. The organization that collected half of all the signatures gathered in the state of New York for President Bush's 1988 primary delegate petitions cannot be ignored by the party hierarchy.

The Patronage Machine

In Nassau County the institutions of government and the Republican party have been inextricably intertwined, with the party employing government jobs of all kinds to reward the faithful. Sometimes the reward is an appointed policymaking position or another type of non-civil service job; sometimes it is the opportunity to run for office with the party's backing; and sometimes it is a "nonpolitical" ostensibly competitive civil service position. The party moves its loyal members up the totem pole from one well-paid job to another and also sees that its members and supporters in the private sector get lucrative government business and other preferments. Public money is used to advance party and private interests. As a Democratic leader once commented, "It's more like the Communist party. Your party position determines your public position. As you move up in the party structure, you move up in public office."[28]

Of course, New York state does have a civil service system. In 1883, the year in which the federal government passed the Pendleton Act, New York established a merit system—the very first state to do so. At present there is a state Civil Service Commission which acts as an overall supervisor of the merit system, but operating authority for personnel administration in local governments is in the hands of separate civil service commissions and personnel departments in the counties, cities, school districts, and other units of local government.[29] In Nassau County the cities of Long Beach and Glen Cove and the town of Hempstead each have their own Civil Service Commission. The other towns, villages, schools and special districts, and all the workers for the county fall under the jurisdiction of the Nassau County Civil Service Commission. These local civil service bodies have to adhere to the state civil service law, but within the boundaries of that law, they are allowed to establish their own rules with the approval of the state commission. The local commissions also need state approval before they can switch a job from competitive to noncompetitive status. The local authorities are free to devise their own examinations for the competitive positions, but for budgetary reasons most of them use the exams provided by the state.

Like most civil service commissions, the New York state commission is supposed to act as a watchdog insuring that appointments and promotions are made, as the State Constitution requires, according to "merit and fitness" determined, insofar as practical, by examinations. The commission has the authority to "conduct investigations concerning any matter touching on the enforcement and effect of the Civil Service Law or Rules,"[30] but as a practical matter it does not have the resources to exercise "day-to-day oversight." In recent years it has only been able to audit individual agencies "once every 10 or 11 years." Nassau County was last audited in 1973.[31] Theoretically, the state commission could make a local commission rescind an appointment and could even remove a local commissioner, but all three members of the bipartisan commission would have to agree to such a move. No one can remember the last time a commissioner anywhere in the state was removed although on very rare occasions the commission has voided an appointment. It seems that the state commission sees itself primarily as a watchdog for the state system and leaves the job of investigating and watching over the lower level governments to the local civil service commissions. These local commissions are required to submit a report to the state each year, but these are no more than a few pages of statistics concerning the number of employees in various categories, plus a list of the local commission's employees and their salaries. The state compiles these reports and issues an annual summary, but does not attempt to determine the validity of the information local agencies choose to submit.

Under New York state law, everyone who works for the state or any of the local governments belongs to either the classified or unclassified service. The latter encompasses elected officials, legislators and their employees, department heads, members and employees of boards of elections and teachers and supervisors in the public schools, the State University and some community colleges. All other positions belong to the classified service, which is divided into competitive, exempt, noncompetitive and labor classes. Policymaking jobs fall in the exempt class and the executive who is the appointing authority can select anyone he or she wants to fill them. Some other jobs for which no examination is practical can also be exempt, but only if the state commission approves. The appointing authority has less leeway in filling the noncompetitive jobs. These are jobs which require that an applicant have certain qualifications regarding education and/or experience, but for which competitive examinations are deemed impractical. Most of the noncompetitive positions are skilled trades jobs although there are some higher level administrative, scientific and technical positions which may involve a "confidential relationship" with the appointing officer or carry influence over policy. The labor class involves the kinds of unskilled labor jobs (which may or may not require some kind of competitive test), that have traditionally been used for patronage purposes because almost anyone can fill the opening.

Any classified job which is neither exempt, noncompetitive or labor is considered a competitive job and has to be filled on the basis of a competition. Applicants have to meet requirements set by the local civil service commission and also generally need to get a minimum, passing score on an examination in order to be placed on the list of eligible candidates which the commission sends to the hiring authority. New York follows the "rule of three," meaning that the appointing officer has to choose among the three highest-scoring candidates, but doesn't necessarily have to give the job to the person who has the best score. Because an eligible list must have three names, when only one or two persons get a passing score, the hiring authority can completely ignore the test results and hire someone else on a provisional basis. There is a time limit of nine months on provisional appointments and of six months on other types of temporary appointments, but there are loopholes in the law which allow such appointments to be extended or allow a person to serve in a succession of nonpermanent appointments. In general much of the state law is loosely formulated and gives the local governments a good deal of discretion in hiring and promoting. Although they have sometimes strayed outside the limits of the state law, most of the time the Nassau County Republicans have been able to maintain the patronage that nourishes the party by artfully stretching and manipulating the legal civil service system. Just how successful they have been can be seen in the remarkable results they have achieved in the Town of Hempstead.

To be sure Hempstead, where Joseph Mondello reigns as the presiding supervisor, is considered the Republican party's stronghold. However, the town does have some registered Democrats. The records show that there is one enrolled or registered Democrat for every two Republicans. If appointments were truly made according to the law on the "basis of merit and fitness without regard to race, religion, sex, age, national origin, disability, marital status or any other nonmerit factor," one would expect that Democrats would hold approximately one third of the town's competitive jobs. Yet, *Newsday*, which conducted an intensive nine-month investigation of the Hempstead Civil Service, found that Democrats held only 16 out of more than 800 competitive jobs. Moreover, the 16 lonely Democrats have stayed near the bottom of the administrative hierarchy and have not been as well paid as their Republican colleagues. In 1990 their average salary was $27,200, while the average for all competitive jobs was $38,000.[32] Through the early 1990s only one Democrat had made it into middle management. Her hiring and subsequent promotion in the 1970s were due primarily to the GOP's need at the time to counteract the negative publicity it was getting because of state and federal investigations of Hempstead's hiring practices and the pressures the Republicans were allegedly putting on the town's workers to contribute 1 percent of their salary to the party. As the sole Democrat in the Sanitation Department, Marilyn Balaban (who is now retired) says she was lonely, but wouldn't change her party registration. She explains that, "It was a matter of principle to me. These people go to meetings at night. They fill envelopes, besides buying tickets (to fund raisers). My husband makes a good living. A few dollars won't make me richer or poorer."[33]

If Mrs. Balaban had tried to complain about her salary being lower than the salaries of registered Republicans in jobs comparable to hers, she undoubtedly would not have gotten far. In Hempstead the Civil Service Commission acts as an agent of the Republican party rather than as a neutral watchdog. Indeed, it is fair to say that the town's Civil Service Commission was established for the purpose of insuring continued, unfettered Republican control of Hempstead's public jobs. Besides Hempstead there is only one other town in the entire state of New York that has its own civil service commission. Most towns fall under the aegis of a county civil service commission as was the case for Hempstead until the late 1960s. When Democrat Eugene Nickerson was elected Nassau County Executive he began, in the words of Joseph Margiotta, to "give us a hard time" about patronage. So Margiotta, who was then chairman of both the Nassau County and Hempstead Town Republican Committees and also sat in the state assembly, used his clout to push a bill through the New York state legislature allowing Hempstead to create its own civil service commission. The three member commission is supposed to be bipartisan, but the Hempstead Democratic leader says he "never heard" of John Connolly, who is the single Democrat on the board and Connolly admits he was appointed (by the town board which is headed by Joseph Mondello) because he's a personal friend of an important local Republican leader.[34]

In its early years the Hempstead Civil Service Commission had not yet perfected its operations and ran into trouble with the New York State Civil Service Commission because it had more provisional employees than any other government in the state. Since then Hempstead has learned to draw less attention to itself and until the 1991 *Newsday* exposé triggered a state investigation, it had managed to work quietly enough to avoid state criticism.

How do the Republicans do it? Many of their techniques are familiar ones that have been used in other patronage havens. In the first place, information about job openings is tightly held within a closed circle of party regulars. While state law requires that job openings be advertised, it does not spell out how this is to be done. Unlike other local governments, Hempstead does not advertise in publications such as the *Civil Service Reporter*. The town does print announcements of job openings, but it doesn't distribute them very widely or in a timely fashion. It uses an outdated mailing list which results in some notices going to closed offices and burned-out buildings. Notices also go to the homes of Republican party officials and to people who have no interest in them, but organizations like the *Circulo de la Hispanidad* or the Nassau Economic Opportunity Council which are anxious to place their people in jobs either do not get notices or get them too late. For example, the *Circulo de la Hispanidad* got a notice of an opening for an engineering aide two days *after* the application deadline. As one would expect, the town also makes no special effort to reach minority organizations like the *Circulo* or the Hispanic Counseling Center. Some well-connected Black Republicans are occasionally asked to help identify minority job candidates, but there is, as the Hempstead affirmative action officer has admitted, no "structured" program. The officer adds that, "What we will do from time to time, if we receive an invitation, we'll participate in a career day. Or a minority job fair."[35]

When Hempstead's civil service administrator was questioned about the town's practices, he said, "I think our distribution within the Town of Hempstead is adequate. I don't know how to expand it. . . . I don't have to advertise in the paper. I get all the recruitment I can possibly use. What do you want me to do? Drag them in by the scruff of their neck?" However, a Republican executive leader, who wanted to remain anonymous, told the newspaper that, "The system isn't a criminal conspiracy. But it doesn't serve our purpose to broadcast news about jobs, if we already have a guy in mind. It's easy to maneuver things when you've been in control for as long as we have."[36]

In case outsiders should happen to hear about openings, Hempstead has another method of discouraging applicants. Although it is probably a violation of state law, Hempstead's notices sometimes list salaries for jobs that are misleadingly low. Presumably, many potential applicants didn't both applying for an administrative assistant's position which was advertised at $24,963. They might well have gone after the job if they had known that the Republican committeewoman who got the job was hired at a salary of $44,196. In another instance a committeeman was paid $68,723 for a job advertised at $29,500. Similarly, committeeman Raymond Graber, who had been convicted in the 1970s of lying to a federal grand jury about the 1% system, was hired as the assistant to the commissioner of planning and development at $55,621 though the job notice said the position paid $28,522.

Because Hempstead has fewer competitive positions than most other New York towns, cities and counties, it can easily keep unwanted applicants from getting most of its jobs. According to the figures submitted to the state Department of Civil Service, in 1990 48 percent of Hempstead's employees held noncompetitive jobs, 2.5 percent were in exempt positions and 20.1 percent in labor slots. This compares to figures for all New York cities of 32.2 percent in noncompetitive, 1.6 percent in exempt and 14.5 percent in labor positions.[37] While noncompetitive jobs do generally carry certain requirements related to education, training and experience, neither they nor the exempt or labor jobs require any testing. Therefore, Hempstead has a pretty free hand in filling these jobs. It is true that all hires have to be approved by the town's personnel director, the head of the department which has the opening, the presiding supervisor and the town board. However, given that the personnel director is a member of the Nassau County Republican party's executive committeeman, the presiding supervisor is Mondello and the town board and department heads are all Republicans, the way is clear for the party to make its influence felt.

Competitive jobs present more of a challenge since state law dictates testing and places some limitations on the construction of eligible lists and the making of appointments. However, it is possible to get around these hurdles too.

Because it is so difficult for anyone not in the Republican party to find out about openings, there are always more Republican than Democratic applicants for jobs. Democrats who do happen to make their way to the town hall are sometimes actively (and illegally) discourged from applying. One Levittown Democrat says she was told outright she'd have a better chance of getting a job if she changed her registration. When Democrats persist and take the test for a job, they are seldom hired even if they score well enough to be placed on the eligible list. Since state law allows the choice of any of the top three candidates, Hempstead officials can legally pass over a first or second place Democrat to choose a third-place Republican. If the person the Republicans want to hire doesn't make it into the top three, the party has ways of whittling down the list so that the favored candidate does advance to that rank. Sometimes the town administrators forget to contact one or two of the top scorers. When Hempstead does contact the candidates, it gives them only four days to answer a letter inquiring about the person's availability. Most other local governments give candidates seven days to reply and the state gives its candidates ten days. At times town and party officials actively discourage high-scoring candidates from taking the job. This was the case when Gary Parisi, a Republican committeeman, placed fifth on a competitive exam for the job of assistant to the purchasing commissioner. The party wanted Parisi to get the job, so several people had to be eliminated from the eligible list, including an employee of the Department of Public Safety named John Meehan. Meehan wanted the purchasing job, which was less strenuous than the work he was doing in Public

Safety, because he had suffered a serious heart attack. Still, he could not resist the pressure put on him by the party. He told his wife that he was "approached and told not to take the job. . . . They just didn't want me. They wanted him (Parisi)." He turned down the purchasing job in August of 1987. Less than a year later, he died of a heart attack.[38]

Parisi did get a passing grade on the test which he took, but it isn't always necessary to pass a test in order to get a job in Hempstead. Under certain circumstances, the town can legally appoint a person who failed the job test or who did not even take it. If only one or two applicants pass the civil service exam for a position, there can be no eligible list since New York law states that an eligible list must have three names. The town can also insure that there is no eligible list by creating a new job title. Whenever there is no eligible list, whatever the reason, the hiring authority can then fill the job provisionally until an exam can be given and graded—a process which sometimes takes years. When there is no list, the law allows the local government to hire anyone it wants on a provisional basis. (*Newsday* found that about 70 percent of the politically connected people working for Hempstead started as provisional appointees.) Once a person is in a job, he or she can get a permanent appointment by taking (or retaking) and passing the test for it at a later date.

In some cases the town has changed the job specifications so that the person the party wants to hire never has to take a written exam. After William Marshall, a Republican committeeman, was provisionally appointed first deputy receiver of taxes, the requirements for the job were changed so that Marshall was the only person who had the required credentials. He applied and then passed the "unassembled" exam—an evaluation of his experience and training—and was given a permanent appointment. (Hempstead's civil service administrator insisted that no matter how it looked, the new job specifications were not tailor-made for Marshall.)

Although provisional appointments are not supposed to last more than nine months, there are techniques for extending them. As noted, a person can be provisionally appointed even if he has taken and failed the job test. If the person has been in the job too long, he or she can be moved to another department and given a provisional appointment there. One party committeeman, who couldn't seem to pass a test, held a series of provisional jobs over a period of 11 years. Mondello has said that he doesn't see anything wrong with this maneuvering. Speaking of one case, he commented, "I approve of a way to keep him on here and keep him working, doing a job for the town and not disrupting this township or his personal life. . . I don't think the test is all-encompassing and should be the final word."[39]

When all else fails, the town has simply created new job titles with specifications that fit the person the party wants or it has added more positions for existing titles. One year the number of assistant superintendents of sanitation was increased from three to nine to accommodate a committeeman who finished sixth on the test for the job. This move cost the town almost $250,000.

Favoritism in Hempstead doesn't end with hiring. Employees who hold party leadership positions and those who contribute generously to the party have higher salaries and advance more rapidly than the average employee does. In 1990 more than half of the 51 top-level civil service employees were members of the Nassau County Republican Committee. Some of the others were relatives of the committeemen or former party officials and most had contributed to the GOP. The politically connected employees earned an average of $57,892 as compared to the $49,426 earned by workers without connections. The few committeemen who work in the lower-level service and maintenance jobs also earn more than others doing similar work; on average the committeemen make almost $13,000 more. Joseph Mondello swears that he doesn't exert pressure on the town's administrators, but clearly, as one insider says, "Politics never hurts."[40]

Union and civil service rules have sometimes been ignored in order to give raises to the politically favored. One committeeman got five "annual" step raises in a single year! Sometimes Hempstead will upgrade a position in order to award someone a higher salary or it will change a job's status from graded to ungraded. In contrast to the graded positions to which union and civil service rules apply, there are no rules governing salaries for ungraded positions so the town board can pay an individual in an ungraded job whatever it wants.

The career of James A. Powers, a former Republican committeeman from Westbury, illustrates how the system can work to help the well-connected individual. According to Newsday:

> After six years as a security officer, Powers was provisionally appointed to licensing inspector trainee, a competitive job, on May 19, 1980. Although the job was advertised as starting at $14,893, he received $19,083. On Oct. 3, 1981, he took the test for the job and came in No. 3. Meanwhile, he had been provisionally appointed to that job on Dec. 21, 1982, after he came in third on a test. Two years later, he was provisionally promoted to his current job of supervisor of licensing. He had just enough experience to qualify and was the only person to take the promotional exam in May, 1985. He was permanently appointed to the job on Jan. 13, 1986. An open exam given simultaneously for the same position required five years as a licensing inspector. In his first 12

months on the job permanently, he skipped five pay steps, increasing his salary by more than $6,000 to $49,980. The skips put him at the top of his grade, which means automatic salary increases were limited by union contract to less than $350 a year. On Dec. 31, 1989, the town board removed the pay limit by making his job ungraded and also gave him a $1,500 raise. Powers said he's had to take tests for every job he's had and wasn't aware of politics playing any part in his promotions or raises.[41]

James Powers must be remarkably blind not to notice how politics helps one get ahead in Hempstead. While some people do walk in off the street and get jobs (usually lower-level ones), those who get the better jobs, promotions, and higher pay follow another route. It's a route similar to the one Chicagoans would have followed twenty years ago. As a Republican from Lynbrook, a village in Hempstead, explained: "Basically to get a job in the town, first you go to the Republican committeeman in your ED (election district). He in turn makes recommendations to the Republican leader who is Bob Becker (in Lynbrook). Becker in turn makes the recommendation, puts his seal of approval on the job."[42]

Promotions and raises, even when they are initiated by a department head putting in a request to the personnel director, have to go through the committeemen and the executive leaders. Peter Schwartz, a former parks employee, says his executive leader told him that if he wanted a promotion he had to "come down to the club, help out, participate. Paying your dues is not enough. The way you get promoted is to participate."[43]

While the lower-level party officials make recommendations, their word is not the final one. The recommendations go through Joseph Mondello, who as presiding supervisor and Republican county chairman, has to approve them. Technically, the town board is the ultimate authority because it must vote on Mondello's recommendations, but it has always rubber stamped all of them.

When Newsday examined civil service jobs in the Towns of Oyster Bay and North Hempstead, it found a pattern similar to Hempstead's. In Oyster Bay in 1990 there was a 95 to 1 ratio of Republicans to Democrats in competitive civil service jobs though there was approximately one registered Democrat for every two registered Republicans. In North Hempstead Republicans outnumbered Democrats in competitive jobs by ten to one though registered Republicans and Democrats are nearly equal with Republicans edging out Democrats by only six to five. As in Hempstead, the committeemen also had better jobs and were paid more than people without political connections.[44]

147

Neither North Hempstead nor Oyster Bay has its own civil service commission. Although town officials decide who they are going to interview among the candidates on the eligible lists and then decide who to hire, the Nassau County Civil Service Commission advertises jobs, processes applications, constructs, administers and grades tests and compiles the eligible lists. It is also responsible for seeing that the towns are in compliance with state law. Neither the Nassau County Personnel Office, which processes the paperwork involved in hiring and functions directly under the County Executive Thomas Gulotta, nor the Nassau County Civil Service Commission seems to offer any interference to the Republican patronage operation. Certainly, the Commission is not willing to discuss its work. My own efforts to get someone at the Commission to talk to me took on comic opera overtones. One official finally agreed to an interview and asked me to come to his office at 5:00 P.M. I arrived at the Commission's building at 4:50 P.M. only to find the building locked. A sign on the door indicated that the office closes at 4:45 P.M.; by 4:50 P.M. there wasn't a soul in sight. I phoned the next morning and was told to call again at a set time a week later since the official didn't have a spare moment until then. When I did call the next week, the official sounded surprised to hear from me. He asked me to call back in ten minutes as he was in the midst of finishing some work. Ten minutes later, I called back. The phone rang and rang, but no one answered. The next morning the official explained that he had been called to a meeting. He apologized, but said he really couldn't talk to me. He also refused to send me a copy of the county's report to the New York State Civil Service Commision. Since the report is public, I was later able to get it from the state.

Many of the government workers in Nassau County are union members, but until the 1992 layoffs and budget cuts, the unions got along well with Nassau's Republican organization. Rita Wallace, the president of the 16,000 member Civil Service Employees Association of Nassau, which is the largest public employee union in the county, said that she didn't have any problem with the hiring authorities choosing among the top three scorers on a political basis and that in general she had no objection to the patronage system as long as "they don't hire people who aren't qualified." She also noted that there were a number of county employees, such as the nurses at the public hospital, who were not in competitive jobs, but were hired on the basis of their qualifications and were completely outside the patronage system.[45]

With the single exception of the 1 percent case (to be discussed shortly), Nassau's workers and their unions have not been inclined to challenge the Republican patronage machine. There have been no

Elrod-Branti suits and no one rushed to court following the Rutan decision. In fact Rutan has had no discernible impact on hiring. Since the initial 1 percent convictions in the late 1970s, the machine has been careful not to leave a paper trail so it would be difficult to win a court battle against it today. Presumably, *Newsday's* research[46] would be useful in a worker's lawsuit, but most workers with a grievance have either been afraid to sue or have lacked the resources to do so. The Democrats have made some use of *Newsday's* reports on the civil service and of its various exposés of machine greed and corruption, but they have not pushed the patronage issue too vigorously. Undoubtedly, this is in part because the Democrats themselves played the patronage game when they were in power (under Nickerson, for example) and because many of them would welcome a share in the spoils of victory. As one elected Democrat remarked, "One of the main reasons for the Republican's success is the way they have refined the art of patronage. I say that not with criticism but with a certain amount of envy."[47] The situation is proof, if anyone really needed it almost 40 years after *Brown v. Board of Education*, that Supreme Court decisions are not self-executing.

The Party Elite: Politics for Fun and Profit

In 1989 when *Newsday* examined the income Republican party leaders realized from their political connections, it found that only two of the 69 members of the Executive Committee of the party were not profiting in some way. As capitalist true believers, Nassau's Republicans have never seen any reason why people whose business is politics should not benefit financially from their calling. In line with this philosophy the party has paid its leaders well. Before he went to jail in 1983, Joseph Margiotta was getting $50,000 a year, a chauffered car and expenses for his work as chairman. The present chairman, Joseph Mondello, gets $75,000[48] annually for running the party. Like many of the leaders, he also earns a government salary and has private business interests which make money because of his political connections. Mondello gets $100,000 as Hempstead's presiding supervisor and draws at least $30,000 a year (plus a share of the annual profits and the use of a car) from his law firm. He gets this bonanza from the firm even though he admits he no longer practices law or goes to his law office. However, he insists that he does look out for the interests of some clients, watching to see that the firm handles their business properly. Therefore, he says, he has not violated the New York Bar Association rule designed to counteract official influence peddling. This rule states that a lawyer is not supposed to let his name be used by a law firm when he is not "actively and regularly practicing law as a member of the firm." Mondello stoutly maintains that he doesn't trade on his political influence; however, his firm receives a $20,000 yearly retainer from the Town of Hempstead's Industrial Development Agency and collects sizable legal fees from both the agency and the companies which receive tax breaks or financing from it.[49]

Most of Nassau's top Republicans hold office in the government as well as in the party. In 1989 forty-seven of the 69 executive leaders held full-time public jobs, including the chief executive and comptroller of the county, the Hempstead presiding supervisor, several town clerks, more than a half-dozen members of three town boards, 26 agency commissioners or other heads of local government bodies, 18 deputy commissioners or other high-level aides, and five members of the New York state legislature. Since 1989 party executives have lost the North Hempstead's supervisor's position, three of the town council slots and one town clerkship, but they still hold an impressive array of offices. These are, on the whole, well paid as well as powerful positions. Party leadership in Nassau County does not require financial sacrifice; in 1989 executive committeemen earned an average of $80,000 a year in their government posts. When Crain's *City and State* surveyed U.S. counties in 1991, it found that Nassau's leaders were near the top of the list. County Executive Thomas Gulotta's $104,433 salary made him the sixth highest paid county executive in the country; the Nassau Comptroller's $103,742 put him in third place on the Comptroller's list; and the Treasurer's $110,354 put him in second place among financial officers.[50]

Nassau's Republicans, like the Democrats in Daley's old Chicago machine, have frequently used their clout to help those near and dear to them. More than 40 of the 69 executive leaders have relatives on the government payroll. Few have done more for their kin and neighbors than the party's patriarch, octogenarian Peter De Sibio. In return for being a top performer in turning out the vote and raising funds, the party has given De Sibio his own private toll bridge. Officially, the Atlantic Beach Bridge is public property and De Sibio is merely the unpaid chairman of the Nassau County Bridge Authority, but the little bridge really seems to exist primarily to serve De Sibio's town organization. Originally, both the tolls and the Authority were scheduled to be abolished once the bridge's bonds were paid off. The bonds have been retired, and three different official reports have urged the elimination of the tolls and the authority, but instead of closing down the toll operation, the bridge was refinanced. As one politician explained, there was a "general feeling . . . that it was his [De Sibio's] bridge and we shouldn't bother him about it."[51] So the tolls continue to be collected with most of the money going to pay for the Bridge Authority's personnel, who mostly spend their time collecting the tolls. De Sibio's son-in-law makes over $43,000 for managing the bridge authority; his nephew gets nearly $40,000 for running the authority's office. At least a dozen of the 36 full-time bridge employees live in De Sibio's home town of Inwood. When a reporter questioned him about this arrangement, De Sibio, who is honored by Inwood's 8,200 inhabitants for his charitable works, said he didn't have to answer since, as he put it, "I'm so good I could pose for holy cards."[52]

De Sibio draws no pay from the Bridge Authority, but that does not mean that he hasn't gained financially from his party position. He gets $30,000 from Hempstead's Industrial Authority for his work as a public relations consultant although no one can say exactly what he does for the money. Joseph Mondello says he thinks that De Sibio "probably does perform some kind of service. I would hope he does."[53] The "holy man's" son Nicholas gets nearly $200,000 a year from Oyster Bay and Hempstead for representing the towns in worker's compensation cases. Joseph Margiotta says he was the one who originally "cleared" Nicholas De Sibio for the legal work.

The patriarch of Inwood is hardly alone in reaping private profits from the public's business. Every government in the United States makes plenty of work for lawyers; in Nassau County this work has often been parcelled out (on a no-bid basis) to firms with political clout, especially those with Republican leaders as partners. When the Oyster Bay town attorney, who just happens to be on the Republican executive committee, needed some help with the town's trial work, he naturally turned to a firm headed by his fellow committeeman. In less than three years the firm earned $175,000 in fees from the town. Similarly, Republican judges (and in Nassau County almost all of the judges are Republicans) have favored members of their party, particularly those in the leadership echelon, with guardianships and other money-making court assignments. Developers and other private businessmen who want something from local government also bring their work to members of the executive committee. For example, one group of developers hired John Dunne's law firm to represent them before the town board. This was a wise choice since at the time every member of the board (which had to give its approval to the developers' project) was a Republican and John Dunne was the Republican leader for the town. Many homeowners trying to have their real estate bill lowered also go to one of the leaders' law firms. Michael Tully's firm, for example, specializes in helping clients obtain lower tax assessments and is quite successful at it—possibly because Tully is a state senator and a member of the Republican executive committee.

In some cases party leaders have had a direct personal financial interest in matters that have come before various Republican controlled governing bodies. A case in point is Easa Easa, an executive committeeman from West Hempstead, who is a partner in a real-estate development company which has profited from zoning changes granted to its properties. The company has also been given the opportunity to buy town land at bargain-basement prices.[54] Easa has denied any wrongdoing and it's quite possible that he sees nothing wrong with his actions. When one party has controlled a government as long as Nassau's Republicans have, there is a tendency to lose sight of the line dividing public from private interests. Even when there is no outright corruption, Nassau's one-party system has, as Burt Neuborne (the attorney for the 1% plaintiffs) notes, fostered a "government culture in which officials automatically favor anything Republican-connected even if nobody explicitly tells them to."[55] Furthermore, one-party domination has fostered a system in which public policy is formulated behind closed doors by the executive leaders. By making decisions at their party meetings rather than at the public sessions of the various government bodies on which they serve, the leaders can sidestep New York's open meetings act. The law applies to meetings of a government body such as the Hempstead Town Board, but does not apply to internal party sessions.

In the final analysis, Nassau's one-party machine politics has tended to produce a nonideological, materialistic individualism which has at times led to ethical lapses. Nowhere is this better illustrated than in the conduct and career of Alfonse D'Amato.

"Senator Pothole"

Over the years people have been drawn to the Nassau County Republican Party for the most practical of reasons. As Alan Eysen has written, Nassau County is populated by homeowners concerned about "a good education for their children and about such things as garbage pickups, good police protection, roads without potholes, property rights and transportation." To a great extent the Republicans have given the voters the services they wanted. Therefore, the voters have supported Republicans for local offices, frequently while voting for Democratic candidates for state and national offices. Undoubtedly, some citizens also cast their ballots for the Nassau Republicans because they feared the encroachment of the big city with its welfare, crime and minorities. The Republicans appealed to these voters by promising to keep out urban evils and problems. A party newspaper sent to every Nassau voter before one election warned that:

Nassau County today faces its most fearsome peril. . . . the very real threat to our suburban way of life posed by the relentless advance of high-rise housing.

Poised like a dagger at the jugular vein of the county, high-rise will surely become a reality if Democratic philosophy is allowed to take hold of our county. And that friends, is what the county executive election is all about. . . . they want to create a "city of Nassau."

Democrats have a tough time trying to justify their existence in suburbia. They flourish best in the teeming wards of the inner cities, exploiting the frustrations of people who live on top of each other, who can't breathe because the air is befouled, who can't swim because the waters reek with slime, who can't travel because the streets are clogged with cars and taxis and buses and trucks. . . .[56]

To be fair, there are many people who have been drawn to the Republican party for more positive reasons. They have supported the party because it was a grass-roots, local organization. The Republican workers who asked for their votes were neighbors who worshipped at the same churches and often shared the same ethnic attachments. The Nassau County Republican Party has always been a locally oriented party concentrating its energies on winning local elections. Federal offices have never been terribly important to the Nassau machine because, unlike county and state legislative posts, they do not produce the jobs and opportunities for making money that are the organization's lifeblood. Reportedly, the party has even had trouble recruiting top people to run for Congress; "many of the GOP's best candidate prospects are unwilling to go to Washington because relocating would require them to abandon the comfort of their suburban Nassau neighborhoods and the security of well-paying county government jobs."[57]

The party's activists are attracted to it for a variety of down-to-earth, practical reasons. Many of them are joiners at heart. They take an interest in their neighborhoods and belong to an array of organizations; they like the hustle-bustle and schmoozing of politics. They are comfortable with the conservative orientation of the Republican party, but are not at all ideological. If they were, they would probably enroll in the New York Conservative party.

There are Republican workers who are content to do their share because they simply enjoy the activity and want to help their party. These are people like the elderly ladies of the Virginia M. Bacon Woman's Republican Club of Oceanside. In the club's early years in the 1940s, the members used to dress in costumes when they were campaigning. They no longer wear their costumes, but they are still an "active force in local politics, staging fund-raisers, doing the leg-work for candidates, and sponsoring candidate forums." As one Republican candidate has said, the club's members, who are active in other community organizations, enable him to "cash in on a lot of the good will they are responsible for in the community."[58]

Naturally, not everyone is so altruistic as the good women of Oceanside. While they may enjoy the social side of politics, a good number of Nassau County Republican activists are drawn to the party by the promise of material rewards. Party activity can lead to money-making opportunities or to a high-paying prestigious job (or both). The party's jobs may not seem desirable to the children of the North Shore rich, but they are very appealing to ambitious young men like the D'Amato brothers of Island Park.

Without the Nassau County machine, Alfonse D'Amato and his younger brother Armand would probably be small-time lawyers, writing wills and handling real estate closings. With the boost provided by the Republican organization, Alfonse has risen to the United States Senate while Armand has gone from the state Assembly to a partnership in a flourishing law firm which counts major corporations among its clients.

Alfonse has always been hard-working, aggressive and determined to get ahead. From an $83 a week patronage job as a law clerk with the county, he rapidly ascended the career ladder, helped along the way by his mentor Joseph Margiotta. At the age of 30 he was the Hempstead Receiver of Taxes; in two years he had advanced to the post of town supervisor and then in 1977, he became the Hempstead presiding supervisor—a position which also made him the head of the Nassau County Board of Supervisors. At the same time he had climbed up through the party ranks to become the Republican leader in Island Park and a member of the executive committee of the county organization.

As he rose, Alfonse brought his little brother along with him. While he was tax assessor, Alfonse asked Margiotta to find something for Armand. At first Armand worked as a legislative aide in Albany, but after two years Margiotta came through with an offer to slate Armand for the state Assembly. Looking back, Margiotta says that "Al had turned Island Park from a marginal area into a Republican stronghold. So when he recommended his brother for the Assembly, that carried some weight."[59] However, Margiotta was not willing to go along with Alfonse's 1982 bid to make Armand the leader of the Republicans in the Assembly. Margiotta felt that Armand, who had a reputation as a lazy, reluctant campaigner and a mediocre, indifferent legislator, was not qualified for the leadership spot. Armand didn't become minority leader; eventually he resigned from the Assembly shortly after being reelected to his seventh term. He explained that, "It just reached a point where I could not justify representing the people of the district in a half-hearted way."[60]

Margiotta's refusal to back Armand broke the last remaining ties between him and his protege Alfonse—the man he once called "my tiger." Their relations were already strained because of Alfonse's actions in 1980. Alfonse, then the presiding supervisor of Hempstead, seemed well on his way to becoming the County Executive in a few years and, in time, possibly the next county chairman. But he wanted more. He saw a chance to break away from the local scene and he grabbed it, even though it meant he had to destroy a respected Republican senator and alienate Margiotta. Ignoring the advice of his friends and of political patrons like Margiotta (who had long supported the liberal-moderate wing of the Republican party), D'Amato mounted a primary challenge to a highly regarded incumbent Senator. Jacob Javits, the 76-year-old Senator, was suffering from a degenerative neurological disease. D'Amato took advantage of Javits' illness and made an issue of the Senator's health and age. The presiding supervisor wrested the Republican nomination from Javits and went on to win the seat in the general election. Ironically, he owed that victory to the man he had humiliated. Javits refused to withdraw as the Liberal Party candidate and as a result the sizeable New York liberal vote was split between Javits and ELizabeth Holtzman who was running on the Democratic ticket. D'Amato won with 45 percent of the vote, just barely enough to beat Holtzman's 44 percent.

Alfonse D'Amato brought the mentality of a parochial machine politician to the lofty chambers of the United States Senate. Although he had won the endorsement of the New York Conservative Party and run as their candidate, even Conservatives recognized that he was more of a pragmatist than a "doctrinaire conservative."[61]

Once in office D'Amato set out to win the loyalty of New York voters one by one, group by group, by doing as much for each person and organization as he possibly could and by making sure that as many people as possible knew that he was delivering the goods for his constitutents. He acquired a reputation as an unprincipled publicity hound, while his aggressive pursuit of local interests earned him the nickname of Senator Pothole. The *Almanac of American Politics* describes him as:

> shrewd to the point of shamelessness in taking practically any position, espousing any cause, and lobbying for any project or program that could be popular with even the smallest segment of

the New York electorate. . . . All the while he remains jovial and good humored—as if he were elbowing erstwhile opponents in the ribs and saying, it's only a game, right? "O.K., I love ya babes," he signs off his phone conversations.[62]

The *New York Times* described D'Amato's efforts to win the pivotal New York Jewish vote as verging on "self parody." As soon as the Iraqis bombed Tel Aviv, D'Amato was on a plane to Israel where he ostentatiously wore a gas mask to show his support for the beleaguered Jews. Although D'Amato is a Catholic, he spends so much time at Jewish services that a bishop once admonished him for going to synagogue more than he goes to church.[63]

D'Amato's style may have dismayed Washington insiders, but it won over the people who counted—the voters. In 1986 he surprised his numerous critics by winning reelection with 57 percent of the vote. No doubt his $12 million war chest also played a role by scaring off challengers and making it possible to buy expensive TV time during the campaign.

D'Amato's millions did not just fall into his lap. He went after the money with a vengeance, pressuring businessmen and others with a stake in government policy to add to his coffers. D'Amato acquired a reputation for being particularly blatant about linking contributions and favors. One Republican strategist commented that New York's junior senator has "raised to a high art the practice of insuring that no good deed goes uncollected."[64]

At the same time that Alfonse—with a 62.6 percent approval rating in 1986[65]—was solidifying his hold on his Senate seat, Armand's law firm was prospering. (The two were not unconnected.) Armand and his partners have denied that they were trading on their connection to the Senator, but surely their clients were aware of the relationship between Armand and Alfonse D'Amato. It seems unlikely that a large defense contractor like Unisys would have paid Armand D'Amato over a hundred thousand dollars if it weren't for his tie to a powerful member of the subcommittee on defense of the Senate Appropriations Committee.

In retrospect the 1986 election may prove to be the high point of Alfonse D'Amato's career. As the 1992 election approached, D'Amato's ratings were in a free fall; by March 1992 only 34 percent approved of his performance. This rating reflected the battering D'Amato's image had taken in the press and on TV from a series of accusations, investigations and indictments of people close to him. The Senate Ethics Committee conducted a two-year investigation of more than a dozen charges including alleged improprieties connected with his fund-raising tactics. D'Amato was accused of using his influence as a member of the Appropriations and Banking Committees to help his contributors. The most serious allegations concerned his relationship with Unisys and letters which had been sent from his office to the Secretary of the Navy urging the Navy to award contracts to the company. The letters were drafted by employees of Unisys and delivered by Armand D'Amato to his brother's office where they were retyped on the senator's stationery and sent out bearing the signature of the senator. Alfonse D'Amato said he knew nothing about the letters and was unaware of his brother's efforts on behalf of Unisys.

In addition to the Unisys case and other allegations involving defense contractors, Senator D'Amato was accused of pressuring the Department of Housing and Urban Development to employ his friends and to approve his contributors' projects. Samuel Pierce, the former Secretary of HUD said he was forced to hire one of D'Amato's neighbors even though "she was not competent for the position."[66] The Senator was also said to have pressured the agency to fund a renovation project which made money for a man who raised thousands of dollars for D'Amato in Puerto Rico. Initially, D'Amato denied that he had even contacted HUD on the man's behalf, but he had to backtrack when letters from him to HUD surfaced. D'Amato has also denied charges that were made concerning his involvement, both before and after he went to the Senate, with a HUD funded housing development in Island Park. The development was supposed to provide low-cost integrated housing, but politically connected Island Parkers were tipped off and got their applications in on 9:00 A.M. of the day the houses were first advertised. As a result none of the houses went to blacks. Instead townspeople, including a cousin of D'Amato's, got subsidized houses at bargain rates. This happened before D'Amato went to the Senate, but a former village official told federal prosecutors that D'Amato continued to exert control over the program after he went to Washington.

In August 1991 the Senate Ethics Committee declared that it hadn't found evidence that Senator D'Amato had broken any federal laws or Senate rules. However, it noted that its work had been hampered because over half of the subpoened witnesses took the Fifth Amendment and refused to testify. Therefore, the Committee reserved the right to reopen the investigation if further information should become available. Although it did not make any formal charges, the Committee did criticize D'Amato's conduct in the Unisys episode. Its report stated that "it is the duty of every United States Senator to conduct his or her office in a manner that precludes its systematic misuse by members of his or her family for personal gain. The activities of Sen. D'Amato's brother on behalf of Unisys constituted such a misuse. Senator D'Amato conducted the business of his office in an improper and inappropriate manner."[67] At his press conference following the issuing of the Committee's report, D'Amato announced that he had forbidden his brother from contacting his Senate office on behalf of any legal clients.[68]

The Committee report was hardly a ringing endorsement; still, the Senator claimed that he had been completely vindicated. In reality it seemed that, in the absence of a smoking gun, the Committee was unwilling to crack down on a fellow senator, particularly when his behavior was not very different from that of some of his colleagues.

D'Amato's troubles did not end when the Senate Ethics Committee finished its work. The Senator's name was again in the headlines when his chief fundraiser in Puerto Rico was indicted on charges related to his involvement with D'Amato. There were even bigger headlines when Armand D'Amato was indicted in March 1992 for fraud in connection with the payments he received from Unisys. The indictment said that the money Armand received for "technical" services was really given to him in order to influence Senator D'Amato.

In the end, Alfonse fared better than his little brother. Instead of uniting, New York's Democrats engaged in a three-way suicidal primary race from which Robert Abrams emerged as victor over Geraldine Ferraro and Elizabeth Holtsman. A particularly inept campaigner, Abrams failed to unite the Democrats and lost by two percentage points to D'Amato.

Alfonce's victory did not, however, save his brother. After the election, Armand was tried and found guilty of seven counts of mail fraud in connectin with the Unisys contract.

Although Alfonce D'Amato managed to escape, it seems clear that the D'Amato brothers were engaged in some form of influence peddling. For years they have used their positions to help themselves politically and financially. In this they have been no different from many Nassau politicians. However, it has been their misfortune to have been caught in the national spotlight at the time that public attitudes and the law were changing. Americans, always suspicious of politicians, have become downright hostile to their elected officials and are no longer willing to accept politics as usual, while the Supreme Court patronage rulings and post-Watergate election laws have made illegal practices that were once legal. These changes have brought trouble for the D'Amatos. Even before his second term had begun, Alfonse D'Amato had found himself at the center of a dramatic trial challenging one of the most time-honored of machine traditions—the "one percent."

The One Percent Case

Corruption and scandal have dogged the Nassau County Republican organization since its beginning. The founder of the modern Republican machine in the county, Russel Sprague, had to resign the party chairmanship because of his questionable dealings in Roosevelt Raceway stock. Sprague's most notable successor, Joseph Margiotta was convicted of mail fraud and extortion and spent a year in a federal prison. As party chairman and the most powerful man in the county, Margiotta was able to direct municipal insurance business to brokers of his choosing. In return for the windfall, the brokers were required to kick back a percentage of their fees to Republican politicians whom Margiotta designated. Although he held no municipal or county office, Margiotta was convicted under federal extortion laws applying to public officials because the jury accepted the prosecution argument that Margiotta had so much influence that he was in effect a public official. The defense argued that Margiotta had done no wrong since fee-splitting was a traditional and legitimate form of patronage. Margiotta's lawyers even called on Jack English, who chaired the Democrats in the years they controlled the county executive's office, to testify that he had also recommended that individuals he termed "political associates" get a cut of municipal insurance commissions.[69] The jury was unconvinced.

The one percent case differed from the actions directed against Margiotta and other individual Republicans because the party itself was put on trial. In the early 1970s *Newsday* investigated the political contributions of public employees and was able to show that the practice of workers giving one percent of their salaries to the Republican party was widespread. Party chairman Margiotta claimed that the party did not coerce employees into giving although it did expect them to donate one percent of their salaries to the organization. He maintained that the donations were entirely voluntary. Despite his denials, investigators from the General Accounting Office began to look into charges that the party had violated national election laws by forcing workers in federally financed programs to donate part of their salaries in order to get, and keep, their jobs. The GAO turned its findings over to the United States Attorney's office in Brooklyn which continued the investigation. Ultimately, Margiotta's executive assistant and six officials of the Town of Hempstead were indicted on a combination of federal and state charges related to the one percent scheme. They were charged under New York statutes of violating the State Civil Service Law prohibiting the solicitation of political contributions from employees on government property. Apparently, some Nassau officials were not aware of this prohibition. One of the Hempstead officials who decided to plead guilty admitted that he had told the workers under his supervision that they should contribute to the Republican party if they wanted to get overtime work or be promoted, but said he had never realized his actions were illegal.

Some of the indicted officials were convicted in federal and Nassau County courts after a trial; others chose to plead guilty. All received light sentences of fines and/or probation; none went to jail.

While these criminal investigations and prosecutions were taking place, the party's one percent was attacked on another front. In late 1974 a public watchdog group called AWARE joined four civil service employees and a union group that had broken away from the Nassau Civil Service Employees Association in filing a civil suit against the Republicans. The employees accused the party of forcing them to make contributions. They asked for the return of the six million dollars "exacted" from them and thousands of other county, town and village employees over the preceding five years. They also demanded compensation for the employees who had been denied raises and promotions because they refused to contribute. However, they failed to convince the justice of the New York State Supreme Court who handled their suit. He said their charges were "speculative" and dismissed the lawsuit.

Regrouping, two of the individual employees joined with the dissident union group, the Civil Service Merit Council, and the Council's president to file a class action suit in federal court. This time, the judge, Jacob Mishler, agreed to hear the case and to give it class action status. In a detailed memorandum of decision he explained that the allegations were serious because they

> "suggest that the defendants have trampled on the First Amendment rights of countless numbers of civil service employees in order to strengthen the financial base of the Nassau County Republican Party. Collectively, the defendants allegedly have the power to appoint individuals in the municipal and county governments. In order to obtain such a position, or to achieve a promotion within the governmental unit, the applicant or employee must contribute a part of his salary to the Nassau County Republican Committee. The pressure to make contributions apparently is generated by party officials acting in concert with elected public officials."[70]

To insure that the vital First Amendment rights of the 22,000 employees in the class were adequately represented, Judge Mishler appointed New York University Law School professor Burt Neuborne as their attorney. The judge felt that Neuborne had the experience and expertise needed and, due to his association with the American Civil

Liberties Association and the law school, would have access to the extensive resources needed to fight a case of such magnitude.

Because of legal technicalities, Judge Mishler ruled that some of the individuals and government bodies who had originally been named as defendants by the plaintiffs could not be sued under federal and state laws. His actions left as defendants the Town of Hempstead, Nassau County, and the Nassau County and Town of Hempstead Republican Committees.

It took eight years from the time Judge Mishler issued his memorandum for the case to finally come to trial. Throughout this period of legal maneuvering, there were numerous attempts to arrive at a settlement. Senator D'Amato, who had unwittingly provided the plaintiffs with a key piece of evidence dating from his days as Hempstead Town supervisor, was particularly anxious to avoid a court appearance and pressured Republican officials to settle with the plaintiffs. But each time it appeared that an agreement was at hand, something happended to undo it. So, on July 29, 1985 the trial began in Uniondale before a six member jury of two Republicans, two Democrats and two independents. As expected, Burt Neuborne introduced as his first piece of evidence a 1971 letter written by Alfonse D'Amato to Donald Woolnough, who was then Margiotta's executive assistant. The letter concerned Robert Marcus, a neighbor of D'Amato's, whose request for a raise had been denied by Hempstead. D'Amato wrote: "I have spoken to Mr. Margiotta and he has indicated to me that the raise for Robert Marcus of the Sanitation Department would be approved if he took care of the 1 percent. Accordingly please find a check for $75 from the Island Park Republican Committeemen's Council." D'Amato's letter was dated June 9th; a second document introduced by Neuborne showed that Marcus was given a raise on June 11th.

Edward Hart, the chief attorney for the Republican party, argued in his opening statement and throughout the trial that the party did not coerce employees into giving. He insisted that if employees gave out of fear, it was fear that they would lose their jobs if the Democrats were elected. Moreover, he maintained that the Nassau Republicans were guilty of "nothing more than political patronage. . . .a time-honored practice dating back to colonial times."[71]

Margiotta's top aide Donald Woolnough was the first witness. He testified that hiring and promotions had indeed gone through Margiotta during the time he was chairman. The County Personnel director would inform Margiotta whenever there was a job opening and the chairman would then ask one of the executive party leaders to send him someone for the job. The candidates would be summoned to Republican party headquarters for an interview with either Woolnough or Margiotta. (The chairman personally saw all candidates for higher paying jobs until the practice was discontinued in 1974). Woolnough said that when he interviewed applicants for the less important jobs, he never discussed money and he further insisted that the one percent was always only a "suggested formula." However, the records Neuborne introduced into evidence showed that employees consistently contributed a sum of money that amounted to approximately one percent of their salary; in some cases they made checks out for exactly one percent down to the last penny.

Following Woolnough's appearance, a number of present and former officials were called as witnesses. Generally, they confirmed Woolnough's account of how the system worked, while adding some new details. For example, one Hempstead Town official testified that whenever an employee was being considered for a raise, he would check with an employee's leader to "see if there was any problem."[72] On the third day of the trial, Joseph Margiotta himself took the stand. Testifying in the same courtroom where he was tried in 1981, Margiotta readily admitted that political factors entered into the recommendations he and other party officials made. He observed that "a political leader who's worth his salt is not going to recommend someone who's not helping the party to win elections," but he averred that an employee's failure to contribute one percent "never entered into any recommendations" of his. However, when he was asked if other party officials might have based their recommendations on contributions, he replied that "It could possibly happen." Furthermore, he conceded that some employees might have felt pressured to contribute especially when the person doing the asking was their boss. He allowed that he could "see where, in a person's subjective frame of mind, where he would feel some pressure."[73]

Neuborne set out to show that workers did in fact feel pressured. He called a number of them to relate their experiences with the system. A woman recalled being interviewed by a party official who asked her a lot of political questions to determine whether she would work for Republican candidates and join the local party club. At the end of the interview the official asked her if he'd left anything out and she said, "I asked him if he was going to ask me if I could type."[74] Another witness drew a laugh from the spectators when he replied to Hart's asking if his contributions were voluntary, "Yes, you *had* to give it voluntarily."[75] Most of the employees said that their fellow workers had told them how the system operated and they hadn't been directly threatened by party representatives. One said, however, that his supervisor had told him he should contribute one percent since, "If you want to get, you have to give." The worker testified that he protested that with four children to support he couldn't afford one percent and offered to pay on installments. He made out a check for $25, but was told it was unacceptable because one percent was "the name of the game."[76] A group of Hempstead security officers also reported that they were forced to buy tickets to fund raisers. The deputy commissioner of Public Safety confirmed that the Commissioner had ordered him to keep track of who gave and who didn't and that "overtime and promotions were directly linked to the sale of tickets." To add insult to injury, the officers were not allowed to eat the $150 dinner they were forced to purchase; instead they were made to "volunteer" to park cars and direct traffic for guests at the fund raiser.[77] Several other supervisors admitted that they had collected money from their workers, but said they were ordered to do so by their bosses.

In rebuttal Republican Attorney Hart offered a parade of witnesses who stoutly maintained they had contributed to the party voluntarily and didn't believe their contributions were connected to promotions and raises. However, all of them indicated that they had been helped to get their jobs and to advance in their careers by their party connections and on cross-examination most of them admitted that they hadn't contributed to the party before they started working for local government.

The defense called witnesses in supervisory positions who denied having pressured anyone. When he testified, Thomas Gulotta insisted he had never been part of the one percent system and that as County Executive he had hired and promoted on the basis of merit.

As the trial drew to a close, Alfonse D'Amato could delay his appearance no longer. On the stand D'Amato tried to put the system and his participation in it in the best possible light. First, he said that in writing his letter he'd only been trying to help a neighbor who was not "sophisticated" enough to know about the one percent. He also attempted to play on the jurors' sympathies by telling them of his own experience following the election of a Democrat as County Executive. He said he was a law clerk in the county attorney's office in November when the "Republicans lost the election. I was fired . . . about February or so. Within about a matter of weeks we had the birth of my first baby. I was making $83 a week. No one came to me and said,'We fired you because you weren't doing a good job'. . . I was fired because I was a Republican." (He didn't add that the party soon got him another job.)

Senator D'Amato conceded that he knew raises for Hempstead and County employees had to be approved by party headquarters and admitted that he personally had made recommendations on hiring, raises and promotions. He agreed that contributions were "obviously a factor" in determining who was recommended, but swore that he had never demanded that workers contribute. D'Amato also told the court that he did not view the system as coercive, but he acknowledged that "there could be some who felt they were being pressured, who weren't giving on a voluntary basis. . . . I gave because . . . if we didn't win, I would be out."[78]

Although Neuborne didn't press D'Amato about contradictions between his testimony at the trial and his earlier statements to a grand jury (before his letter had become known) that he was "not aware" of the one percent policy, the whole episode tarnished D'Amato's reputation. According to the jurors, D'Amato's letter and his testimony also critically influenced their verdict. As one woman explained, D'Amato's letter "was pretty persuasive . . . the fact that the . . . supervisor of Hempstead knew the one percent scheme existed."[79]

On September 4, 1985 the jury delivered its verdict that the Town of Hempstead and the Nassau County and Hempstead Town Republican organizations had "coercively solicited" contributions from government workers and that all three had "knowingly and willfully engaged in a pattern of illegal activity." Further, the jury found that a "substantial number of public employees" were afraid that if they didn't contribute to the Republican Party they would "lose opportunities for promotions, overtime and other requests for favorable consideration." However, the jury also ruled that the coercive practices did not continue after January 1, 1976; therefore the defendants would only be liable for damages up to that date.[80] Finally, the jury ruled in favor of one of the individual plaintiffs and against the other. It found that one had been denied a promotion because he hadn't contributed, but that the other person's failure to win a promotion wasn't related to a refusal to donate.

Ironically, the jury cleared the Nassau County government of having been part of the one percent operation. For that the county probably had Judge Mishler to thank. The judge was anxious to conclude the trial and made it clear to the attorneys that he would not be happy if they persisted in calling all of the witnesses they had scheduled. The lawyers took the hint and cut short their presentations. Consequently there was not much testimony dealing with the county; one juror stated after the trial that the jury felt it couldn't be certain of the county's involvement because the plaintiffs "just didn't bring enough people in to prove the case."[81]

In December Judge Mishler upheld the jury's verdict, but this did not mean the case was at an end; it only set the stage for further rounds of legal activity. Over the next few years there were numerous appeals on various points from both sides. In addition, a second set of trials was held to determine the validity of individual complaints and the amount of money each worker should get. It had been decided that workers who had contributed to the party would have their money refunded, but there was no agreement on how much, if anything, should be given to those employees who said they were denied promotions and raises because they had *not* contributed. Four test cases were randomly selected for trial to settle these questions of causation and damages. In two instances, the workers lost because they could not show that they deserved to be promoted. In the other two cases the workers appeared to have a good chance of winning. But one case had to be dropped because at the last minute the claimant confessed that he had contributed to the Republican party. The final test case involved a man who had done an excellent job of running a power station, but had never advanced because he didn't donate to the party. There was a highly credible witness who would testify to the man's competence and the worker, a diabetic who had lost his eyesight, was certain to win the jury's sympathy. Unfortunately, the strain was too much for the man; he had a heart attack and died just before the trial was set to begin.

In 1989 Neuborne and the Republicans were finally able to settle the case. They negotiated an agreement which required the Republicans to pay $1.3 million in three separate installments. Approximately half of the money would go to the claimants and half would pay for Neuborne's legal work. It was also agreed that the 21 individuals whose claims had already been certified by the court would get triple damages of approximately $3.10 for every dollar they were forced to give.

With its usual efficiency, the party set about raising the money for the settlement. They began with a $500 inaugural dinner for County Executive Thomas Gulotta which was attended by more than 700 people. Even Joseph Margiotta, who had been persona non grata in party circles, was allowed to take a prominent role in the affair. He ended up selling 70 tickets—more than anyone else except for Joseph Mondello, the reigning party chariman.[82]

By the end of 1991 the party had made all of the payments and Neuborne, as administrator of the funds, had distributed all of the money to the claimants. Approximately 1,000 people came forward to claim refunds for the money they had contributed to the party. Another 100 or so received payments ranging from $1,000 to $10,000 to compensate for promotions and raises they lost because they didn't contribute.

After the One Percent

In the beginning it was as if the one percent trial never happened. The verdict, like Margiotta's earlier conviction and jailing, had no immediate impact at the polls. The Republicans did as well, if not better, than ever. Nor, it seemed, did the trial and its revelations fundamentally affect the Republican patronage and funding operation. Job candidates were no longer interviewed at party headquarters and the computer print-outs giving the names and salaries of town workers were no longer distributed to party leaders, but the leaders still provided recommendations and hiring and advancement were still correlated with contributions and party activities. As one worker observed, "The only thing that's changed is that they don't ask you for the 1 percent anymore. I know for a fact that the only way to get any place in the town of Hempstead is through donations . . . they also want you to work for the party."[83]

After the trial the Republicans stopped mailing appeals for contributions to everyone on the computer lists of public employees. But, as Burt Neuborne noted, their new mailing lists are keyed to past contributors so a "disproportionately high number of recipients are public employees."[84] Not surprisingly, a disproportionately high percentage of Republican contributors are also public employees.

It is possible that the one percent together with the exposés which appear regularly in the pages of Long Island's one major daily newspaper—*Newsday*—finally began to register on Nassau's voters and played a role in the Democratic election victories of November 1991. However, it is more likely that the voters were primarily responding to other developments. By 1991 the recession had come to Long Island. The unemployment rate climbed as thousands of workers in the defense plants which had been the backbone of the Island's economy were laid off. The Island, like so many other parts of the nation, began to suffer the effects of the rapid growth and the excesses of the 1980s. It found itself with "an overburdened, outmoded transportation system; burdensome taxes, energy, housing and garbage-disposal costs that are among the highest in the country; a Byzantine structure of overlapping, inefficient governments, and a growing rift between environmental and economic interests that tends to discourage business and stall development."[85]

For years voters accepted the costs of the Nassau machine's patronage and preferments because the local governments delivered. But, as services deteriorated and taxes went up, some of the machine's middle-class core constituency began to desert it. There was increasing resentment of the big salaries and perks of Nassau politicians and of the Republican organization's lock on good public jobs which seemed more and more desirable as jobs became scarce. As one Republican politician said after the 1991 election, "The Republican organization used to be perceived as the neighborhood network. I don't think it's perceived that way anymore. Now it's a very distant thing. People think the organization is not interested in the quality of their life but in the quality of life of their own.[86]

For years the public employee unions and their members had played ball with the machine, but with the prospect of furloughs, layoffs and stagnant salaries, the unions began to turn against it. Even some employees who owed their jobs to the Republicans turned against the party as layoffs loomed. In their complacency the Republicans took the workers for granted while Democrats like Yevoli in Oyster Bay courted town and county employees. Yevoli sent out a mailing to public employees which asked what the Republicans had ever done besides ask for contributions and urged the workers to "Promise anything but when the curtain closes. . . .vote for yourself."[87]

The Democrats have benefited from voter disaffection with the Republicans, but their triumph may be short lived. They have taken office in a time of austerity. Democratic officials will have to cut budgets and will inevitably make enemies. Moreover, the Democrats show few signs of mending their fractious ways and working to build their party. By the time the next election rolls around, the voters may turn against the Democrats they voted for in 1991.

If the Republicans don't tear themselves apart with the internal feuding that heated up after the 1991 election, the organization might live on in some form for years. It still has loyal adherents and campaign workers to continue the labor-intensive door-to-door campaigning suited to the Island where the TV and radio rates of the New York metropolitan area are too high for the electronic media to be a realistic campaign option. The machine's patronage army is shrinking, but even a few thousand jobs will take care of the committeemen and other key personnel. Even if Gulotta is ousted as County Executive in 1993, the Republicans should be able to hold on to many of their thousands of jobs for the forseeable future. Given the prohibitions on politically motivated firing of nonpolicy-making public employees, those who now hold those jobs cannot be ousted. The situation could be drastically changed as a result of a lawsuit brought by the New York Civil Liberties Union. In April of 1993 U.S. District Court Judge Arthur Spatt ruled that the Nassau County Board's system of weighted voting is unconstitutional because it violates the 14th Amendment's "one person-one vote" requirement. The county will now have to revise its charter, probably replacing the Board of Supervisors with a legislature. Whatever the final form of the new government, it will have to increase minority representation which will affect the balance between the two parties. However, the process of revision will take time. For now, Nassau's patronage army is battered and smaller than it was in its glory days, but it's still alive.

CHAPTER 5
PATRONAGE AFTER RUTAN:
IS THE PARTY OVER?

Patronage may be the last secret in America. Every day people go on the Phil Donahue or Oprah Winfrey show and reveal the most intimate details of their lives. But it's unlikely you'd ever get a group of elected officials to tell tales of patronage. Virtually no one in political office is talking, as the bosses of yesterday did, about the jobs they control. It's hardly respectable to be a politician; to be an old-fashioned spoils politician is clearly beyond the pale. So we are left to make educated guesses about patronage, gathering bits of evidence here and there, never knowing for sure if we are on the mark.

The patronage armies of the nineteenth and twentieth century machines appear to be marching out of contemporary political life. The combination of the Supreme Court decisions in Elrod, Branti and Rutan; tight budgets and taxpayer revolts which make for fewer government jobs; public employee unions and contracts mandating job posting, seniority and all manner of other restrictions on hiring and promotion; tightened conflict-of-interest laws and other anticorruption measures; the public's anti-politics mood and its heightened intolerance of traditional politics; campaigns in which TV commercials have replaced precinct workers; and the changing nature of government jobs with fewer unskilled laborer positions and more professional posts demanding specific training and skills, makes it impossible to continue to raise and maintain armies of patronage workers. There are still some battalions left in places like Nassau

County, but they are shrinking and it's hard to imagine new ones taking their place. *But,* that doesn't mean patronage is dead. Previous pronouncements of its death were, as the earlier chapters document, premature. Patronage didn't die with the first Mayor Daley. There is less of it today, and it is sometimes different in form, but it is still part of the political scene.

It is not wise to believe the pious pronouncements of politicians on patronage. It is fashionable today for governors to proclaim themselves to be modern managers and to express their disdain for patronage. The former governor of Utah, for one, told an interviewer that it was "much better to have the employee morale that comes from tenure than to be able to put your people in."[1] As candidates, some governors promise to rid their states of patronage. Once in office, they proudly announce that patronage has been banished. Young Evan Bayh, for example, campaigned as a self-proclaimed enemy of Indiana's notorious patronage politics. After the election he said that there would be no more "politics as usual." But Bayh made a political operative named Robert Boxell the personnel director of the traditionally patronage heavy Indiana Department of Transportation. Boxell had "no significant personnel experience," but he did know how to run a patronage operation. According to Judge John Tinder of the United States District Court of Southern Indiana, who presided at a bench trial involving a fired INDOT subdistrict superintendent, "because of his decades of experience in the wars of partisan politics in Indiana, if Boxell did not personally know the political affiliation of all of the incumbent subdistrict superintendents and candidates, he knew how to learn that information from others through simple telephone calls. Thus, it was not necessary to require the incumbents or candidates to declare their political affiliation. Plaintiff introduced Boxell's notes which contained "R" and "D" notations next to the names of candidates for subdistrict superintendent positions."

Boxell stayed at INDOT long enough to fire "all 37 out of 37 Republican subdistrict superintendents." Although the Bayh administration claimed that "they sought out the most qualified applicants" as replacements, they didn't contact anyone with experience in highway construction for recommendations. They *did* ask key members of the Democratic party throughout the state to make recommendations. At the trial the Governor's Executive Assistant for Transportation admitted that politics was a factor in filling the 37 positions.

As soon as he had finished firing and hiring at INDOT, "Boxell was moved to the Indiana Bureau of Motor Vehicles, another state agency that was being reconstructed pursuant to promises made by candidate Bayh during the 1988 campaign."[2]

Boxell did his work at the Indiana Department of Transportation before Rutan, but only the naive could believe that the mere issuance of a Supreme Court decision will put an immediate end to political hiring. Court decisions have to be implemented by others—in this instance thousands of local hiring authorities. Rutan will make these authorities more cautious. At the very least they will be more careful about leaving a paper trail. However, they will not abandon patronage simply because the Supreme Court has spoken.

Court decisions have their greatest impact when the people who have the power to implement them have their own reasons for obeying the court—as Harold Washington did in Chicago. Washington's cooperation only went so far. He continued to use patronage in some agencies which were not party to the Shakman decrees and in the Chicago First program it appeared that he was also trying to get around the decrees by working through private businesses. In Nassau County, where the Republicans in power were not interested in ending patronage, Rutan had no discernible impact.

Rutan's restrictions on political hiring are relatively easy to evade. By necessity hiring authorities have to be given some flexibility. Except for completely mechanical, low-level jobs, hiring criteria have to have some "play" in them. Since it's impossible to eliminate an element of human judgment in the making of hiring decisions, the door will always be open to manipulation of the hiring process.

Of course, one can always go to the courts. But, it's one thing to suspect political manipulation and another thing to prove it. Moreover, the rejected applicants who would have the standing to sue generally don't have the resources and it's difficult to find a lawyer who will take these cases on a contingency basis. And, putting aside monetary considerations, not many lawyers want to take on the "powers that be." It's usually not a good idea to offend the most influential officials in the local area. Even when some workers find the courage to file a lawsuit, get good legal representation and eventually win in court, their victory will not necessarily signal the end of the patronage system. This was clearly true in Nassau County. The system might have changed if the judge had been willing to appoint a referee to reform the county personnel system and to exercise ongoing supervision of it. But Judge Mishler was not willing to take such an activist stance and it's not to be expected that many federal judges today—when over 60 percent of the sitting federal judges are Reagan-Bush appointees—would be willing to do so. And, irrespective of their ideological predilections, judges may hesitate to impose a referee and an elaborate set of rules on a personnel system knowing that the Shakman Hiring Provisions have been very cumbersome and have caused such extensive delays in the hiring process that the city of Chicago has been at a competitive disadvantage in attracting the best applicants.[3]

It is conceivable that Rutan will gradually penetrate personnel policies around the country. However, there may not be enough time for that to happen since there is some possibility that Rutan will be overturned. Before the 1992 term many lawyers felt quite certain that there would be a reversal as soon as the court got around to taking another patronage case. With the retirements of Justices Brennan, Marshall and White, only Justices Blackmun and Stevens are left of the five who voted for the majority in Rutan. No one knows how Justices Souter and Thomas feel about the patronage cases, but it's not unreasonable to suppose that one of them, most probably Justice Thomas, would find Justice Scalia's arguments more persuasive than Justice Brennan's. Justice Thomas, added to the original four who were in dissent on Rutan, would produce a majority for reversal. However, after the 1992 term it appeared that Justice Scalia could no longer count on Justices O'Connor and Kennedy to support his position. In *Planned Parenthood v. Casey*, the Pennsylvania abortion case, Justices O'Connor, Kennedy and Souter made it clear that they were reluctant to reverse an established precedent, particularly one involving the fundamental liberties guaranteed by the First Amendment, even if they would not have voted with the majority initially.

The "New" Patronage

With or without Rutan, patronage will not disappear. There are probably thousands of small pockets of patronage lodged in the 80,000 plus units of local government in the United States. The small units often have no professional personnel office or civil service system of any kind. In Pennsylvania alone there are 2,574 general local governments, including 1,459 townships of the second class with populations ranging from 29 to 5,200 which are not subject to state civil service requirements. Pennsylvania even permits the members of the governing Boards of Township Supervisors to hire themselves for the jobs of roadmaster, laborer, township secretary or treasurer.[4]

America's legislators and political executives will continue to have some patronage. No court has tried to take control of staff jobs away from legislators nor deny executives the power to make appointments to policymaking jobs. While there are not enough of these policymaking positions to build a patronage army, their numbers can be considerable; the mayor of Chicago is allowed almost 900 appointments and the governor of Illinois has several thousand. In addition to cabinet and other high-level administrative positions, mayors, county executives, governors and the like are usually able to make appointments to various councils and commissions. Although these jobs are often part-time and/or unpaid, they can be valuable political capital. Many people covet the honor or influence such posts confer and a savvy mayor or governor can use them to reward followers and contributors, or as bargaining chips with legislators. Sometimes the "little" jobs can, as Alan Rosenthal observes, count more than big ones since they are the "plums legislators want to secure for constituents in their districts and/or contributors to their campaigns. . . . they provide governors with the kind of patronage that helps keep legislators in line."[5] Even in California, where Progressivism was supposed to have eliminated patronage more than fifty years ago, there are nearly 4,000 slots on assorted boards and commissions, which governors have used to "secure support from the legislature and key interest groups. For example, the 477 appointments to the District Agricultural Association are typical patronage. Appointments to many minor commissions, councils, and boards are often used to reward the party faithful and the governor's supporters or to gain support from various organizations and groups."[6]

Politically astute mayors have also been able to use their ability to control appointments to build their own personal organizations. The old style Tammany Hall type of machine may be nearly extinct, but in a number of cities a new form of personal "mayor-centered"[7] political organization based on machine-like material incentives has risen to fill the void. During his sixteen years (1967-83) as mayor of Boston, Kevin White was able to fashion such a machine.

When he first was elected, White fostered his progressive image by appointing some good government types to highly visible positions in his administration. In key, but less visible jobs, he placed loyal political operatives whom he could depend on to help him solidify his control of the city's government and increase his personal power. His man at the head of the Assessing Department could, for example, use tax abatements to reward the mayor's contributors. White also made use of "holdover" appointments to increase his leverage over administrators. Instead of making a formal appointment, he would "holdover" the person who already occupied the position. Without an official appointment, the person served "at the pleasure of the mayor" and could be summarily dismissed. Naturally, White could control these "holdovers" more easily than he could someone with a fixed tenure. Once he had gained control over his high-level appointees, White was able to "affect personal practices within city government. The control he exercised over job hirings and promotions, two things requiring the cooperation of department heads, gave White a supply of patronage that he used to build a political organization composed of city workers.''[8] White offered city jobs to campaign workers and, conversely, recruited individuals who were already working for the city for his campaign organization. Although they may have genuinely liked the mayor, the city workers were also drawn to the organization and were kept working for it over the years by promises of promotions and salary increases (in their city jobs) for doing a good job in the campaign.

Of course there was a civil service system in Boston but, with the help of his loyal administrators and a cooperative personnel department, the mayor was able to circumvent civil service restrictions. The state Civil Service Commission which was supposed to act as a watchdog was ineffectual and didn't interfere with White's patronage operation. Actually, it unwittingly helped the mayor by being so slow in giving examinations that White was frequently able to hire provisional workers. In one election White put more than 1,600 campaign workers into provisional slots.

In addition to the provisional and full-time civil service jobs he controlled, White was also able to create jobs through an assortment of mayoral agencies and programs that operated outside of civil service. Federal money was used to finance much of this patronage; at one point CETA (Comprehensive Employment and Training Act) money was funding more than 1,300 jobs in 38 city agencies. In all White had about 4,000 jobs at his disposal.

In many respects White's organization operated like the first Mayor Daley's Cook County organization. The precincts were worked and jobs and city services were used to win support. However, the Cook County Democratic organization was a party operation while White's organization was strictly personal. White could not transfer his backing to other candidates and when he left the mayor's office, his organization disintegrated.

Kevin White was more successful than many other mayors of the period in building an effective political organization. Barbara Ferman, who compared him with San Francisco's mayors, argues that his success was partly due to his superior political skills, but that it was also a function of Boston's political system and political culture. White governed within a relatively unfragmented centralized government which facilitated strong executive leadership. His leadership and his practice of a machine type of materialistic politics were more acceptable in Boston than they would have been in a city with a reformist, issue-oriented political culture. In Boston the working class and ethnic populations tend to see politics as a means for achieving individual goals rather than as an instrument of public policy. There is an assumption the individuals are in politics for what they can get out of it and the populace expects (and generally tolerates) backroom deals and corruption. Such a culture provides a fertile soil for patronage; it is simply considered a normal part of politics.

The man who followed Kevin White, Raymond Flynn, projects himself as an urban populist. He had tried to distinguish himself from his predecessor by concentrating on bringing neighborhood leaders into his organization. However, he has also used government jobs as a tool, placing most of his neighborhood coordinators (who are akin to Daley's ward committeemen) on the municipal payroll. Twenty-two of the 26 neighborhood coordinators have jobs as city administrators. Flynn has also put his operatives in the mayoral agencies which are not covered by civil service. There they can prod the line bureaucrats in the traditional city departments to respond to citizen complaints. In this way Flynn's organization manages to give voters much the same service that the old machines did.[9]

Detroit's Coleman Young is another mayor who has put together an effective personal organization. Young has gotten the maximum mileage out of the 150 appointments the law allows him by filling the slots with loyal political operatives, These appointees form the core of his organization. They play a key role in organizing the many fund-raising events which provide the money that pays for the organization's campaign activities. Like traditional party bosses, Young also has a one-percent club for city hall staffers. Many city workers contribute to Young's campaign and work for his organization even though they are hired and promoted under civil service. Di Gaetano and Klemanski speculate that the employees feel obligated to help the mayor as a "sign of loyalty."[10]

Young uses some of the money he collects to make up for the dearth of government jobs under his control. He recruits campaign workers by offering them pay for doing political work at election time. In impoverished Detroit these "jobs" are very attractive and are effective in drawing workers.

Both the Young and Flynn campaign operatives indicate that the day of the precinct workers may not be completely gone. The two mayoral machines are "hybrids" which blend "old-style personal contact machine techniques of electioneering with high technology methods." They "muster large numbers of political workers to canvass neighborhoods block by block" while also using polling, phone banks and sophisticated media campaigns.[11]

To maintain his populist purity, Flynn has eschewed pinstripe patronage. He refuses to accept contributions from individuals connected with businesses that are seeking (or have) city contracts or franchises or want some favor such as a zoning variance from the city. The bulk of his contributions have come from individuals who have given small amounts. Because he had his neighborhood networks to rely on, he has also needed less money than candidates who use TV and high tech methods exclusively. In 1987 the Flynn campaign committee reported that it raised about $740,000. This compares to the $4 million it took for Richard Phelan, a political unknown with no organizational support, to get himself elected to the presidency of the Cook County Board.[12] A millionaire lawyer, Phelan provided much of his campaign money himself. Once in office he began to use pinstripe patronage, dispensing lucrative contracts to law firms, vendors and consultants, to build an even bigger war chest for a future try at the governorship.

Phelan's pinstripe patronage is not illegal and given the cost of campaigning in the 1990s, more and more elected officials can be expected to use it. In the absence of government financing, politicians have to raise the massive funds needed for today's campaigns from private sources. As New York University Law School professor Burt Neuborne has noted, there will continue to be a "below-the-line" underground system for getting money, until the nation recognizes that the "cost of running the political system has to be an above-the-line expense."[13] For years machines relied on collecting one, two or three percent from government workers. Now that the courts have ruled that assessing employees violates the constitution, political organizations and candidates running on their own will have to find money elsewhere. Contractors, lawyers, developers and others who want some preferment from government are the most obvious source of money. Jonathan Katz has observed that "many elected officials, at both the state and local levels, are more interested these days in steering lucrative contracts and consulting jobs to wealthy contributors than they are in getting rank-and-file campaign workers onto the public payroll.[14] For the highly ambitious governor, pinstripe can even provide the crucial edge needed in a race for a presidential nomination. The *New York Times* reports that Arkansas governor Bill Clinton won the 1992 Democratic nomination in part because he raised more money than his rivals. He was able to do this because he could "draw donations from people who rely on the business he controls as the state executive." The list of his donors is "especially rich with people involved with state contracting, lucrative state bond work and the state's pension funds, as well as their friends and relatives. Many others are executives of businesses that are regulated by state agencies."[15]

Although finding jobs for campaign workers no longer has priority, many politicians will continue to put them on the payroll whenever it appears safe to do so. They will also appoint contributors and members of their campaign team to government posts when possible. Some of the very governors who told researchers they weren't interested in patronage later changed their minds.

Certainly, patronage has its downside. It takes time and energy; it can make enemies of those who are passed over; and evidence of patronage can be used against a politician by a crusading newspaper or an election opponent. To the extent that patronage increases the costs and inefficiencies of government, it may also lead to a loss of voter support. The thousands of lower-level appointments are particularly bothersome. Many of them have elaborate clearance mechanisms which "consume inordinate quantities of staff time." Recommendations have to be "solicited and/or acknowledged" and "appropriate legislators, campaign coordinators, relevant county party chairmen, affected professional or interest groups" all may have to be consulted.[16]

While all these drawbacks are real, it still can be a costly mistake for an executive to turn his back on patronage. Michael Dukakis, for one, found this out the hard way. In his first term Dukakis made enemies by renouncing patronage. Legislators, in particular, were upset with the governor for failing to play by Massachusetts' rules and "helping his friends." Dukakis was not reelected. When he did regain the governorship, he embraced patronage so fervently that the president of the state senate was led to remark that "Dukakis has raised patronage to a fine art." He gave jobs to his campaign workers and used some top-level appointments to strengthen his standing with the legislature.[17] Like Clinton after him, Dukakis also tapped the beneficiaries of state business for contributions to his presidential campaign.

Patronage can also help a governor establish control over the state's bureaucracies. There's some indirect evidence that "governors who reward departments on the basis of political criteria are more likely to influence departmental decisions than if they rely on objective, rational criteria."[18] Even elected officials who are not interested in building their own campaign organizations may, as Frank Thompson has written, "strive to place people loyal to them in strategically sensitive positions" in order to keep the "bureaucracy responsible and accountable." Though the line between the two can become fuzzy, these "elected executives view leverage over personnel administration more as a tool for allowing them to govern than as a means of building electoral machinery."[19]

On the federal level the increased politicization of the bureaucracy under the Reagan administration appears to have been motivated more by ideological than partisan concerns. In the states too, governors have successfully pushed for more control over appointments to overcome the rigidities and resistance of the civil service bureaucracy. Since 1970 more than half the states have revised their personnel systems, "almost all in the direction of increasing the number of exempt top managers and policymaking careerists, and giving elected and appointed administrative superiors more personnel discretion."[20] A new class of employees has been created who are "neither wholly political appointees nor neutral protected civil servants." Although they can be removed at will, "new governors coming into office have not generally fired them en masse."[21] All the same, taking tenure and other civil service protections from career professionals probably makes them more attuned to their governor's wishes. As Deborah Roberts observes "the key point is not the very few who are fired or leave, but the measures taken to keep their superior's goodwill by the many who are retained." However, while exemptions are supposed to make administrators "more responsive and cooperative . . . they may also negatively affect creativity, initiative, morale, program advocacy and self-expression."[22]

These exempt employees may represent a third way in public personnel. The many flaws of the current merit and civil service systems have often been used to justify the practice of old-fashioned patronage politics. But bringing back or enshrining spoils simply substitutes one bad system for another. Instead, political executives and public personnel administrators should focus their energies on developing other alternatives. It's true, for example, that civil service systems generally so overprotect jobholders that it becomes almost impossible to fire anyone. But the cure is not to strip government employees of all job protection and put them at the mercy of a party chairman who cares only about working the precincts or a governor who is determined to push an ideological agenda. While it won't be easy, it should be possible to adopt reforms which would balance the protection of the employee's rights with organizational efficiency and responsiveness.[23]

Final Thoughts

Patronage armies with tens of thousands of foot soldiers are a thing of the past, but patronage is not dead and gone and is unlikely to be in the forseeable future. As long as politicians need to raise money and find workers for their campaigns, as long as elected officials have to bargain with legislators and interest groups and work to establish control over the bureaucracy, patronage will exist in one guise or another. The reformers would seem, as Theodore Lowi argues, to have forgotten that "reform did not eliminate the need for political power. It simply altered what one had to do to get it." Lowi has also cautioned that where reforms do succeed in eliminating patronage and otherwise tying the hands of elected heads of government, power may shift to the permanent bureaucracy. To the extent that these bureaucracies are "professionally organized career agencies" whose leadership "is relatively self-perpetuating and not readily subject to the controls of any higher authority," the political system will have become "less democratic, less responsive to the people's wishes as expressed in their electoral decisions."[24]

On balance it is unlikely that the passing of the machines and their armies and the scaling down of patronage everywhere will have the disastrous consequences that either Lowi or Justice Scalia have envisioned. In his Rutan dissent Justice Scalia asserted that without patronage political participation would decline, party discipline would evaporate and with it the "strength of the two-party system" would "wane." "It is folly," he warned, "to think that ideological conviction alone will motivate sufficient numbers to keep the party going through the off-years." Candidates who could not rely on "patronage-based party loyalty" would, he feared, be forced to "attract workers and raise funds by appealing to various interest groups." He maintained that the Elrod and Branti decisions had "by contributing to the decline of party strength . . . also contributed to growth of interest-group politics in the last decade."[25]

Historical experience and the data accumulated by social scientists do not support Scalia's contentions. Far from fostering a two-party system, patronage politics at its height suppressed opposition and maintained a strong one-party system. During the machine years, the Republican party virtually ceased to exist within the borders of Chicago. When machine chronicler Milton Rakove asked the students in his university classes to collect information about Chicago Republicans, the students literally could not find the party. Some of the ward committeemen didn't have offices; others had no listed telephone number either at home or in an office; some were unavailable at all times; and others refused to answer the students' "questions or make comments on any matters pertaining to their wards." A student researcher who was trying to locate the 24th ward Republican headquarters was given an address which turned out to be in the middle of the Douglas Park lagoon. In the 11th ward a student found the outside doors to the Republican headquarters were boarded up. A few of the Republican committeemen turned up in the offices of the ward Democrats who supported the GOP representatives in order to maintain the semblance of a two-party system.[26]

Justice Scalia also overlooks evidence that patronage, both past and present, has not necessarily strengthened party organizations. Patronage can be used to support individual politicians like Kevin White or factions within the parties and thus may even weaken the two parties.[27] Nor is it clear that the decline of patronage has brought about a decline in party organizational strength. The evidence on this question is mixed, but there are some scholars who find reason to believe that on the whole "the prophets of party demise . . . have been proven wrong." In the states "since the 1960s . . . party organizations have become more professionalized and organizationally stronger."[28] Having reviewed the literature on parties, Michael Margolis concluded that the "national and (to a lesser extent) state party organizations seem to be adapting successfully to modern circumstances." While the "so-called boss ruled city and county organizations have virtually disappeared," local organizations still function; they have revived since the late 1970s though they seem to have lost political clout.[29] Leon Epstein also reports that studies indicate that parties continue to be active on the local level in a number of cities and that people are often attracted to party work today by "largely nonpatronage incentives." Many people are motivated to do party work by their policy commitments.[30] Certainly many of the Reaganites who revived the Republican party in the 1980s were drawn to politics by ideology. Moreover, their ideological commitment has sustained them over the long haul. Justice Scalia clearly underestimates the power of ideology to motivate participation.

Surveying the party scene, Denise Baer and David Bositis go so far as to call the parties "resurgent." They argue that:

> In organizational terms the two parties are flourishing. Party identification is undergoing a process of readjustment—from one based on inherited group loyalties to one based on a substantive political consensus. Turnout has declined, but primarily due to the increasing structural costs of participation, not because of a lesser attachment to parties. In fact, all other measures of party participation are up. Issue voting has increased. . . .[31]

There is no denying that the parties today are different from the parties that existed when patronage was at its zenith, but the changes reflect a multitude of social, political and technological changes. (If Justice Scalia really wants to return to the old days, he'd have to begin by abolishing television!) It's naive to think that the Supreme Court could, by reversing itself in Elrod, Branti and Rutan, bring back the parties of yesterday or produce the programmatic, responsible parties for which Justice Scalia appears to yearn.

It's equally naive to think that reversing the patronage decisions and allowing patronage of the sort that once existed in Cook County or in Illinois in the Thompson years would stem the "growth of interest group politics" and make it easier for parties to enact their programs into law. It is true, as Cynthia Bowman notes in the *Northwestern University Law Review*, that a strong patronage-based party organization like the Cook County machine of the 1950s and 1960s "can resist the demands of interest groups." However, the Cook County Democratic Organization did not use its power to bring diverse interests together and enact its programs into law. It didn't have any programs and it didn't try to broker the interests of all the groups on the scene. Rather, it "simply tried to ignore the interests of large numbers of minority groups for a very long period of time."[32]

Similarly, the Illinois Republican party in the Thompson years was neither a programmatic nor an issue-oriented party. Nor did it act as a counterweight to interest groups. Instead Thompson brought interest groups into the fold. They provided him (and his successor Jim Edgar) with contributions and occasionally with manpower by lending their executives to help in campaigns. Over the course of Thompson's fourteen years as governor, special interest contributions to his campaigns increased. By 1986 they accounted for 46 percent of the total with the biggest givers being (in order) construction, banking/financial, labor, manufacturing and medical interests.[33] Two leading experts on Illinois, Samuel Gove and James Nowlan, report that interest groups have been growing in influence and have to be rated a "strong" power in Illinois politics. They note that the "leading players in the Illinois political process provide the major interest groups important places at the table at which public policy issues are bargained . . . (which) is consistent with a dominant political culture . . . that accepts government and politics as a kind of marketplace."[34]

Justice Scalia's argument that patronage contributes to the democratization of American politics rests on a shaky foundation. Patronage did not always lead to increased participation in politics. Steven Erie has convincingly shown that once they were entrenched in power, the Irish machines did not try to draw new groups into their coalition, but used their resources to mobilize their core constituencies. If anything the machines actively kept other groups out of the political process because they didn't have enough jobs and benefits for their Irish supporters *and* newcomers to the cities. As Erie explains, "once minimal winning coalitions had been constructed, the machines had little incentive to naturalize, register, and mobilize the votes of later ethnic arrivals."[35] In the 1990s governments are retrenching; there are fewer jobs and a patronage-based party would have even less incentive to share the spoils with new groups.

Even for the Irish, patronage did not necessarily provide the best path to economic and social advancement. To be sure, the Irish got jobs, but the jobs were mostly poorly paid positions as laborers, clerks, firefighters and policemen. Erie argues that "by channeling so much economic energy into the public sector, the Irish forsook opportunities in the private sector, save for industries such as construction that depended on political connections."[36] While public jobs today can help individual members of a minority group, patronage is unlikely to be the engine of advancement for a group as a whole. There are fewer unskilled jobs which could help the uneducated at the bottom of the social scale; increasingly government jobs require professional training and are likely to be filled by individuals who have already begun the climb out of poverty and lower-class status. Conversely, the abolition of large-scale patronage in Chicago did not harm Black job seekers; the percentage of Blacks in city jobs at present is greater than it was in the days of the machine.

At every turn Justice Scalia *overestimates* the cost of implementing Elrod, Branti and Rutan, and *underestimates* the costs of large-scale patronage to society. For example, he is quite right in stating that the appeals courts have had difficulty in implementing the Branti standard for separating political from nonpolitical jobs. However, there are reasonable ways to deal with the problem short of reversing the patronage decisions. The vast majority of government jobs are not difficult to categorize; they are patently routine, nonpolicymaking and nonconfidential in character. For those that are not, Steven G. Heinen suggests "allowing state legislatures to determine which jobs are appropriate for patronage practices, subject only to rational-relationship review of the courts." The government would have to show only that its decisions were not "patently arbitrary or discriminatory" and that they are "rationally connected" to the government's purposes.[37] For her part, Cynthia Bowman points out that many cities, including Chicago, have already classified some positions as exempt from their civil service systems. These cities can easily declare that all such positions will also be considered "political" and will be exempt from the Supreme Court's strictures on patronage.[38]

Justice Scalia would leave it to the "people's representatives" to decide whether patronage is desirable. Since he does not believe patronage is unconstitutional, he sees not call for Supreme Court action. When he balances the negative impact of patronage on the individual against the benefits to society, Justice Scalia finds the benefits far outweigh the costs. If only Justice Scalia could talk to some of the "little people" who were harmed by the Illinois patronage system that was at issue in Rutan, he might change his mind. Individuals did feel they were forced to vote in the Republican primary and work for the Republican party. There are many people in Springfield who could tell Justice Scalia that they did not feel free to risk losing the only good jobs available to them by openly supporting the Democratic party. For all intents and purposes, the First Amendment was a dead letter.

It is difficult to find any benefits which would balance such a denial of the individual's constitutional rights. In fact, when it is examined closely, the impact of patronage on the government's functioning appears to be more negative than positive. Patronage does not really increase governmental accountability and responsiveness to the electorate as its proponents claim. During the Chicago machine years, there were many employees who did little work or did very poor work for the city. Yet they kept their jobs year after year because they did their party work well. Patronage employees are not necessarily unqualified or lazy. But when political considerations take precedence, it is likely that there will be fudging and compromises and the city or state will not get as good a work force as it otherwise could. As New York's Commission on Government Integrity concluded after intensive investigation:

> [H]ard-working public servants are demoralized when they see appointments made mainly for political reasons. . . . the professionalism of the government's work force is debased. . . . Patronage insidiously attacks the best government employees. The most professional public servants, the ones that are deeply committed to the mission of their agency, experience that much more frustration when they see the mission obscured by political considerations. These employees feel ethically compromised when they "play ball," and are forced to participate in the patronage practices they find offensive. Cynicism, resentment and resignation are the sure results.[39]

When the work force isn't the best it could be, when the best employees are demoralized, the taxpayer is cheated because government isn't as efficient or as effective as it might be.

Everyone bears the costs of patronage, but only those in the "right" party get the benefits. All taxpayers support the government, but only taxpayers in the "right" party get government jobs and contracts. Understandably, those in power come to believe the government belongs to them. They find it hard to distinguish between their private and partisan interests and the public interest. Patronage politics and corruption have gone hand in hand throughout our history. Because of that, patronage undermines the public's confidence in its government. As Professor David Rosenbloom told the New York Commission, "patronage leads people to believe that government is corrupt, that it is not serving the public interest generally, that it is serving the interests of one party or one set of people, rather than the community as a whole."[40]

Presidents, governors and mayors should be able to have their own team. We can only hope that they will pick qualified people who are not chosen simply to repay a political debt. And, until the political system—especially the financing of campaigns—is changed, there will be some patronage here and there throughout the government. It is probably fruitless to try to eliminate patronage completely. We should instead concentrate on trying to reduce it.[41] In this, Chicago and the Shakman decree have shown the way. Where there is political will (without political will, any system can be circumvented), a number of relatively simple steps such as widespread advertising of jobs and lotteries for unskilled positions can reduce the patronage army to a few platoons.

NOTES

Chapter 1

1. Donald R. Harvey, *The Civil Service Commission* (Evanston, Illinois: Row, Peterson, 1958), p. 43.

2. Elrod v. Burns, 427 U.S. 347 (1976).

3. Rutan v. Republican Party of Illinois, 848 F.2d 1396 (7th Cir. 1988).

4. Rutan v. Republican Party of Illinois, 110 S. Ct. 2734 (1990)

5. Ibid., 2738.

6. The actual words are a quote from Justice Brennan's Elrod opinion. In Rutan the Justice refers back to this opinion.

7. Branti v. Finkel, 445 U.S. 518 (1980).

8. Dirk Johnson, "Court Ruling on Patronage Gets Some Mixed Reviews," *New York Times*, June 23, 1990, p. A6.

9. Nina Burleigh, "Lawyer Triumphs over Political Patronage," *Chicago Tribune*, July 22, 1990, Sec. 6, p. 2.

10. Lynn Sweet and Ray Hanania, "Court 'naive'—Thompson," *Chicago Sun-Times*, June 22, 1990, p. 5.

11. Johnson, p. A6.

12. Sweet and Hanania, p. 5.

13. Johnson, p. A6.

14. All of the quotations in this and the following three paragraphs are from Justice Scalia's dissent in Rutan.

15. Cherry Collis, "Cleaning up the Spoils System," *State Government News*, 33 (1990), p. 6.

16. Jeffrey L. Katz, "The Slow Death of Political Patronage," *Governing*, 4 (1991), p. 62.

17. Collis, p. 9.

18. Katz, pp. 58 and 62.

19. Katz, p. 62.

20. Johnson, p. 6.

21. Rita Ciolli and Carol Eisenberg, "Patronage Jobs Illegal," *Newsday* June 22, 1990, p. 19.

22. Quoted in Martin Tolchin, "Why Patronage is Unlikely to Fade Away," *New York Times*, July 1,1990, Sec. 4, p. 2.

23. Rutan, p. 4881.

24. Rutan, pp. 4880 and 4887. Justice Stevens is quoting from his earlier opinion in Illinois State Employees Union, Council 34, American Federation of State, County and Municipal Employees, AFL-CIO v. Lewis, 473 F.2d (1972) at 568, n.14.

25. Ari Hoogenboom, *Outlawing the Spoils* (Urbana: University of Illinois Press, 1961), pp. 209-13.

26. Martin and Susan Tolchin, *To the Victor* (New York: Random House, 1972), p. 322.

27. Richard Hofstadter, *The Idea of a Party System* (Berkeley: University of California Press, 1970), pp. 2-3. The passage is quoted by Justice Stevens in Rutan, p. 4877.

28. Frederick C. Mosher, *Democracy and the Public Service*, 2d. ed. (New York: Oxford University Press, 1982), p. 60.

29. Hoogenboom, p. 4.

30. Leonard D. White, *The Federalists* (New York: Macmillan, 1948), p. 46.

31. Ibid., p. 273.

32. Hofstadter, pp. 156-57.

33. Carl R. Fish, *The Civil Service and the Patronage* (Cambridge: Harvard University Press, 1920), p. 51.

34. Mosher, pp. 61-62.

35. Leonard D. White, *The Jeffersonians* (New York: Macmillan, 1951), pp. 387-90.

36. White, *Jeffersonians*, pp. 555-56. Also see Michael Nelson, "A Short Ironic History of American National Bureaucracy," *Journal of Politics*, 44 (1982), pp. 757-59.

37. See Mathew Crenson, *The Federal Machine* (Baltimore: Johns Hopkins University Press, 1975), Ch. 2.

38. Robert V. Remini, *The Life of Andrew Jackson* (New York: Harper and Row, 1988; Penguin Books, 1990), p. 184.

39. All of the quotations from Jackson's message to Congress on December 8, 1829 are taken from Paul P. Van Riper, *History of the United States Civil Service* (Evanston, Il.: Row, Peterson, 1958), pp. 36-37.

40. Remini, p. 185. The 20 percent estimate is from Nelson, p. 760.

41. Ibid., pp. 184-85.

42. Stephen Skowronek, *Building a New American State* (Cambridge: Cambridge University Press, 1982), pp. 31-32.

43. Crenson, pp. 170-173; Nelson, pp. 760-61.

44. Hofstadter, p. 250.

45. Ibid., Ch. 6.

46. Hoogenboom, p. 7.

47. Leonard D. White, *The Jacksonians* (New York: Macmillan, 1954), p. 314.

48. Hofstadter, p. 270.

49. Van Riper, p. 60.

50. Van Riper, p. 44.

51. See Fish, pp. 79-104 and White, *Jeffersonians*, pp. 394-98.

52. William L. Riordon, ed. *Plunkitt of Tammany Hall* (New York: Dutton, 1963), p. 37.

53. Ibid., pp. 11-12.

54. Van Riper, p. 62. Also see Van Riper, chapter 4 and Hoogenboon for a detailed account of the reform movement.

55. Skowronek, p. 68.

56. White, *Jeffersonians*, p. 349.

57. Crenson, p. 173.

58. Ibid., p. 349.

59. Alexander Callow, *The Tweed Ring* (London: Oxford University Press, 1965), p. 166.

60. Riordon, pp. 3-4.

61. Van Riper, p. 417 and Crenson, pp. 224-25 and Fish, p. 180.

62. See Van Riper, Chapter 5 for a discussion of the Pendleton Act.

63. Skowronek, pp. 68-74.

64. Hoogenboon, p. 261.

65. All of the quotations and the information on FDR are from Van Riper, pp. 312-61.

66. Paul Volcker, Chairman, National Commission on the Public Service, *Leadership for America* (Lexington, Mass.: Lexington Books, 1990), p. 17.

67. Bradley H. Patterson, Jr. *The Ring of Power* (New York: Basic Books, 1988), pp. 239-40.

68. Patricia W. Ingraham, "Building Bridges or Burning Them," *Public Administration Review*, 47 (1987), p. 426.

69. Volcker, p. 18.

70. On the relationship between career and political appointees, see James P. Pfiffner, *The Managerial Presidency* (Belmont, California: Wadsworth, 1991) and the books cited in endnote 71. For the argument that the president should use his appointees to control the career service and advance his policy goals see Richard Nathan, *The Administrative Presidency* (New York: John Wiley, 1983). In *Presidential Influence and the Administrative State* (Knoxville: University of Tennessee Press, 1989) Richard Waterman uses case studies to evaluate the Nathan thesis. The Waterman book also has a useful bibliography.

71. See Patterson, pp. 239-59; the National Academy of Public Administration report by John W. Macy, Bruce Adams and J. Jackson Walter, *America's Unelected Government* (Cambridge, Mass.: Ballinger, 1983); Hugh Heclo, *A Government of Strangers* (Washington: Brookings Institution, 1977); G. Calvin Mackenzie, ed. *The In-and-Outers* (Baltimore: John Hopkins, 1987); G. Calvin

Mackenzie, *The Politics of Presidential Appointments* (New York: The Free Press, 1981).

72. Dom Bonafede, "The White House Personnel Office from Roosevelt to Reagan," in *The In-and-Outers*, p. 33.

73. James P. Pfiffner, "Nine Enemies and One Ingrate: Political Appointments during Presidential Transitions," in *The In-and-Outers*, pp. 60-61.

74. Hugh Heclo, "The In-and-Outer System: A Critical Assessment," in *The In-and-Outers*, p. 196.

75. Ibid.

76. Linda L. Fisher, "Fifty Years of Presidential Appointments," in *The In-and-Outers*, pp. 12-13.

77. Chester N. Newland, "A Mid-Term Appraisal—The Reagan Presidency: Limited Government and Political Administration," *Public Administration Review*, 43 (1983), p. 3.

78. Ann Devroy, "Missing a Chance to Hire 300,000 Political Patrons," *Washington Post Weekly Edition*, October 30, 1989, p. 13.

79. Hoogenboom, p. 256.

80. Albert H. Aronson, "State and Local Personnel Administration," in Frank J. Thompson, ed. *Classics of Public Personnel Policy*, 2d ed. (Pacific Grove, California: Brooks/Cole, 1991), pp. 134-37.

81. Ibid., pp. 136-37.

82. Advisory Commission on Intergovernmental Relations, *The Question of State Government Capability* (Washington, D.C.: Government Printing Office, 1985), pp. 161-65.

83. Aronson, p. 141. According to Jay M. Shafritz, Albert C. Hyde and David H. Rosenbloom less than 12% of the cities with over 50,000 people lack merit systems. See their *Personnel Management in Government*, 3rd ed. (New York: Marcel Dekker, 1986), p. 48.

84. As Shafritz, et.al., point out, the statistics are suspect because they are generally compiled by official groups using mailed questionnaires inquiring if a jurisdiction has a merit system. There is no attempt to verify the answers, *Personnel Management*, p. 48.

85. Raymond Wolfinger, "Why Political Machines Have Not Withered Away and Other Revisionist Thoughts," *Journal of Politics*, 34 (1972), pp. 365-98.

86. Martin Shefter, *Political Crisis/Fiscal Crisis* (New York: Basic Books, 1987), pp. 90, 99.

87. Tolchin and Tolchin, p. 99.

88. Shefter, pp. 97-100.

89. *New York Times*, January 19, 1975, p. 1 as quoted by Shefter, p. 100.

90. Shefter, pp. 174-75.

91. Edward I. Koch with William Rauch, *Politics* (New York: Simon and Schuster, 1985), pp. 18-19.

92. Ibid., pp. 28-31.

93. Ibid., p. 19.

94. See for example Shefter; the various contributors to Jewell Bellush and Dick Netzer, *Urban Politics: New York Style* (Armonk, New York: M.E. Sharpe, 1990); Arthur Browne, Dan Collins and Michael Goodwin, *I, Koch* (New York: Dodd, Mead 1985) and Jack Newfield and Wayne Barrett, *City for Sale* (New York: Harper and Row, 1989). Browne was with the *Daily News*, Collins was U.P.I. City Hall Chief, and Goodwin was the *New York Times* City Hall chief. Newfield and Barrett are associated with the *Daily News* and the *Village Voice*. They offer detailed accounts of patronage in the Koch administration, but their work has to be treated with caution because they do not identify many of their sources and because Newfield, an important figure in New York politics, has been an enemy of Koch for years.

95. Joyce Purnick and Martin Tolchin, "Doling Out Jobs Under Koch: The Mayor Kept His Distance," *New York Times*, April 22, 1986, pp. 1, 13.

96. Edward I. Koch with William Rauch, *Mayor* (New York: Warner Books, 1985), p. 83.

97. Howard Kurtz, "Biaggi Influence-Peddling Trial to Open," *Washington Post*, August 24, 1984, p. A9 as quoted by Richard Wade, "The Withering Away of the Party System," in Bellush and Netzer, p. 283.

98. The report is in Bruce A. Green, ed. *Government Ethics Reform for the 1990's* (New York: Fordham University Press, 1991). The account which follows is drawn from this volume and from testimony quoted by the *New York Times*.

99. DeVincenzo eventually pleaded guilty to three counts of perjury. He admitted he lied when asked whether there was political screening and whether he had ordered evidence destroyed. Because some of the hearing records were lost, the prosecutor agreed to a sentence of five years probation. Ronald Sullivan, "Ex-Aide to Koch Admits He Lied About Job Bank," *New York Times*, April 5, 1991, p. B3.

100. Wade, p. 286. Also see J. Phillip Thompson, "David Dinkins' Victory in New York City: The Decline of the Democratic Party Organization and the Strengthening of Black Politics," *PS*, 23 (1990), pp. 145-48.

101. Philip Russo, "The Patronage Police," *Empire Report*, 15 (1989), p. 19.

102. Tolchins, p. 125.

103. J. Christine Altenburger, "Patronage: Ethics Gone Amok," in Peter Madsen and Jay M. Shafritz, eds., *Essentials of Government Ethics* (New York: Penguin, 1992), pp. 259-62.

104. All the material on this episode is from the *New York Times*. See Joseph Berger, "School Official Tells of Patronage Scheme," October 24, 1989, p. A24 and "Nine Suspended at School Board Over Patronage," October 25, 1989, p. A28 and Andrew L. Yarrow, "Stress Forces Whistleblower to Retire From the Schools," November 13, 1990, p. B12.

Chapter 2

1. Quoted in Steve Johnson, "Gift of Gab Helped Make Him Master of the Quick Quip," *Chicago Tribune* (December 8, 1987), Section 7, p. 17.

2. Robert J. McClory, "Shakman: The Man and His Battle Against Patronage," *Illinois Issues*, vol. 9 (September 1983), p. 9.

3. Shakman v. Democratic Organization of Cook County, 435 F.2d 267 (7th Cir. 1970).

4. McClory, p. 9.

5. The original suit was brought against the Cook County Democratic Organization and various party officials including Daley who was the Chairman; the City of Chicago, and a number of officials of Chicago and Cook County. The suit was expanded to include Republicans in 18 northern Illinois counties, the Republican governor and Attorney General, and the Cook County Republican Central Committee. In all, 42 officeholders signed the 1972 consent decree. Several officials held out and did not sign the decree until much later. The last two of these, the Chicago Park District and the Cook County Sheriff, signed in 1980. The text of the consent decree is printed as an appendix in 481 F. Supp. 1315 (1979).

6. 481 F. Supp. 1315 (1979). In 1984 Judge Bua further extended his ruling to apply to promotions, declaring that promotions among existing city employees were not to be based on political sponsorship or other political considerations. Herron v. City of Chicago, 591 F. Supp. 1565 (1984).

7. Judge Bua's 1979 decision and 1983 order applied only to the Democratic Party and Democratic officials of the City of Chicago and of Cook County. Of the defendants named in the 1983 order, the Clerk of the Circuit Court was the first to submit a plan of compliance, followed by the City of Chicago which developed its detailed hiring plan in 1984. The Cook County State's Attorney Richard M. Daley, the son of Mayor Daley, signed a consent decree detailing hiring procedures and naming exempt positions in 1981. The Sheriff of Cook County and the Chicago Park District did not develop hiring plans until 1986.

8. U.S. Court of Appeals for the Seventh Circuit, Numbers 85-1870, 85-1911, and 85-1912, decided August 5, 1987. According to the U.S. Supreme Court, in order to have standing, a "plaintiff must allege a personal injury fairly traceable to the defendants's allegedly unlawful conduct and likely to be redressed by the requested relief" [Justice O'Connor in Allen v. Wright, 486 U.S. 737 (1984)]. The question of standing had been a key issue in the case from the beginning. U.S. District Court Judge Abraham Marovitz initially dismissed Shakman's suit on the grounds that Shakman and Lurie did not have the standing to assert the rights of employees, 310 F. Supp. 1398 (1969), but the Seventh Circuit Court of Appeals reversed Judge Marovitz's ruling, 435 F.2d 267 (1970). The U.S. Supreme Court denied certiorari, 4042 U.S. 909 (1971). Because of the Allen decision and other changes in the legal and political "landscape," in 1987 the Court of Appeals backed away from its 1970 decision and found that the plaintiffs lacked standing to challenge the constitutionality of political hiring.

9. Shakman later served as the head of the Independent Voters of Illinois, one of the major reform organizations in Chicago. See James Q. Wilson, *The Amateur Democrat* (Chicago: The University of Chicago Press, 1962).

10. Abraham Chayes, "The Role of the Judge in Public Law Litigation," *Harvard Law Review*, vol. 89 (May 1976), pp. 1281-1316.

11. David H. Rosenbloom, "Public Administration and the Judiciary: The 'New Partnership,' " *Public Administration Review*, vol. 47 (January/February 1987), p. 75.

12. For accounts of how the machine operated, see Milton Rakove, *Don't Make No Waves, Don't Back No Losers* (Bloomington: University of Indiana Press, 1975) and *We Don't Want Nobody Nobody Sent* (Bloomington: University of Indiana Press, 1979); Thomas M. Guterbock, *Machine Politics in Transition* (Chicago: University of Chicago Press, 1980); Harold F. Gosnell, *Machine Politics, Chicago Model*, 2nd ed. (Chicago: University of Chicago Press, 1968); John M. Allswang, *Bosses, Machines and Urban Voters* (Baltimore: John Hopkins University Press, 1986); Mike Royko, *Boss* (New York: E.P. Dutton, 1971); and Len O'Connor, *Clout* (New York: Avon Books, 1976).

13. Lois Wille, "Ald. Vito Marzullo: Dispenser of Jobs," *Chicago Daily News*, February 7, 1967.

14. C. Richard Johnson, "Successful Reform Litigation: The Shakman Patronage Case," *Chicago-Kent Law Review*, 64 (1988), p. 482.

15. Wille, February 7, 1967.

16. Lois Wille, "The South Side Job Story," *Chicago Daily News*, February 8, 1967.

17. John Camper, "The Road to City Hall," *Chicago Tribune Magazine*, November 16, 1986, pp. 36-37.

18. Rakove, *Don't Make No Waves*, p. 116.

19. 481 F.Supp. 1315 (1979) at p. 1325.

20. Rakove, *Don't Make No Waves*, pp. 112-113.

21. Ibid., p. 118.

22. Ibid., p. 123.

23. Ibid., pp. 123-24.

24. Guterbock, pp. xix, 173-74.

25. Arnold R. Hirsch, "Martin H. Kennelly: The Mugwump and the Machine," in Paul M. Green and Melvin G. Holli, eds., *The Mayors* (Carbondale, IL: Southern Illinois University, 1987), pp. 130-32.

26. Quoted by Peter Knauss in *Chicago: A One Party State* (Champaign, IL: Stripes Publishing Co., 1974), p. 105.

27. Lois Wille, *Chicago Daily News*, Series on "Patronage and Power," February 2-11, 1967.

28. *Chicago Sun-Times*, September 14, 1975.

29. Hay Associates, "Review of the Personnel Department/Executive Summary/Employment Categories and Processes," May 1981, p. 12.

30. The phrase "dual employment system" was used by Charles Pounian, head of personnel from 1960 to 1985, in an affidavit filed with the U.S. District Court.

31. Royko, *Boss*, p. 17.

32. Len O'Connor, *Requiem* (Chicago: Contemporary Books, 1977), p. 24.

33. *Official Report of The Task Force on Affirmative Action of the City of Chicago,* December 1985, pp. 4-6; Wille, *Chicago Daily News,* February 10, 1967.

34. A group of city workers won a lawsuit in which they charged that the city manipulated the civil service process to give promotions to individuals with powerful political sponsors. In one instance, when political sponsors requested that individuals not on the eligibility list be given appointments, examinations were privately held for these persons and they were subsequently given jobs. Herron v. City of Chicago, 591 F. Supp. pp. 1565-68. (1984).

35. For the text of the ordinance, see the *Journal of the City of Chicago,* Chicago, October 24, 1975, pp. 1443-1446. For discussions of the ordinance, see the *Wall Street Journal,* December 22, 1975, and the Chicago *Daily News, Sun-Times* and *Tribune,* September and October 1975.

36. For the text of the ordinance, see the Municipal Code of Chicago, Chapter 25; for the Hay report, see City of Chicago, "Review of the Personnel Department/Executive Summary/Employment Categories and Processes," May, 1981.

37. Notice to all employees issued by Abraham L. Marovitz of the U.S. District Court for the Northern District of Illinois, May 5, 1972. The text of the consent judgments attached as an appendix to Judge Bua's 1979 opinion. 481 F. Supp. 1315 (1979).

38. Paul Kleppner, *Chicago Divided* (Dekalb, Illinois: Northern Illinois University Press, 1985), p. 87.

39. See Leah M. Bishop, "Patronage and the First Amendment After Elrod v. Burns," *Columbia Law Review,* vol. 78 (1978), pp. 478-80; and Marita K. Marshall, "Will the Victor Be Denied the Spoils? Constitutional Challenge to Patronage Dismissals," *Hastings Constitutional Law Quarterly,* vol. 4 (1977), pp. 182-83.

40. Alfredo S. Lanier, "Disabling the Patronage Army," *Chicago,* vol. 32 (December 1983), p. 234.

41. Quoted in the *Reader,* "Reader's Digest of Neighborhoods" (June 18, 1976), p. 3.

42. Ibid.

43. Shakman, 481 F. Supp. 1315 (1979), p. 1355.

44. The words are capitalized in the notice which is printed in the order, Shakman, 569 F. Supp. 177 (1983), pp. 183-84.

45. According to the City Law Department, as of April 1988, some 810 positions were in Schedule G, the list of exempt positions subject to mayoral appointment. This does not include employees on the mayor's staff and others on Schedule A through F (such as City Council employees) who are also exempt.

46. The City Law Department could not give exact figures, but one attorney working on Shakman asserted that there were "no more than 50" challenges of exempt positions and the number was more likely "about 25."

47. While the revised agreement on exempts was being worked out, Judge Bua barred Mayor Washington from firing any of the 900 employees whose positions were to be placed on the exempt list, saying "these people

have families, they have homes, and to allow the mayor to engage in whole-sale firing of these people would be a travesty and it would, in effect, turn the Shakman decree on its head." *Chicago Tribune* (May 25, 1983), p. 5.

48. Since the official's job title had been eliminated, the city had to find a comparable position for him. He was appointed to a position in the Department of Streets and Sanitation which carried a Deputy Commissioner's pay but which did not, according to his attorney, "involve meaningful duties." *Chicago Tribune* (May 1, 1984).

49. Tomczak v. City of Chicago, 765 F.2d 633 (7th Cir. 1985).

50. Nekolny v. Painter, 653 F.2d 1164 (7th Cir. 1981).

51. Shakman, 569 F. Supp. 177 (1983), p. 178.

52. The following discussion is based on the *Principles for Plan of Compliance with Shakman Judgment*, as submitted to the United States District Court for the Northern District of Illinois, May 1984.

53. The following discussion is based on the *Detailed Hiring Provisions for Compliance with the Shakman Judgment*, October 31, 1984, and the Revised Provisions of August 20, 1986.

54. Eligible lists may remain active for a year or more. The Commissioner of Personnel has the authority to decide how long a list will remain active. When there is an active eligible list, it must be used as a "preliminary source of applicants for the class titles for which it was created."

55. The assessment is based on city reports, affidavits, and other documents that are filed with the Court, the Court-ordered compliance audit for the year 1985-1986, various city documents (such as the Department of Personnel's rulings), newspaper reports, and extensive interviewing of the lawyers for the plaintiffs in the Shakman case, representatives of the city's Department of Law, numerous officials and former officials in the Department of Personnel, various heads of other city departments, expert observers of Chicago politics, and other individuals active in Chicago and Cook County politics. Because Shakman and the general subject of patronage are sensitive matters in Chicago politics, most interviewers would only speak on the condition that they would not be quoted by name. Therefore, with a few exceptions in cases where permission was given to attribute a statement to a particular individual, specific sources are not cited. The findings from my own interviews are bolstered by the auditor's summary of his findings from interviews with key staff members of the Department of Personnel and other departments and from a focus group interview with 16 Department of Personnel examiners. In addition, the auditors' report includes results from a mail survey of 69 newly hired/promoted city employees and 76 rejected applicants for city jobs. The Shakman Compliance Audit for the Year 1985-1986 was completed by the Human Resources Consulting Group of Arthur Young in December of 1986, but it was not made public until July 1987 because of wrangles between the city and the auditor. It is probably not accidental that the city's objections to various aspects of the audit delayed its release until after the April 1987 mayoral election.

56. For example, job seekers have to fill out separate applications for each job title. The new Commissioner of Personnel is trying to put in place a

system which will make it possible to require a single application for multiple positions. In part because the burdens imposed by Shakman have forced the Department of Personnel to try to do more with limited resources, the department is attempting to streamline its procedure and to automate as much as possible, but its progress has been slowed by the lack of funds to hire additional staff or outside consultants.

57. Shakman Compliance Audit for the Year 1985-1986 (Chicago: Human Resource Consulting Group, Arthur Young, December 1986), Part II, p. 7.

58. Audit, Section V, p. 4.

59. Audit, Section V, pp. 12-19.

60. Audit, Section V, p. 10.

61. Audit, Section VII, p. 7.

62. City of Chicago, Compliance Audit of the Implementation of the Detailed Hiring Provisions Under the Shakman Judgment 55 (1989), pp. 3-4, 40-41, 47-49.

63. Illinois Commission of the Future of Public Service, *Excellence in Public Service: Chicago's Challenge for the '90's.* (Chicago Community Trust/Government Assistance Project, August 1991), pp. 4-6, 8.

64. Story by Fran Spielman in the *Chicago Sun-Times*, May 23, 1991, p. 1.

65. Story by John Kass and Robert Davis in the *Chicago Tribune*, May 23, 1991, p. 1.

66. *Sun Times*, May 23, 1991, p. 1.

67. Fran Spielman, "Shakman Shackles Hiring: Report," *Chicago Sun-Times*, September 13, 1991, p. 16.

68. Bill and Lori Granger, *Fighting Jane*, (New York: Dial Press, 1980), p. 93.

69. Rakove, *We Don't Want Nobody*, pp. 320-21.

70. Guterbock, pp. 38-39.

71. Rakove, *We Don't Want Nobody*, pp. x, xi.

72. See Michael Preston, "The Election of Harold Washington: An Examination of the SES Model in the 1983 Chicago Mayoral Election," in Michael B. Preston, Lenneal J. Henderson, Jr., and Paul L. Puryear, eds., *The New Black Politics*, 2nd ed. (New York: Longman, 1987), pp. 139-71 and Melvin G. Holli and Paul M. Green, *Bashing Chicago Tradition* (Grand Rapids, Michigan: W.B. Erdmans, 1989). For analyses of the state of the machine in the 1970s and 1980s and its loss to Harold Washington in 1983, see Louis H. Masotti and Samuel K. Gove, eds., *After Daley* (Urbana: University of Illinois Press, 1982); Melvin G. Holli and Paul M. Green, eds., *The Making of the Mayor* (Grand Rapids, MI: William B. Erdmans Publishing Company, 1984); Paul Kleppner, *Chicago Divided* (DeKalb: Northern Illinois University Press, 1985); and Paul M. Green and Melvin G. Holli, eds., *The Mayors* (Carbondale: Southern Illinois University Press, 1987). For a general analysis of The Irish Machines, see Steven P. Erie, *Rainbow's End* (Berkeley: University of California Press, 1988).

73. The Principles state that the plan "will provide for excluding hiring procedures which discriminate by race, color, sex, religion, national origin,

age, or handicap status, and will promote the City's ability to meets its affirmative action objectives." Principle 4, section 3).

74. Figures from Pierre deVise, "Mayor Washington's Second Term: Dividing the Spoils," Chicago Regional Inventory Working Paper No. II, 92 (May 1987), p. 6. In 1986, whites still held 65 percent of all city jobs, although they constituted only 43 percent of the population. Under Mayor Bilandic, in 1978 whites had held 71.5 percent; thus, affirmative action was slowly having an impact on the overall composition of the city's workforce.

75. *Chicago Tribune*, April 27, 1987.

76. *Chicago Tribune*, January 22, 1987.

77. The constitutionality of patronage contracting has been challenged, but so far the federal appeals courts have been reluctant to extend to public contractors the first amendment protections that the U.S. Supreme Court gave public employees in Elrod, Branti, and Rutan. See Thomas G. Dagger, "Political Patronage in Public Contracting," *University of Chicago Law Review*, vol. 51 (Spring 1984), pp. 518-58.

78. Erie, pp. 156-162. Also see Arnold R. Hirsch, "Chicago," in Richard M. Bernard, ed., *Snowbelt Cities* (Bloomington, Indiana University Press, 1990), pp. 76-81. And Barbara Ferman, "Chicago: Power, Race, and Reform," in H.V. Savitch and John Clayton Thomas, eds., *Big City Politics in Transition* (Newbury Park California: Sage, 1991), pp. 50-55.

79. John M. Allswang, "Richard J. Daley: America's Last Boss," in Green and Holli, *The Mayors*, p. 163.

80. Holli and Green, *Bashing Chicago Tradition*, pp. 139-41 and Larry Bennett, "Beyond Urban Renewal: Chicago's North Loop Redevelopment Project," *Urban Affairs Quarterly*, 22: (1986), pp. 249-50.

81. Neighborhood Bulletin (Chicago: Mayor's Office of Inquiry and Information, February 15-March 15, 1987), p. 2.

82. Ray Gibson, "Daley had Investments in 26 Wards." *Chicago Tribune*, March 14, 1991, see p. 1.

83. Hirsch, "Chicago", p. 83. Also see William J. Grimshaw, "The Political Economy of Machine Politics," *Corruption and Reform*, 4 (1989), pp. 23-37.

84. Dempsey J. Travis, *An Autobiography of Black Politics*, (Chicago: Urban Research Press, 1987), p. 235.

85. See Steven Erie, pp. 161-69.

86. Hirsch, "Chicago," p. 84.

87. Robert T. Starks and Michael B. Preston, "Harold Washington and the Politics of Reform in Chicago: 1983-1987," in Rufus P. Browning, Dale Rogers Marshall and David H. Tabb, eds., *Racial Politics in American Cities*, (New York: Longman, 1990), p. 97. Also see Michael B. Preston, "The Election of Harold Washington: An Examination of the SES Model in the 1983 Chicago Mayoral Election," in *The New Black Politics*, 2nd ed. (New York: Longman, 1987), pp. 139-63.

88. Melvin G. Holli, "Daley to Daley," in Paul M. Green and Melvin G. Holli, eds., *Restoration 1989* (Chicago: Lyceum Books, 1991), p. 205.

89. Paul M. Green, "Chicago's 1991 Mayoral Elections: Richard M. Daley wins Second Term," *Illinois Issues*, 17 (June 1991), pp. 17-20 and *Chicago Tribune*, April 13, 1991, p. 15.

90. Richard Day and Jeff Andreasen, "Chicago's 1991 and 1983 Democratic Mayoral Primaries," *Illinois Issues*, 17 (1991), p. 28.

91. Paul M. Green, "Mayor Richard M. Daley: His Views of the City and State," *Illinois Issues*, 17 (1991), p. 22.

92. Robert Davis, "Daley's Privatization Plans Raise Patronage Army Fears," *Chicago Tribune*, November 4, 1990, Sec 2, p. 1.

93. Mark Brown and Chuck Neubauer, "Real Insiders Reap Rewards," *Chicago Sun-Times*, October 11, 1990, p. 16.

94. Ray Gibson, "Daley Fuels Patronage in Pinstripes," *Chicago Tribune*, July 29, 1990. Sec. 2, p. 1. Also see Roger Flaherty and Harlan Draeger, "Daley-linked Law Firm Gets A Plum," *Chicago Sun-Times*, November 4, 1991, p. 18.

95. John Kass, "Democrats Set Their Priorities Locally," *Chicago Tribune*, March 15, 1992, Sec. 1, p. 1.

Chapter 3

1. John H. Fenton, *Midwest Politics* (New York: Holt, Rinehart Winston, 1966), pp. 115-16.

2. Ibid., p. 224.

3. Ibid., pp. 226-27.

4. Jim Gempel, "Vulnerability to Reform: Why the Eastern Style Machine Could Not Take Hold in the West," Paper delivered at the Midwest Political Science meeting in Chicago, April 18-20, 1991, pp. 10-18.

5. David Mayhew, *Placing Parties in American Politics* (Princeton: Princeton University Press, 1986), p. 11. Also see Chapter 8, especially pp. 236-37.

6. Jack H. Knott and Gary J. Miller, *Reforming Bureaucracy* (Englewood Cliffs, New Jersey: Prentice Hall, 1987), pp. 44-47.

7. Neal R. Peirce and Jerry Hagstrom, *The Book of America*, rev. ed. (New York: Warner Books, 1984), p. 267.

8. Neal R. Peirce and John Keefe, *The Great Lake States of America* (New York: Norton, 1980), p. 135.

9. *The Capital Times*, Madison, Wisconsin, editorial of March 7, 1989. This section is based on *The Capital Times* articles by Mike Hill appearing on March 4, 6 and 7, 1989.

10. Communication from the Association of Career Employees, March 20, 1991 and stories in *The Capital Times*, March 20 and 21, 1989.

11. Richard Eggleston, "Thompson patronage rampant, critics say," *Wisconsin State Journal*, October 14, 1990, p. 1, 11.

12. Ibid., p. 11.

13. Dan Allegretti, "Gov's patronage: a legacy of trouble," *Capital Times*, November 1, 1990, p. 12A.

14. Frank J. Munger, *Two-Party Politics in the State of Indiana* (Ph.D dissertation, Harvard University, 1955), p. 6 as quoted by Mayhew, p. 94.

15. Fenton, p. 165.

16. The account of the license bureaus is drawn from Raymond H. Scheele, "Political Parties in Indiana," in William P. Hojnacki, ed. *Politics and Public Policy in Indiana* (Dubuque, Iowa: Kendall/Hunt, 1983), p. 20 and E.R. Shipp, "Political Use of Auto Fee is Challenged in Indiana," *New York Times*, May 29, 1984, p. A12.

17. I interviewed present and former governement officials, party leaders, lawyers, newspapermen, personnelists and academics. Because patronage is a sensitive issue (especially now that Rutan has declared most patronage unconstitutional), nearly all asked not to be identified.

18. Kyle Niederpruen and Susan Hanafee, "Political spoils still the rule for 7,000 jobs," *Indianapolis Star*, July 10, 1988, pp. A1, 12, 13. The clearance card is reprinted on p. A12. The last statement is based on material from interviews.

19. Governor Evan Bayh, *Message of March 15, 1990*. The preceding section draws on interviews and on Kyle Niederpreun, "State police now allowing officers to re-declare party," *Indianapolis Star*, July 31, 1990, pp. A1, 8 and Patrick J. Traub, "Bipartisan hiring rules facing repeal," *Indianapolis Star*, February 4, 1991.

20. Interview, September 23, 1991.

21. Mayhew, p. 99.

22. Some of this money went back to patronage workers in the form of payments for election day expenses. See Scheele, p. 21.

23. I had several conversations with national and state AFSCME officials. None indicated that attacking patronage and supporting worker suits was a major concern in Indiana.

24. Cheri Collis, "Cleaning up the Spoils System," *State Government News*, 33 (September 1990), p. 8.

25. Terry Horne, "No policy role, supervisor says," *Indianapolis News*, July 26, 1990, p. D8. Also see Kyle Niederpreun and Susan Hanafee, "Five lawsuits claim state jobs lost to politics," *Indianapolis Star*, July 7, 1990, p. A10 and James A. Gillaspy, "Aide admits politics part of highway hiring," *Indianapolis Star*, July 27, 1990, p. C1.

26. Susan Hanafee and Kyle Niederpreun, "Some fall through the cracks of hiring reform, *Indianapolis Star*, July 30, 1990, p. A1.

27. Kyle Niederpreun and Susan Hanafee, "Fired workers dispute end of political hiring," *Indianapolis Star*, July 29, 1990, p. A1.

28. Ibid., p. A10.

29. See Fenton, pp. 194-218 and Edgar G. Crane, "Illinois Government and Politics: An Overview, pp. 8-10 and Peter W. Colby, "Illinois Politics and the Ideal of Responsible Party Government," p. 180. Both are in Edgar G. Crane, ed., *Illinois: Political Processes and Governmental Performance* (Dubuque, Iowa: Kendall/Hunt, 1980.

30. Quoted (with approval) by Peirce and Hagstrom, p. 283.

31. Ibid., p. 234.

32. David Kenney, *Basic Illinois Government*, rev. ed. (Carbondale: Southern Illinois University Press, 1974), p. 264.

33. Thomas Page, *State Personnel Reorganization in Illinois* (Urbana, University of Illinois Institute of Government and Public Affairs, 1961), p. 9.

34. See John Barlow Martin, "The Blast in Centralia No. 5: A Mine Disaster No One Stopped," reprinted in Richard J. Stillman, ed., *Public Administration*, 4th ed. (Boston: Houghton Mifflin, 1988), pp. 16-36.

35. Milton Rakove, *We Don't Want Nobody Nobody Sent* (Bloomington: Indiana University Press, 1979), pp. 10-11. Also see Rakove, *Don't Make No Waves, Don't Back No Losers* (Bloomington: Indiana University Press, 1975), pp. 144-46 and Robert P. Howard, *Mostly Good and Competent Men: Illinois Governors 1818-1988* (Springfield, Il.: Sangamon State University Press, 1988), pp. 276-77.

36. John Barlow Martin, *Adlai Stevenson of Illinois* (Garden City, N.Y.: Doubleday, 1976), pp. 366-67.

37. Ibid., p. 512.

38. Ibid., pp. 355-61.

39. Ibid., p. 376.

40. Ibid., p. 400.

41. David Kenney, *A Political Passage: The Career of Stratton of Illinois* (Carbondale: Southern Illinois University Press, 1990), p. 19.

42. Howard, p. 283.

43. This account of the 1955 Personnel Code and its implementation is based on Page, especially Chapter 4, pp. 26-33.

44. Howard, p. 283.

45. Kenney, p. 115.

46. Kenney, p. 131.

47. Kenney, p. 156. In an interview on July 31, 1991 Stratton told me that the appointment of his aide, an educated man who had at one time been the principal of Springfield High School, was "non-political." He also said that the purpose of the new personnel code was to "formalize" the personnel system, not to reform it.

48. Kenney, p. 112.

49. Kenney, pp. 131-32.

50. See Page, Chapter 6, especially pp. 96-106.

51. Kenney, p. 172.

52. Oral History Office, Sangamon State University, "Stories of The Governorship," *Illinois Issues*, 8 (December 1982), p. 17.

53. See Howard, esp. p. 172 and George Bliss, "We're forced to help Walker: state workers," *Chicago Tribune*, March 5, 1976; George Bliss, "Walker may face suit on coercion of highway aides," *Chicago Tribune*, March 6, 1976. Also see Carolyn Toll and Charles N. Wheeler III, "6 state workers politick on public time," *Chicago Sun-Times*, March 1, 1974.

54. As quoted by Peirce and Keefe, p. 94.

55. Robert E. Hartley, *Big Jim Thompson of Illinois* (Chicago: Rand McNally, 1979), p. 25. All the information about Thompson before he become governor comes from this book.

56. The definition is from Charles N. Wheeler III, "Gov. James R. Thompson, 1977-1991: The complete campaigner, the pragmatic centrists," *Illinois Issues* (December 1990), p. 16.

57. Robert P. Howard, "Thompson v. Stevenson: A Long View," *Illinois Issues* (December 1990), p. 16.

58. Hartley, p. 118.

59. Basil Talbott Jr., "Thompson promises no firings for political reasons," *Chicago Sun-Times*, January 12, 1977, p. 40.

60. Ibid., pp. 134-38.

61. Wheeler, p. 16.

62. Hartley, p. 138.

63. Peter W. Colby, "Illinois Politics and the Ideal of Responsible Party Government," in Crane, ed. p. 182.

64. Mildred A. Schwartz, *The Party Network: The Robust Organization of Illinois Republicans* (Madison: University of Wisconsin Press, 1990), p. 152.

65. David Kenney, Written Communication, October 28, 1991. Professor Kenney, a political scientist, served as head of the Department of Conservation in the Thompson administration.

66. Edgar G. Crane, "The Office of Governor," in Crane, ed., *Illinois*, p. 81.

67. William Griffin and Michael Sneed, "State aides still on 'ghost payroll'," *Chicago Tribune*, August 7, 1977 and John Elmer, "Aide admits Thompson didn't end ghost payrolls," *Chicago Tribune*, July 27, 1977. For the January statement see, "Thompson admits he'll use 'ghost payrollers' for staff," *Chicago Tribune*, January 28, 1977.

68. Bob Wiedrich, "Bureaucrats a curse on elected officials," *Chicago Tribune*, October 7, 1979; "Thompson removes 1,000 jobs from civil service protection," *Chicago Tribune*, September 28, 1979, Sec. 1, p. 1; Basil Talbott, Jr., "Governor signs bill for 800 'clout' jobs," *Chicago Sun-Times*, September 28, 1979.

69. The statistics and quotations are from James D. Nowlan, William S. Hanley and Donald Udstuen, "Personal and Patronage," in James D. Nowlan, ed. *Inside State Government in Illinois* (Chicago: Neltnor House, 1991), pp. 51-52.

70. James R. Thompson, Office of the Governor, *Executive Order Number 5*, Springfield, November 12, 1980.

71. Not all Illinois employees work for the governor. Some work for one of the five other elected state officials or for such separate authorities as the State Universities Civil Service System or the Illinois Toll Highway Authority. In 1991, Nowlan, Hanley and Udstuen estimated that 73,000 persons worked for the governor and that 62,000 of these were covered by the Illinois Personnel Code (see p. 51). The governor's press conference is reported in Daniel Egler and Mitchell Locin, "Thompson puts freeze on hiring," *Chicago Tribune*, November 13, 1980 and G. Robert Hillman, "Thompson orders state hiring freeze," *Chicago Sun-Times*, November 13, 1980.

72. With a few exceptions such as Professor Kenney and Mary Lee Leahy, the Rutan plaintiffs' lawyer, most of the people I interviewed were

only willing to speak if guaranteed confidentiality. I spoke to newsmen, legislators, former state officials and a few still in state government, union officials, and Democratic party officials. I was not able to talk to anyone at a high level in the Republican party or in the Thompson or Edgar administrations. Some of the state's lawyers told me that they would like to talk to me, but were under orders not to discuss anything to do with Rutan or patronage. Gene Reineke, the executive director of the Republican State Central Committee (who had been one of Thompson's patronage chiefs and subsequently headed state personnel) cancelled an appointment his secretary had given me. Governor Edgar's office told me that no one could talk to me about patronage because there is "no patronage anymore." Former Governor Thompson was too busy with his work as a high-paid lobbyist and lawyer to see me.

73. Thomas Hardy, "New era for state brings in new GOP leader," *Chicago Tribune*, April 17, 1991, Sec. 2, p. 8.

74. Robert Rich and James M. Banovetz, "Issues Facing the Future of the Public Service in Illinois," October 1990 (Background paper prepared for the Illinois Commission on the Future of the Public Service), p. 4.

75. Nowlan, Hanley and Udstuen, p. 56.

76. Ibid., pp. 56-57. According to the Civil Service Commission, a total of 1,545 provisional, emergency and temporary appointments were made in fiscal 1990 (July 1, 1989 through June 30, 1990). Of these appointments 83, or 5.37 percent, exceeded the statutory time limits. See Civil Service Commission, *83 Annual Report*, pp. 11-12.

77. David K. Hamilton, "The Staffing Function in Illinois State Government After Rutan," (Paper prepared for the American Society for Public Administration Conference, Chicago, April 13, 1992), p. 6.

78. Nowlan, Hanley and Udstuen, pp. 53-56.

79. Hamilton, p. 6.

80. Petitioner's Brief on the Merits, Rutan v. Republican Party of Illinois, 110 S.Ct. 2729 (1990), p. 12.

81. See Nowlan, Hanley and Udstuen, pp. 58-59.

82. Nowlan, Hanley and Udstuen, p. 53. It also might be noted that one of my informants stressed that patronage was used primarily to obligate the county chairman rather than to secure the loyalty of the individual workers. This is partly because the workers turn over fairly rapidly, especially in such low-level jobs as prison guard, but also because money for TV, phone banks and such is more critical than party workers in today's elections.

83. James W. Fossett and J. Fred Giertz, "Money, Politics and Regionalism in Allocating State Funds in Illinois," in Peter F. Nardulli, ed. *Diversity, Conflict and State Politics: Regionalism in Illinois* (Urbana: University of Illinois Press, 1989), pp. 242-44. On the legislature and governor also see Jack R. Van Der Slik and Kent D. Redfield, *Lawmaking in Illinois* (Springfield: Sangamon State University, 1989), pp. 152-70.

84. James D. Nowlan, *A New Game Plan for Illinois* (Chicago: Neltnor House, 1989), p. 132.

85. Mike Lawrence, "The Rematch: Thompson v. Stevenson," *Illinois Issues* (October 1986), p. 13.

86. Paula Wolff, Presentation at the American Society for Public Administration National Conference, Chicago, April 13, 1989.

87. See Illinois Commission on the Future of Public Service, *Excellence in Public Service: Illinois' Challenge For The 90s* (Chicago: Chicago Community Trust/Government Assistance Project, January 1991), especially pp. 11-13, 24-25, and 35.

88. Samuel K. Gove, "The Illinois Public Service—Some Preliminary Observations" (Background paper prepared for the Illinois Commission on the Future of Public Service, undated), p. 4.

89. Lynn Sweet, "Jubilant lawyer savors victory in 5-year battle," *Chicago Sun-Times*, June 22, 1990, p. 5.

90. Interview, March 11, 1991.

91. Sweet, p. 5.

92. The form is part of the brief submitted by the plaintiffs to the Supreme Court. Unless otherwise noted, the discussion of the plaintiffs' case is based on material in this brief and in the petition for a writ of certiorari which the plaintiffs submitted to the Supreme Court.

93. William H. Freivogel, "Political Hiring in Illinois is Challenged," *St. Louis Post-Dispatch*, October 8, 1989. All of the quotations from Moore and the people he dealt with are from this article.

94. The defendants were sued in their official capacities and as individuals. Greg Baise was also sued as a "representative of a purported defendant class consisting of all 'directors, heads or chief executive officers . . . since February 1, 1981, of departments, boards, and commissions under the jurisdiction of the Governor" and Lynn Quigley was sued as a representative of all " 'liasons' between the Governor's Office of Personnel and the departments, boards" etc. The action against the defendants was filed on behalf of the five plaintiffs and on behalf of six "asserted plaintiff classes" consisting of all voters (1); and taxpayers in Illinois (2); all Illinois employees who desire a promotion (3); a transfer (4); or have been laid off, but not rehired (5); and all persons who desire employment with the state of Illinois (6). Rutan v. Republican Party of Illinois 641 F. Supp. 249 (C.D. Ill. 1986), p. 251. Although it went all the way to the Supreme Court, the case was never certified as a class action.

95. The two decisions are: 848 F.2d 1396 (7th Cir. 1988) and 868 F.2d 943 (7th Cir. 1989).

96. David Heckelman, "Lawyer wins case that could end 'spoils system' in state government," *Chicago Daily Law Bulletin*, 136 (July 11, 1990), pp. 1, 18.

97. Oral Argument in the Supreme Court of the United States, Rutan (1990), No.: 88-1872 and 88-2074. The dialogue is on pp. 37 and 38 of the official transcript.

98. See Chapter 1 for a discussion of the majority opinion by Justice Brennan and the dissent by Justice Scalia.

99. Petitioner's Brief, Rutan, p. 21. Leahy conceded that friends and relatives, including some Democrats, were given jobs, but argued that the motivation in these instances was clearly political and it could therefore be said

that the benefits of state employment were limited to "those who are politically favored."

100. Thomas Hardy and Rick Pearson, "Court ruling: Thompson legacy?" *Chicago Tribune*, June 22, 1990, p. 8.

101. James R. Thompson, *Executive Order Number Three*, June 22, 1990.

102. Hamilton, p. 14.

103. James R. Thompson, *Administrative Order Number Two*, October 1, 1990, p. 1.

104. James R. Thompson, *Administrative Order Number One*, July 17, 1990.

105. Thompson, *Administrative Order Number Two*.

106. Michael D. Klemens, "Jim Edgar, Illinois' 38th governor: transition from Republican to Republican," *Illinois Issues*, 17 (January 1991), p. 13. The biographical data on Edgar come from this article and from Lynn Sweet, "Gov. Edgar's first 100 days," *Chicago Sun-Times*, April 25, 1991, p. 36.

107. According to DCMS, agencies don't have to adhere to the prescribed procedures in filling temporary, emergency, seasonal student appointments or positions covered under the provisions of a collective bargaining agreement. DCMS, "Clarification of Issues"—Administrative Order Number 1 (1991), May 15, 1991.

108. DCMS, May 15, 1991. In November of 1991 DCMS reported that it had established an Office of Employment Counseling and Recruitment in September, but it's not clear if these counsellors are functioning as Field Advisors.

109. "Governor Jim Edgar's Charge to the Human Resources Advisory Council," September 25, 1991.

110. Dennis Conrad, "State urges dismissal of damage claim in patronage case," *Chicago Daily Law Bulletin*, February 7, 1991, pp. 1, 20.

111. She was made an acting supervisor in December 1990. By the terms of the settlement she will be appointed to the "full-time certified, civil service position of Disabilities Claims Supervisor I in the Department of Rehabilitation Services." All quotations are from the settlement accepted by Judge Baker. Mimeographed copy provided to me by Mary Lee Leahy.

112. Jim Ritter, "State reaches settlement in patronage hiring case," *Chicago Sun-Times*, January 21, 1992, p. 4.

113. This was the word used by Mary Lee Leahy in a telephone interview, May 7, 1992.

114. Ritter, Ibid.

115. A number of affadavits filed in the Shakman case speak to the difficulties individuals have in finding a lawyer who will take employment discrimination cases on a contingency fee basis. In a February 1991 affadavit Roslyn C. Lief notes that one of the few firms in Chicago which took these cases recently closed down because of the financial difficulty of maintaining a practice based on nonpaying clients where it is necessary to rely on court fee awards.

116. See Hamilton.

117. Paula Wolff claims that Thompson was able to get better people into policymaking jobs before Rutan. Presentation to the American Society of Public Administration conference, April 13, 1992.

118. Charles Bosworth Jr., "GOP Official is Indicted," *St. Louis Post-Dispatch*, December 18, 1991, p. 1 and Jay Fitzgerald, "2 accused of selling-state jobs," *State Journal Register*, December 18, 1991, p. 1.

119. Dennis Conrad, "Despite court ruling, Republicans top Democrats in getting prison jobs," *Taylorville Breeze-Courier*, March 24, 1991, pp. 1, 3.

120. Jenni Davis, "County politicians may be working around Rutan," *State Journal Register*, March 30, 1992, p. 1.

121. Rick Pearson, "Edgar patronage aide given new state post," *Chicago Tribune*, October 27, 1991, Sec. 2, p. 2.

122. Tim Jones, "Edgar vows ethics law changes," *Chicago Tribune*, September 5, 1991, Sec. 2, p. 2.

123. Charles N. Wheeler III, "Edgar's plan to put Illinois on new road," *Illinois Issues*, 17 (March 1991), p. 8.

124. Telephone interview, May 13, 1992.

125. The information on the Springfield fund-raiser comes from Jay Fitzgerald, "Edgar's office: Fund-raising rules may have been broken," *State Journal-Register*, April 14, 1992, pp. 1, 3. The figures on 1990 are from a report issued by the State Board of Elections in Springfield, January 30, 1992.

126. Edgar also promised appointments to some leaders and saw that hundreds of thousands of dollars in campaign funds were deposited in black banks. His campaign also made a point of buying from black businesses. See Ann Marie Lipinski and Hanke Gratteau, "Edgar shows GOP can win black votes," *Chicago Tribune*, December 16, 1990, Sec. 1, pp. 1, 8.

127. Mark Brown and Chuck Neubauer, "Real insiders reap rewards," *Chicago Sun-Times*, October 11, 1990, p. 16.

128. Ibid.

129. As one political writer told me, after a campaign is over, the governor (and other elected officials) sometimes will find a place for the key people on their own staffs or in some agency where they can stay until they are needed in the next campaign. Sometimes these people continue to do political work while on the state payroll in a job that is essentially a sham.

130. Kenney, Written Communication, October 28, 1991.

131. Jay Fitzgerald, " 'Pinstripe patronage' not out of business under Edgar," *State Journal-Register*, December 9, 1991, pp. 1, 3.

132. Kevin McDermott, "Contract questions," *State Journal-Register*, February 28, 1992.

133. Kevin McDermott, "DCFS Funds go to Suter supporters," *State Journal-Register*, March 29, 1992, pp. 1, 7.

134. Kevin McDermott, "Private legal fees for DCFS hiked to $1.6 million in 1991," *State Journal-Register*, February 9, 1992. The figures on fees come from the state comptroller's office. All state contracts are a matter of public record.

135. Kevin McDermott, "State paying millions to private law firms," and "Politics plays a role in portion of private legal fees," *State Journal-Register*,

February 9, 1992, pp. 1, 4, 5; Kevin McDermott, "Patronage stretches state's legal padding," and "Legal services firms know who to know," *State Journal-Register*, February 10, 1992, pp. 1, 3; Rick Pearson, "More state funds may go for Thompson patronage case," *Chicago Tribune*, April 3, 1991, Sec. 2, p. 6.

136. Hanke Gratteau and Ray Gibson, "State's cookie jar: Contracts," *Chicago Tribune*, December 27, 1992, p. 1.

137. Ibid., p. 16.

138. Ray Gibson and Hanke Gratteau, "Helping their cronies is the lease politicians can do," *Chicago Tribune*, December 29, 1992, pp. 1, 10. The front page December 28, 1992 article by Gibson and Gratteau, "Savvy don't retire, they consult," and another on December 30, 1992 by Laurie Cohen, "Bonds are patronage of different pinstripe," completed the series. On January 3, 1993 Gibson and Gratteau discussed the chances for reform in "Government reform in the air; will it land on the books," while the editors called for change in "the land that reform forgot" in an editorial on "The costly culture of clout," Section 4, p. 2.

139. LaFalce v. Houston 712 F.2d 292 (1983), p. 294.

140. Nowlan, Hanley and Udstuen, p. 57.

141. Peirce and Keefe, p. 90.

Chapter 4

1. *Newsday* used this label for its August 21, 1989 feature section on the county Republican party. That section reported by Brian Donovan, Alan Eysen, Dena Bunis, Walter Fee and Celeste Hadrick is one of the major sources for this chapter. I have also relied heavily on *Newsday*'s September 1991 series on patronage and civil service in the town of Hempstead which was the work of staff writers Lou Dolinar, Alan Eysen, Celeste Hadrick and Michelle Slatalla and research assistant Laura Kim Hoslund. In addition to these two major series, I have used dozens of other articles from *Newsday*. Some of these, particularly the older ones, were from the files of Alan Eysen and from the clipping file maintained at the Long Island Studies Institute collection at Hofstra University. The *Newsday* articles and some of the other materials in these files did not always give complete bibliographic information. Therefore, I will only give specific (and as complete as possible) information on the exact article used when I am quoting directly.

In addition to the material from *Newsday* and the Long Island Studies Institute, I have also relied on a number of interviews I conducted in the summer of 1991. With some exceptions, such as Burt Neuborne, the attorney for the plaintiffs in the 1 percent case, most of these people—Democratic and Republican party officials, union officials and workers, civil service commission people, academic and other expert observers of Nassau County politics—requested confidentiality.

2. Office of the County Executive, *Nassau County: a Profile*. Undated, circa 1988, pp. 11-13.

3. The terms city, town and village are legal ones and are not necessarily correlated with population. In political terms, in New York state everyone

who lives outside a city or an Indian reservation lives in a town. The towns may vary in size from Hempstead (the largest) to Montague, which had 32 residents in 1980. Peter W. Colby, "The Government of New York State Today," in Peter W. Colby, ed., *New York State Today: Politics, Government and Public Policy* (Albany: SUNY Press, 1985), pp. 107-14.

4. Irving Long, "2 Town Races Key for Dems," *Newsday*, September 16, 1991, p. 3.

5. Alan Eysen, "Mantle of GOP Power Shifts," *Newsday*, November 7, 1991.

6. Michael Barone and Grant Ujifusa, *The Almanac of American Politics, 1992* (Washington, D.C.: National Journal, 1992), p. 843.

7. Gwen Young, "For Oyster Bay's Yevoli a thousand thank-you's," *Newsday*, November 7, 1991, p. 5.

8. Ibid., p. 136.

9. Bryan K. Marquard and Maureen Fan, "In N. Hempstead, cheer coexists with GOP gloom," *Newsday*, November 7, 1991, p. 136.

10. Michelle Slatalla, "No-Party Rule," *Newsday*, November 7, 1991, p. 3.

11. The quotations are from *Nassau County*, p. 9 and p. 11. Other data is from Barone and Ujifusa, p. 845.

12. Sarah Lyall, "Nassau County Sued over Rights of Minorities to Representation." *New York Times*, September 25, 1991, p. A16.

13. Sarah Lyall, "After Decades of Prosperity, Long Island Confronts a Stagnant Economy," *New York Times*, December 21, 1991, p. 10.

14. *Nassau County*, pp. 17-18.

15. This account of the history of the Nassau Republican party draws on Dennis S. Ippolito, "Political Perspectives and Party Leadership: A Case Study of Nassau County, New York," (Ph.D. dissertation, University of Virginia, 1967) and material in the files of Alan Eysen and the Long Island Studies Institute.

16. Sidney C. Schaer, "Political Pioneer Watches in the Wings," *Newsday*, October 25, 1991, p. 31.

17. Robert A. Caro, *The Power Broker* (New York: Vintage Books, 1975), p. 208.

18. Ibid., pp. 152, 209.

19. Tom Watson, "All-Powerful Machine of Yore Endures in New York's Nassau," *Congressional Quarterly*, August 17, 1985, p. 1623.

20. This section and the others on party structure draws heavily on the work of Alan Eysen.

21. Watson, p. 1623.

22. Barone and Ujifusa, p. 847.

23. Watson, p. 1624.

24. Alan Eysen, "The GOP's Enduring Structure," *Newsday*, August 21, 1989, p. 38.

25. Nicholas Goldberg, "Mondello and the Machine," *Newsday*, July 15, 1990, p. 13. The entire discussion of Mondello draws from this article.

NOTES

26. Frank Lynn, "Life after Jail: Politicians Get Help From Their Friends," *New York Times*, October 23, 1987, p. B1. Information on Margiotta also comes from Alan Eysen, "Margiotta's Newest Tune: 'R-e-s-p-e-c-T'," *Newsday*, December 8, 1989, p. 20.

27. Goldberg, p. 13.

28. Frank Lynn, "At Last, a Last Hurrah for Margiotta?" *New York Times*, May 8, 1983, p. E6.

29. Georgia C. Delaney, "The New York State Civil Service Law and its Administration in Ontario County, State of New York," *Public Personnel Management*, 14 (Summer 1985), p. 198.

30. New York State Department of Civil Service, *Summary of New York State Civil Service Law*. Albany, circa 1987.

31. Interview with high-level official of the New York State Civil Service Commission, June 28, 1991.

32. The figures on salaries appear in *Newsday*, September 22, 1991, p. 51. The entire discussion of Hempstead is largely drawn from the *Newsday* series on the town's Civil Service Commission of September 22, 23, 24.

33. *Newsday*, September 23, 1991, p. 23.

34. *Newsday*, September 22, 1991, p. 52.

35. *Newsday*, September 24, 1991, p. 37.

36. *Newsday*, September 24, 1991. The first quote is on p. 37; the second is on p. 6.

37. Municipal Service Division, New York State Department of Civil Service, *Municipal Civil Service in New York State Summary of Annual Reports*, Albany, 1990.

38. *Newsday*, September 22, 1991, p. 52.

39. *Newsday*, September 23, 1991, p. 22.

40. *Newsday*, September 23, 1991, p. 22.

41. *Newsday*, September 22, 1991, p. 51.

42. Ibid., p. 51.

43. Ibid., p. 51.

44. Lou Dolinar, Alan Eysen and Celeste Hadrick, "Jobs Spelled G-O-P," *Newsday*, December 29, 1991, pp. 5, 48, 49.

45. Interview, June 17, 1991.

46. For its study of the Hempstead civil service *Newsday* conducted a nine-month investigation. The paper developed a data base drawing on many sources. The paper "obtained 1990 computer tapes of employment records from Hempstead, along with additional tapes from the Nassau County Board of Elections identifying party affiliation and party committee members. These were supplemented by data from the county Civil Service Commission, and records of contributors to the Nassau Republican Party in the past four years. The people identified from these sources were matched with payroll records to produce lists of town workers who were committee people, contributors and others with known ties to the party." September 22, 1991, p. 52.

47. *Newsday*, August 21, 1989, p. 32.

48. Unless otherwise noted, the figures on salaries and other financial benefits are from 1989.

206

49. Celeste Hadrick and Brian Donovan, "Mondello's Legal Connections Questioned," *Newsday*, August 21, 1989, pp. 33, 39.

50. Charles V. Zehren, "Even in Hard Times, They Earn Top Dollar," *Newsday*, September 28, 1991, p. 20.

51. Dena Bunis, " 'The Last of a Vanishing Breed'," *Newsday*, August 21, 1989, p. 39.

52. Ibid., p. 39.

53. Ibid., p. 33.

54. Brian Donovan, Stephanie Saul and Celeste Hadrick, "The Easa Advantage," *Newsday*, October 16, 1988, p. 7.

55. *Newsday*, August 21, 1989, p. 32.

56. Samuel Kaplan, *The Dream Deferred* (New York: Seabury Press, 1971), pp. 138-39.

57. Watson, p. 1624. In the 1960s Dennis Ippolito's research on party committeemen indicated that both Democrats and Republicans worked primarily for locally based candidates. Also see Dennis S. Ippolito and Lewis Bowman, "Goals and Activities of Party Officials in a Suburban Community," *Western Political Quarterly*, 22:3 (1969), pp. 575-77.

58. *Newsday*, March 8, 1989.

59. Nicholas Goldberg, "Armand D'Amato: In Kin's Shadow," *Newsday*, March 27, 1992, p. 6. The discussion of the D'Amatos draws primarily on the coverage in *Newsday* and *The New York Times*.

60. Ibid.

61. Frank Lynn, "D'Amato and GOP on L.I. Share Common Toughness," *New York Times*, October 29, 1980, p. B4.

62. Barone and Ujifusa, pp. 832-33.

63. Elizabeth Kolbert, "Senator Pothole," *New York Times Magazine*, October 27, 1991, p. 36.

64. Ibid., p. 38.

65. Nicholas Goldberg and Alan Eysen, "Consensus: A Bad Blow to Senator's Campaign," *Newsday*, March 4, 1992, p. 4.

66. Philip Shenon, "H.U.D. Hired D'Amato Ally Under Pressure, Report Says," *New York Times*, November 2, 1990, p. A12.

67. Robert W. Greene, "Senator's Brother Indicted," *Newsday*, March 12, 1992, pp. 5, 33.

68. Lindsey Gruson, "Senate Panel Finds No Evidence to Warrant Action on D'Amato," *New York Times*, August 3, 1991, pp. 1, 11.

69. Rita Ciolli, "Witness Tells of 60s Patronage," *Newsday*, April 15, 1981, p. 7. Outside the courtroom English also revealed that his law firm had given $500 to the Margiotta defense fund.

In a letter dated January 29, 1982 the Nassau County Republican Committee argued that the New York State Superintendent of Insurance had found that prior to 1978 "sharing of commissions with brokers who performed no services was approved." However, the Committee did not mention that the SIC had also said the practice was an "unconscionable waste" of public money.

70. 435 F. Supp. 546 (1977), p. 550.

71. John T. McQuiston, "Federal Trial Begins in Suit over Kickbacks in Nassau," *New York Times,* July 30, 1985, B.2. The description of the trial which follows is based on McQuiston's articles in the *New York Times* and the coverage of the trial in *Newsday,* much of it by Irving Long.

72. Irving Long and Patrick Brasley, "Town Consulted GOP on Raises, Court Told," *Newsday,* July 31, 1985, p. 3.

73. The Margiotta quotations are from John T. McQuiston, "Margiotta Says He Checked Applicants for County Jobs," *New York Times,* August 2, 1985, p. B.2 and "Margiotta: Employee Raises Tied to Party Considerations," *Newsday,* August 2, 1985.

74. "Caso at 1% Trial, Asserts GOP Called Shots on Jobs, Raises," *Newsday,* August 8, 1985.

75. Irving Long, "Data on Guilt Ok'd in 1% Case," *Newsday,* August 6, 1985, p. 6.

76. Marie Cocco, "GOP Told Me 'To Get, You Must Give,' Worker Testifies," *Newsday,* August 1, 1985, p. 3.

77. John T. McQuiston, "Guard Testifies Boss Demanded Work for G.O.P.," *New York Times,* August 17, 1985.

78. "D'Amato: 1% Existed, But I Never Sought Donations," and "Exerpts from D'Amato's Testimony," *Newsday,* August 17, 1985.

79. Larry Light and Patrick Brasley, "D'Amato Letter a Key to the Verdict: Jurors," *Newsday,* September 5, 1985, p. 5.

80. During the trial Judge Mishler ruled that the class of plaintiffs would be limited to employees whose claims fell between December 12, 1973 when the statute of limitations expired and June 27, 1977 when the class was certified. The jury's decision placed a further limitation by restricting claims to the period ending January 1, 1976.

81. Light and Brasley, p. 5.

82. Irving Long, "$500-a-Person Inaugural for Gulotta," *Newsday,* November 29, 1989, p. 3; Nicholas Goldberg, "Margiotta Back in Party's Graces," *Newsday,* January 18, 1990, pp. 7, 33; and Irving Long, "Main Course at Gala: 1% Case," *Newsday,* January 18, 1990, pp. 7, 33.

83. Marie Cocco, "Patronage Outlives 1% System," *Newsday,* August 25, 1985, p. 23. Also, Burt Neuborne told me he tried to get a decree setting up a "real personnel department," but the judge refused to grant this (and a number of Neuborne's other requests). Telephone Interview, June 21, 1991.

84. Ibid.

85. Sarah Lyall, *New York Times,* December 21, 1991, p. 10.

86. Celeste Hadrick, "Experts: GOP Out of Touch," *Newsday,* November 7, 1991, p. 4.

87. Ibid, p. 136.

Chapter 5

1. Larry Sabato, *Goodbye to Goodtime Charlie,* 2nd ed. (Washington, D.C.: Congressional Quarterly, 1983), p. 69. Sabato also comments that the

"governors seem to believe . . . that on balance civil service is vastly more desirable than patronage."

In their essay on gubernatorial appointment powers, Thad L. Beyle and Robert Dalton note that scholars have reported that contemporary governors support civil service reform and the reduction of patronage powers and that the fifteen former governors they interviewed also feel positively on balance about the trend towards less patronage and a more professional state bureaucracy. "Appointment Power: Does it Belong to the Governor?," in Thad L. Beyle and Lynn R. Muchmore, eds. *Being Governor: The View From the Office* (Durham, North Carolina: Duke University Press, 1983), p. 112.

2. All quotations concerning the INDOT episode are from Judge Daniel Tinder, "Memorandum Following Bench Trial," John V. Selch vs. Christine W. Letts et al, June 3, 1992.

3. Cynthia Grant Bowman, " 'We Don't Want Anybody Anybody Sent': The Death of Patronage Hiring in Chicago," *Northwestern University Law Review*, 86:1 (1991), p. 93. However, Bowman argues that courts should intervene where necessary, but should keep remedial measures simple. She notes that the "Chicago experience suggests that the best remedy may simply be to publicize job vacancies widely, to disseminate information about the First Amendment rights of job applicants, and then to rely upon a professionalized personnel department, coupled with the threat of litigation by individuals whose rights are violated."

4. J. Christine Altenburger, "Patronage: Ethics Gone Amok," in Peter Madsen and Jay M. Shafritz, eds, *Essentials of Government Ethics* (New York: Penguin Books, 1992), pp. 361-62.

5. Alan Rosenthal, *Governors and Legislatures* (Washington, D.C.: Congressional Quarterly, 1990), p. 14.

6. Charles G. Bell and Charles M. Price, *California Government Today*, 4th ed. (Pacific Grove, California: Brooks/Cole, 1992), pp. 208-09.

7. This is Alan Di Gaetano's label. See the discussion of his ideas in Bernard H. Ross, Myron A. Levine and Murray Stedman, Jr., *Urban Politics*, 4th ed. (Itasca, Illinois: F.E. Peacock, 1991), p. 130.

8. Barbara Ferman, *Governing the Ungovernable City* (Philadelphia: Temple University Press, 1985), p. 92. The entire account of White's actions is drawn from Ferman's book.

9. Alan Di Gaetano and John S. Klemanski, "Urban Regimes: The Electoral Connection," Unpublished paper, pp. 21-23. All the information on mayors Flynn and Young comes from this paper which Professor Di Gaetano kindly made available to me.

10. Ibid., p. 21.

11. Ibid., pp. 23-24.

12. David Moburg, "Richard Phelan," *North Shore*, 15: July (1992), p. 36.

13. Telephone Interview, June 21, 1991.

14. Jonathan Katz, "The Slow Death of Political Patronage," *Governing* (April 1991), p. 60.

15. Neil A. Lewis, "Being Governor Helps Clinton Raise Money at Home," *New York Times*, April 27, 1992, p. A14.

16. Diane Kincaid Blair, "The Gubernatorial Appointment Power: Too Much of a Good Thing," in Beyle and Muchmore, pp. 118-21.

17. Rosenthal, p. 78. Rosenthal draws on Robert L. Turner, *Dukakis: An American Odyssey* (Boston: Houghton, Mifflin, 1988), pp. 118-19.

18. Glenn Abney and Thomas P. Lauth, *The Politics of State and City Administration* (Albany: State University of New York Press, 1986), p. 57.

19. Frank J. Thompson, "The Politics of Public Personnel Administration," in Steven W. Hays and Richard C. Kearney, eds., *Public Personnel Administration*, 2nd ed. (Englewood Cliffs, New Jersey: Prentice Hall, 1990), p. 5.

20. Deborah D. Roberts, "A New Breed of Public Executive Top Level Exempt Managers in State Government," *Review of Public Personnel Administration*, 8:2 (1988), p. 23.

21. Deborah D. Roberts, "A Personnel Chameleon Blending the Political Appointee and Careerist Traditions: Exempt Managers in State Government," in Carolyn Ban and Norma M. Riccucci, eds., *Public Personnel Management* (White Plains, New York: Longman, 1991), p. 191.

22. Ibid., p. 201.

23. Carolyn Ban has suggested that hiring methods in government agencies are in fact becoming more flexible. See "The Realities of the Merit System," in Ban and Riccucci, pp. 17-27. It is far beyond the scope of this book to analyze in detail current government personnel systems or to suggest how they might be changed. The National Commission on the State and Local Public Service which was created in 1991 is conducting extensive research on this topic and expects to publish its recommendations in 1993.

24. Theodore J. Lowi, "Gosnell's Chicago Revisited via Lindsay's New York," Foreword to Harold Gosnell, *Machine Politics, Chicago Model*, 2nd ed. (Chicago: University of Chicago Press, 1968), pp. x, xv.

25. Rutan v. Republican Party of Illinois, 110 S.Ct., pp. 2753-54.

26. Milton Rakove, *Don't Make No Waves, Don't Back No Losers* (Bloomington: Indiana University Press, 1975), pp. 166-73.

27. See for example Alan Ware, *The Breakdown of Democratic Party Organization 1940-1980* (New York: Oxford University Press, 1985), especially p. 35.

28. John F. Bibby, "Party Organization at the State Level," in L. Sandy Maisel, ed., *The Parties Respond* (Boulder, Colorado: Westview Press, 1992), p. 27.

29. Michael Margolis, "The Importance of Local Party Organization for Democratic Governance," Paper presented at the American Political Science Association meeting, Washington, D.C., August 1991, pp. 3-4.

30. Leon D. Epstein, "Overview of Research on Party Organization," paper presented at the American Political Science Association meeting, Washington, D.C., August 1991, p. 5.

31. Denise L. Baer and David A. Bositis, *Elite Cadres and Party Coalitions* (New York: Greenwood Press, 1988), p. 122.

32. Bowman, p. 86.

33. Common Cause/Illinois, "The Influence of Money in Illinois Politics," in Dick Simpson, ed. *Chicago's Future*, rev. ed. (Champaign, Illinois: Stipes Publishing, 1988), pp. 336-40.

34. Samuel Gove and James Nowlan, "Politics in Illinois," unpublished manuscript, pp. 20-22.

35. Steven P. Erie, *Rainbow's End* (Berkeley: University of California Press, 1988), p. 218 and Chapter 3.

36. Erie, p. 90.

37. Steven G. Heinen, "Political Patronage and the First Amendment," *Harvard Journal of Law and Public Policy* 14:1 (Winter 1990-91), pp. 302-03.

38. Bowman, p. 88. Bowman also points out, as has been observed in previous chapters, that hiring suits are very difficult to win and that Chicago's experience indicates that Rutan will not lead to the flood of litigation which Justice Scalia envisages. Since 1979 there have only been two political discrimination cases brought by job applicants against the city of Chicago. See pp. 93-95.

39. New York State Commission on Government Integrity, "Restoring the Public Trust: A Blueprint for Government Integrity," *Fordham Urban Law Journal*, 18:2 (Winter 1990), p. 201.

40. Ibid., p. 200.

41. Christopher Daniel makes this point in "Curbing Patronage Without Paperasserie." Paper presented at the American Society for Public Administration meeting, Chicago, April 1992.

INDEX

213